STUDENT BOOK

STECK-VAUGHN

SCIENCE

TEST PREPARATION FOR THE 2014 GED® TEST

- Life Science
- Physical Science
- Earth and Space Science
- Science Practices

POWERED BY
PAXEN

Houghton
Mifflin
Harcourt

POWERED BY
PAXEN

Reading Level:	**9 - 12**
Category:	**GED Material**
Subcategory:	**GED–Science**
Workbook Available:	**Yes**
Teacher Guide Available:	**Yes**
Part of a Series:	**Yes**
CD / CD ROM / DVD Available:	

Acknowledgments

For each of the selections and images listed below, grateful acknowledgment is made for permission to excerpt and/or reprint original or copyrighted material, as follows:

Text

9 Used with permission of MayoClinic.com. **36** Used with permission of the U.S. Fish and Wildlife Service.

Images

Cover (bg) © Chen Ping-hung/E+/Getty Images; **cover (inset)** © Design Pics/John Short/Getty Images. **Opener** Alex Wong/Getty Images. **1** © Wolfgang Flamisch/Corbis. **40** © Ralph Lauer/AP/Corbis. **41** iStockphoto. **80** Roger Ressmeyer/Corbis. **81** iStockphoto.

Science

Table of Contents

About the GED® Test

Welcome to the first day of the rest of your life. Now that you've committed to study for your GED® credential, an array of possibilities and options—academic, career, and otherwise—awaits you. Each year, hundreds of thousands of people just like you decide to pursue a GED® credential. Like you, they left traditional school for one reason or another. Now, just like them, you've decided to continue your education by studying for and taking the GED® Test.

Today's GED® Test is very different from previous versions of the exam. Today's GED® Test is new, improved, and more rigorous, with content aligned to the Common Core State Standards. For the first time, the GED® Test serves both as a high-school equivalency degree and as a predictor of college and career readiness. The new GED® Test features four subject areas: Reasoning Through Language Arts (RLA), Mathematical Reasoning, Science, and Social Studies. Each subject area is delivered via a computer-based format and includes an array of technology-enhanced item types.

The four subject-area exams together comprise a testing time of seven hours. Preparation can take considerably longer. The payoff, however, is significant: more and better career options, higher earnings, and the sense of achievement that comes with a GED® credential. Both employers and colleges and universities alike accept the GED® credential as they would a high school diploma. On average, GED® graduates earn at least $8,400 more per year than those with an incomplete high school education.

The GED® Testing Service has constructed the GED® Test to mirror a high school experience. As such, you must answer a variety of questions within and across the four subject areas. For example, you may encounter a Social Studies passage on the Reasoning Through Language Arts Test, and vice versa. Also, you will encounter questions requiring varying levels of cognitive effort, or Depth of Knowledge (DOK) levels. The following table details the content areas, number of items, score points, DOK levels, and total testing time for each subject area.

Subject-Area Test	Content Areas	Items	Raw Score Points	DOK Level	Time
Reasoning Through Language Arts	**Informational Texts**—75% **Literary Texts**—25%	*51	65	80% of items at Level 2 or 3	150 minutes
Mathematical Reasoning	**Algebraic Problem Solving**—55% **Quantitative Problem Solving**—45%	*46	49	50% of items at Level 2	115 minutes
Science	**Life Science**—40% **Physical Science**—40% **Earth and Space Science**—20%	*34	40	80% of items at Level 2 or 3	90 minutes
Social Studies	**Civics/Government**—50% **U.S. History**—20% **Economics**—15% **Geography and the World**—15%	*35	44	80% of items at Level 2 or 3	90 minutes

*Number of items may vary slightly by test.

Because the demands of today's high school education and its relationship to workforce needs differ from those of a decade ago, the GED® Testing Service has moved to a computer-based format. Although multiple-choice questions remain the dominant type of item, the new GED® Test series includes a variety of technology-enhanced item types: drop-down, fill-in-the-blank, drag-and-drop, hot spot, short answer, and extended response items.

The table to the right identifies the various item types and their distribution on the new subject-area exams. As you can see, all four tests include multiple-choice, drop-down, fill-in-the-blank, and drag-and-drop items. Some variation occurs with hot spot, short answer, and extended response items.

2014 ITEM TYPES

	RLA	Math	Science	Social Studies
Multiple-choice	✓	✓	✓	✓
Drop-down	✓	✓	✓	✓
Fill-in-the-blank	✓	✓	✓	✓
Drag-and-drop	✓	✓	✓	✓
Hot spot		✓	✓	✓
Short answer			✓	
Extended response	✓			✓

Moreover, the new GED® Test relates to today's more demanding educational standards with items that align to appropriate assessment targets and varying DOK levels.

- **Content Topics/Assessment Targets** These topics and targets describe and detail the content on the GED® Test. They tie to the Common Core State Standards, as well as state standards for Texas and Virginia.
- **Content Practices** These practices describe the types of reasoning and modes of thinking required to answer specific items on the GED® Test.
- **Depth of Knowledge** The DOK model details the level of cognitive complexity and steps required to arrive at a correct answer on the test. The new GED® Test addresses three levels of DOK complexity.
  - **Level 1** You must recall, observe, question, or represent facts or simple skills. Typically, you will need to exhibit only a surface understanding of text and graphics.
  - **Level 2** You must process information beyond simple recall and observation to include summarizing, ordering, classifying, identifying patterns and relationships, and connecting ideas. You will need to scrutinize text and graphics.
  - **Level 3** You must explain, generalize, and connect ideas by inferring, elaborating, and predicting. For example, you may need to summarize from multiple sources and use that information to develop compositions with multiple paragraphs. Those paragraphs should feature a critical analysis of sources, include supporting positions from your own experiences, and reflect editing to ensure coherent, correct writing.

Approximately 80 percent of items across most content areas will be written to DOK Levels 2 and 3, with the remainder at Level 1. Writing portions, such as the extended response item in Social Studies (25 minutes) and Reasoning Through Language Arts (45 minutes), are considered DOK Level 3 items.

Now that you understand the basic structure of the GED® Test and the benefits of earning a GED® credential, you must prepare for the GED® Test. In the pages that follow, you will find a recipe of sorts that, if followed, will guide you toward successful completion of your GED® credential.

GED® Test on Computer

Along with new item types, the 2014 GED® Test also unveils a new, computer-based testing experience. The GED® Test will be available on computer and only at approved Pearson VUE Testing Centers. Along with content knowledge and the ability to read, think, and write critically, you must perform basic computer functions—clicking, scrolling, and typing—to succeed on the test. The screen below closely resembles a screen that you will experience on the GED® Test.

The **INFORMATION** button contains material vital to the successful completion of the item. Here, by clicking the Information button, you would enable a map about the American Revolution. On the Mathematical Reasoning exam, similar buttons for **FORMULA SHEET** and **CALCULATOR REFERENCE** provide information that will help you answer items that require use of formulas or the TI-30XS calculator. You may move a passage or graphic by clicking it and dragging it to a different part of the test screen.

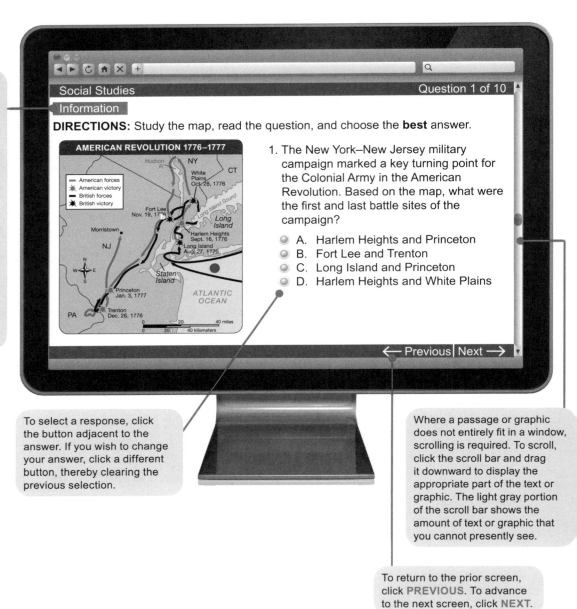

To select a response, click the button adjacent to the answer. If you wish to change your answer, click a different button, thereby clearing the previous selection.

Where a passage or graphic does not entirely fit in a window, scrolling is required. To scroll, click the scroll bar and drag it downward to display the appropriate part of the text or graphic. The light gray portion of the scroll bar shows the amount of text or graphic that you cannot presently see.

To return to the prior screen, click **PREVIOUS**. To advance to the next screen, click **NEXT**.

Some items on the new GED® Test, such as fill-in-the-blank, short answer, and extended response questions, will require you to type answers into an entry box. In some cases, the directions may specify the range of typing the system will accept. For example, a fill-in-the-blank item may allow you to type a number from 0 to 9, along with a decimal point or a slash, but nothing else. The system also will tell you keys to avoid pressing in certain situations. The annotated computer screen and keyboard below provide strategies for entering text and data for fill-in-the-blank, short answer, and extended response items.

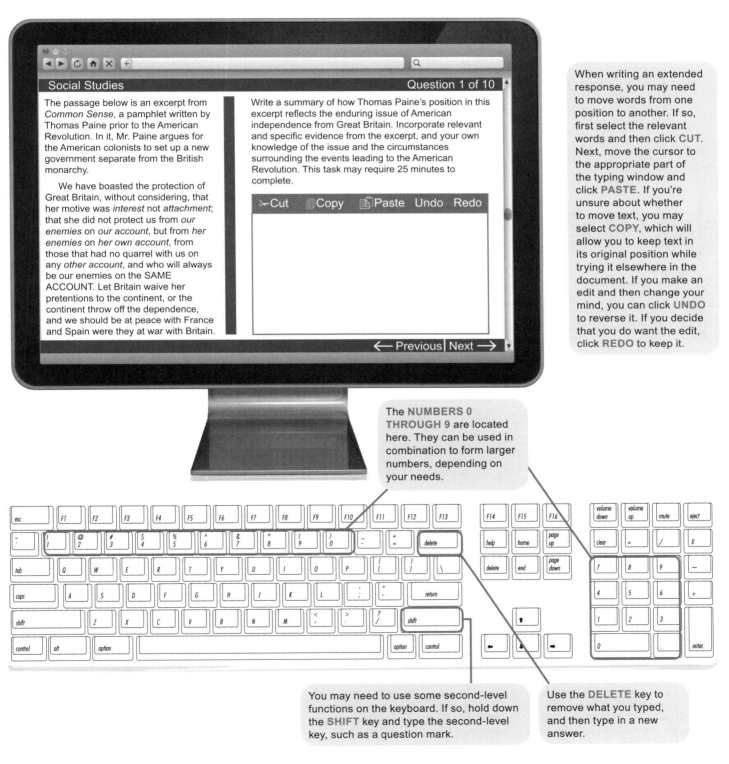

Social Studies   Question 1 of 10

The passage below is an excerpt from *Common Sense*, a pamphlet written by Thomas Paine prior to the American Revolution. In it, Mr. Paine argues for the American colonists to set up a new government separate from the British monarchy.

We have boasted the protection of Great Britain, without considering, that her motive was *interest* not *attachment*; that she did not protect us from *our enemies* on *our account*, but from *her enemies* on *her own account*, from those that had no quarrel with us on any *other account*, and who will always be our enemies on the SAME ACCOUNT. Let Britain waive her pretentions to the continent, or the continent throw off the dependence, and we should be at peace with France and Spain were they at war with Britain.

Write a summary of how Thomas Paine's position in this excerpt reflects the enduring issue of American independence from Great Britain. Incorporate relevant and specific evidence from the excerpt, and your own knowledge of the issue and the circumstances surrounding the events leading to the American Revolution. This task may require 25 minutes to complete.

✂Cut   ▤Copy   ▤Paste   Undo   Redo

← Previous | Next →

When writing an extended response, you may need to move words from one position to another. If so, first select the relevant words and then click **CUT**. Next, move the cursor to the appropriate part of the typing window and click **PASTE**. If you're unsure about whether to move text, you may select **COPY**, which will allow you to keep text in its original position while trying it elsewhere in the document. If you make an edit and then change your mind, you can click **UNDO** to reverse it. If you decide that you do want the edit, click **REDO** to keep it.

The **NUMBERS 0 THROUGH 9** are located here. They can be used in combination to form larger numbers, depending on your needs.

You may need to use some second-level functions on the keyboard. If so, hold down the **SHIFT** key and type the second-level key, such as a question mark.

Use the **DELETE** key to remove what you typed, and then type in a new answer.

About *Steck-Vaughn*
Test Preparation for the 2014 GED® Test

Along with choosing to pursue your GED® credential, you've made another smart decision by selecting *Steck-Vaughn Test Preparation for the 2014 GED® Test* as your main study and preparation tool. Our emphasis on the acquisition of key reading and thinking concepts equips you with the skills and strategies to succeed on the GED® Test.

Two-page micro-lessons in each student book provide focused and efficient instruction. For those who require additional support, we offer companion workbooks, which provide *twice* the support and practice exercises. Most lessons in the series include a *Spotlighted Item* feature that corresponds to one of the technology-enhanced item types that appear on the GED® Test.

The **LEARN THE SKILL** section provides information about the skill to be studied.

Each lesson includes correlations to **ASSESSMENT TARGETS** that will help focus your studies.

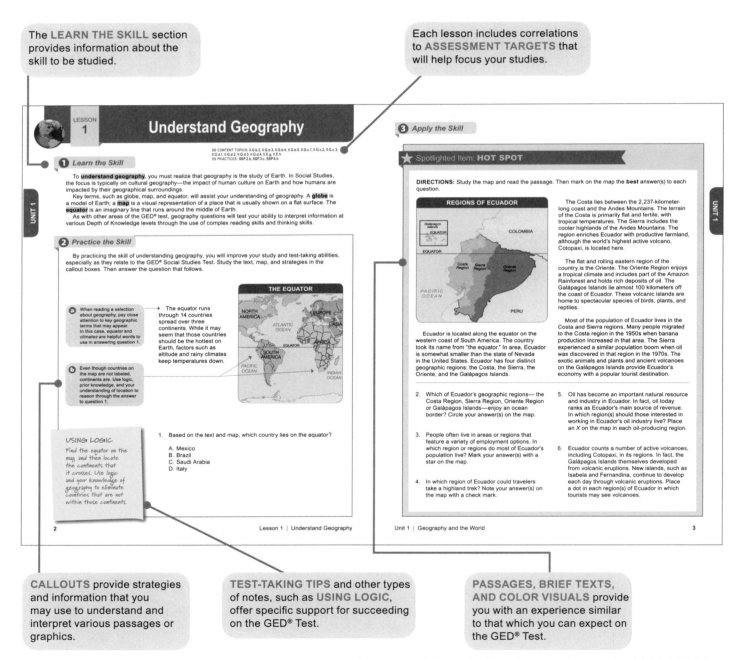

CALLOUTS provide strategies and information that you may use to understand and interpret various passages or graphics.

TEST-TAKING TIPS and other types of notes, such as **USING LOGIC**, offer specific support for succeeding on the GED® Test.

PASSAGES, BRIEF TEXTS, AND COLOR VISUALS provide you with an experience similar to that which you can expect on the GED® Test.

Every unit in *Steck-Vaughn Test Preparation for the 2014 GED® Test* opens with the feature GED® Journeys, a series of profiles of people who earned their GED® credential and used it as a springboard to success. From there, you receive intensive instruction and practice through a series of linked lessons, all of which tie to Content Topics/Assessment Targets, Content Practices (where applicable), and DOK levels.

Each unit closes with an eight-page review that includes a representative sampling of items, including technology-enhanced item types, from the lessons that comprise the unit. You may use each unit review as a posttest to gauge your mastery of content and skills and readiness for that aspect of the GED® Test.

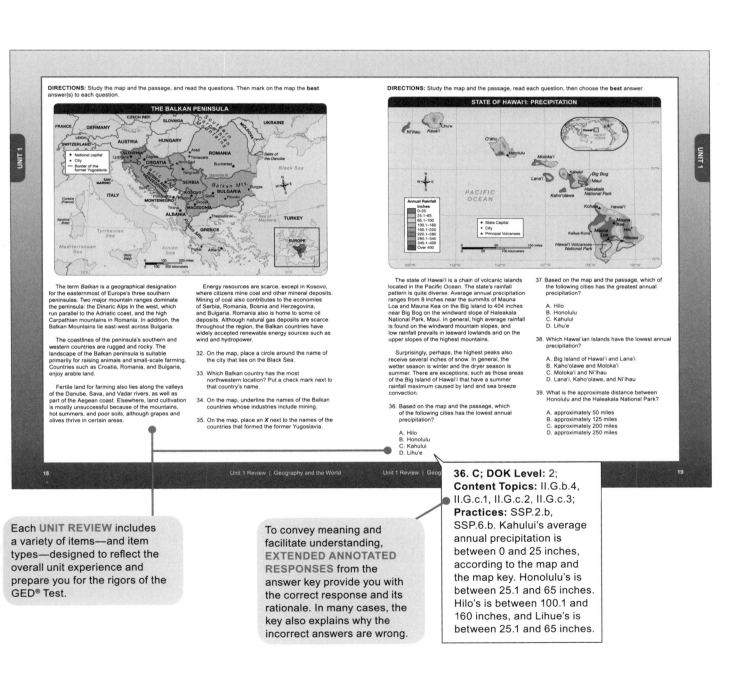

Each **UNIT REVIEW** includes a variety of items—and item types—designed to reflect the overall unit experience and prepare you for the rigors of the GED® Test.

To convey meaning and facilitate understanding, **EXTENDED ANNOTATED RESPONSES** from the answer key provide you with the correct response and its rationale. In many cases, the key also explains why the incorrect answers are wrong.

36. C; DOK Level: 2; **Content Topics:** II.G.b.4, II.G.c.1, II.G.c.2, II.G.c.3; **Practices:** SSP.2.b, SSP.6.b. Kahului's average annual precipitation is between 0 and 25 inches, according to the map and the map key. Honolulu's is between 25.1 and 65 inches. Hilo's is between 100.1 and 160 inches, and Lihue's is between 25.1 and 65 inches.

About the GED® Science Test

The new GED® Science Test is more than just a set of investigations and procedures. In fact, it reflects an attempt to increase the rigor of the GED® Test to better meet the demands of a 21st-century economy. To that end, the GED® Science Test features an array of technology-enhanced item types. All the items are delivered via computer-based testing. The items reflect the knowledge, skills, and abilities that a student would master in an equivalent high school experience.

Multiple-choice questions will remain the majority of items on the GED® Science Test. However, a number of technology-enhanced items, including drop-down, fill-in-the-blank, drag-and-drop, hot spot, and short answer questions, will challenge you to master and convey knowledge in deeper, fuller ways.

- Multiple-choice items assess virtually every content standard as either discrete items or as a series of items. Multiple-choice items on the new GED® Test include four answer options (rather than five), structured in an A./B./C./D. format.
- Drop-down items include pull-down menus of response choices, enabling you to complete statements on the GED® Science Test.
- Fill-in-the-blank items allow you to type in one-word or short answers. For example, you may be asked to describe in a word or a short phrase a trend on a graph or to demonstrate understanding of an idea or vocabulary term from a text passage.
- Drag-and-drop items involve interactive tasks that require you to move small images, words, or numerical expressions into designated drop zones on a computer screen. On the GED® Science Test, you may be asked to assemble data, compare and contrast, or sequence information. For example, you may be asked to place organisms in specific locations on a food web or sequence the steps in a scientific investigation.
- Hot spot items consist of a graphic with virtual sensors placed strategically within it. They allow you to demonstrate understanding of information presented visually or in text or relationships between data points in a passage or graphic. For example, a hot spot item could ask you to demonstrate your understanding of heredity by selecting offspring with a particular trait.
- Short answer items on the GED® Science Test feature two 10-minute tasks in which you compose brief responses to science content. Such responses may include providing a valid summary of a passage or model, creating and communicating a valid conclusion or hypothesis, or deriving evidence from a passage or graphic that supports a particular conclusion.

You will have a total of 90 minutes in which to answer about 34 items. The science test is organized across three main content areas: life science (40 percent), physical science (40 percent), and Earth and space science (20 percent). All told, 80 percent of the items on the GED® Science Test will be written at Depth of Knowledge Level 2 or 3.

About *Steck-Vaughn Test Preparation for the 2014 GED® Test: Science*

Steck-Vaughn's student book and workbook help unlock the learning and deconstruct the different elements of the test by helping you build and develop core reading and thinking skills. The content of our books aligns to the new GED® science content standards and item distribution to provide you with a superior test preparation experience.

Our *Spotlighted Item* feature provides a deeper, richer treatment for each technology-enhanced item type. On initial introduction, a unique item type—such as drag-and-drop—receives a full page of example items in the student book lesson and three pages in the companion workbook lesson. The length of subsequent features may be shorter depending on the skill, lesson, and requirements.

A combination of targeted strategies, informational callouts, sample questions, assorted tips and hints, and ample assessment help focus study efforts in needed areas.

In addition to the book features, a highly detailed answer key provides the correct answer and the rationale for it so that you know exactly why an answer is correct. The *Science* student book and workbook are designed with an eye toward the end goal: success on the GED® Science Test.

Along with mastering key content and reading and thinking skills, you will build familiarity with alternate item types that mirror in print the nature and scope of the technology-enhanced items included on the GED® Test.

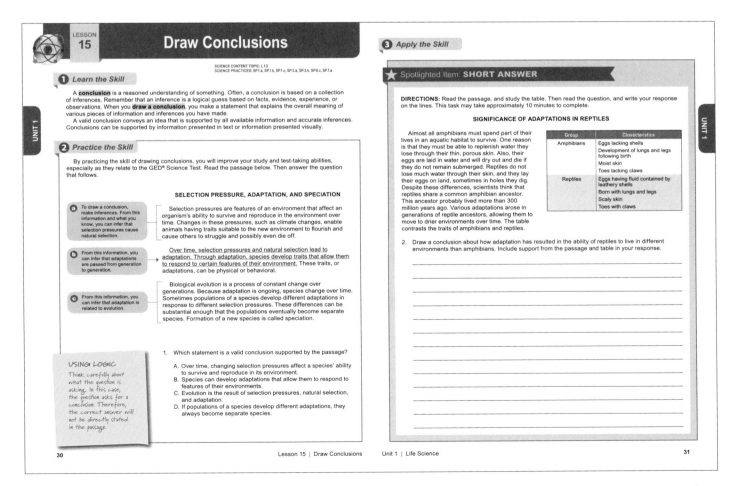

Calculator Directions

Certain items on the GED® Mathematical Reasoning Test allow for the use of a calculator to aid in answering questions. That calculator, the TI-30XS, is embedded within the testing interface. The TI-30XS calculator will be available for most items on the GED® Mathematical Reasoning Test and for some items on the GED® Science Test and GED® Social Studies Test. The TI-30XS calculator is shown below, along with callouts of some of its most important keys. A button that enables the calculator reference sheet is located in the upper right corner of the testing screen.

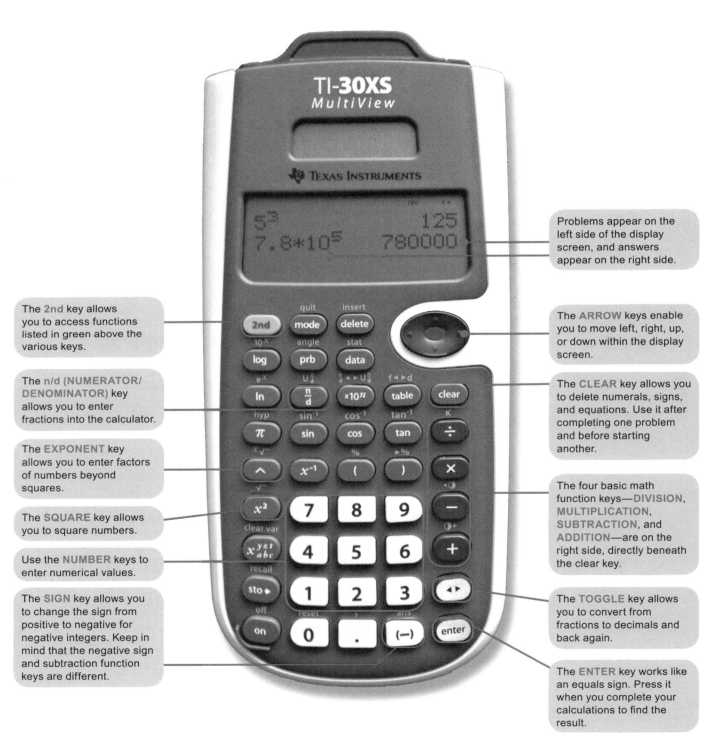

The 2nd key allows you to access functions listed in green above the various keys.

The n/d (NUMERATOR/ DENOMINATOR) key allows you to enter fractions into the calculator.

The EXPONENT key allows you to enter factors of numbers beyond squares.

The SQUARE key allows you to square numbers.

Use the NUMBER keys to enter numerical values.

The SIGN key allows you to change the sign from positive to negative for negative integers. Keep in mind that the negative sign and subtraction function keys are different.

Problems appear on the left side of the display screen, and answers appear on the right side.

The ARROW keys enable you to move left, right, up, or down within the display screen.

The CLEAR key allows you to delete numerals, signs, and equations. Use it after completing one problem and before starting another.

The four basic math function keys—DIVISION, MULTIPLICATION, SUBTRACTION, and ADDITION—are on the right side, directly beneath the clear key.

The TOGGLE key allows you to convert from fractions to decimals and back again.

The ENTER key works like an equals sign. Press it when you complete your calculations to find the result.

Getting Started

To enable the calculator for a question that allows it, click the upper left portion of the testing screen. If the calculator displays over the top of a problem, you may move it by clicking it and dragging it to another part of the screen. Once enabled, the calculator will be ready for use (no need to push the **on** key).

- Use the **clear** key to clear all numbers and operations from the screen.
- Use the **enter** key to complete all calculations.

2nd Key

The green **2nd** key is located in the upper left corner of the TI-30XS. The **2nd** key enables a second series of function keys, which are located above other function keys and noted in green type. To use the 2nd-level function, first click the numeral, next click the **2nd** key, and then click the 2nd-level function key you need. For example, to enter **25%**, first enter the number [**25**]. Then click the **2nd** key, and finally click the 2nd-level **%** key (1st-level *beginning parenthesis* sign).

Fractions and Mixed Numbers

To enter fractions, such as $\frac{3}{4}$, click the **n/d (numerator/denominator)** key, followed by the numerator quantity [**3**]. Next, click the **down arrow** button (upper right corner of the calculator), followed by the denominator quantity [**4**]. To calculate with fractions, click the **right arrow** button and then the appropriate function key and other numerals in the equation.

To enter mixed numbers, such as $1\frac{3}{8}$, first enter the whole number quantity [**1**]. Next, click the **2nd** key and the **mixed number** key (1st level **n/d**). Then enter the fraction numerator [**3**], followed by the **down arrow** button and then the denominator [**8**]. If you click **enter**, the mixed number will convert to an improper fraction. To calculate with mixed numbers, click the **right arrow** button and then the appropriate function key and other numerals in the equation.

Negative Numbers

To enter a negative number, click the **negative sign** key (located directly below the number **3** on the calculator). Keep in mind that the **negative sign** key differs from the **subtraction** key, which is found in the far right column of keys, directly above the **addition (+)** key.

Squares, Square Roots, and Exponents

- **Squares:** The x^2 key squares numbers. The **exponent** key ($\wedge$) raises numbers to powers higher than squares, such as cubes. For example, to find the answer to 5^3 on the calculator, first enter the base number [**5**], then click the exponent key ($\wedge$), and follow by clicking the exponent number [**3**] and then the **enter** key.
- **Square Roots:** To find the square root of a number, such as 36, first click the **2nd** key, then click the **square root** key (1st-level x^2), then the number [**36**], and finally **enter**.
- **Cube Roots:** To find the cube root of a number, such as **125**, first enter the cube as a number [**3**], followed by the **2nd** key and **square root** key. Finally, enter the number for which you want to find the cube [**125**], followed by **enter**.
- **Exponents:** To perform calculations with numbers expressed in scientific notation, such as 7.8×10^9, first enter the base number [**7.8**]. Next, click the **scientific notation** key (located directly beneath the **data** key), followed by the exponent level [**9**]. You then have 7.8×10^9.

Test-Taking Tips

The new GED® Test includes more than 160 items across the four subject-area exams of Reasoning Through Language Arts, Mathematical Reasoning, Science, and Social Studies. The four subject-area exams represent a total test time of seven hours. Most items are multiple-choice questions, but a number are technology-enhanced items. These include drop-down, fill-in-the-blank, drag-and-drop, hot spot, short answer, and extended response items.

Throughout this book and others in the series, we help you build, develop, and apply core reading and thinking skills critical to success on the GED® Test. As part of an overall strategy, we suggest that you use the test-taking tips presented here and throughout the book to improve your performance on the GED® Test.

> ➤ **Always read directions thoroughly so that you know exactly what to do.** As we've noted, the 2014 GED® Test has an entirely new computer-based format that includes a variety of technology-enhanced items. If you are unclear of what to do or how to proceed, ask the test provider whether directions can be explained.

> ➤ **Read each question carefully so that you fully understand what it is asking.** For example, some passages and graphics may present information beyond what is necessary to correctly answer a specific question. Other questions may use boldfaced words for emphasis (for example, "Which statement represents the **most** appropriate revision for this hypothesis?").

> ➤ **Manage your time with each question.** Because the GED® Test is a series of timed exams, you want to spend enough time with each question, but not *too* much time. For example, on the GED® Mathematical Reasoning Test, you have 115 minutes in which to answer approximately 46 questions, or an average of about two minutes per question. Obviously, some items will require more time and others will require less, but you should remain aware of the overall number of items and amount of testing time. The new GED® Test interface may help you manage your time. It includes an on-screen clock in the upper right corner that provides the remaining time in which to complete a test.

Also, you may monitor your progress by viewing the **Question** line, which will give you the current question number, followed by the total number of questions on that subject-area exam.

> ➤ **Answer all questions, regardless of whether you know the answer or are guessing.** There is no benefit in leaving questions unanswered on the GED® Test. Keep in mind the time that you have for each test, and manage it accordingly. If you wish to review a specific item at the end of a test, click **Flag for Review** to mark the question. When you do, the flag will display in yellow. At the end of a test, you may have time to review questions you've marked.

> ➤ **Skim and scan.** You may save time by first reading each question and its answer options before reading or studying an accompanying passage or graphic. Once you understand what the question is asking, review the passage or visual for the appropriate information.

> ➤ **Note any unfamiliar words in questions.** First attempt to re-read the question by omitting any unfamiliar word. Next, try to use other words around the unfamiliar word to determine its meaning.

> ➤ **Narrow answer options by re-reading each question and re-examining the text or graphic that goes with it.** Although four answers are *possible* on multiple-choice items, keep in mind that only one is *correct*. You may be able to eliminate one answer immediately; you may need to take more time or use logic or make assumptions to eliminate others. In some cases, you may need to make your best guess between two options.

> ➤ **Go with your instinct when answering questions.** If your first instinct is to choose **A** in response to a question, it's best to stick with that answer unless you determine that it is incorrect. Usually, the first answer someone chooses is the correct one.

Study Skills

You've already made two very smart decisions in studying for your GED® credential and in purchasing *Steck-Vaughn Test Preparation for the 2014 GED® Test: Science* to help you do so. Following are additional strategies to help you optimize your possibilities for success on the GED® Test.

4 weeks out ...

> **Set a study schedule for the GED® Test.** Choose times in which you are most alert and places, such as a library, that provide the best study environment.

> **Thoroughly review all material in *Steck-Vaughn Test Preparation for the 2014 GED® Test: Science*.** Use the *Science* workbook to extend understanding of concepts in the *Science* student book.

> **Keep a notebook for each subject area that you are studying.** Folders with pockets are useful for storing loose papers.

> **When taking notes, restate thoughts or ideas in your own words rather than copy them directly from a book.** You can phrase these notes as complete sentences, as questions (with answers), or as fragments, provided you understand them.

2 weeks out ...

> **On the basis of your performance on the unit reviews, note any troublesome areas.** Focus your remaining study around those areas.

The days before ...

> **Map out the route to the test center, and visit it a day or two before your scheduled exam.** If you plan to drive to the test center on the day of the test, find out where you will need to park.

> **Get a good night's sleep the night before the GED® Test.** Studies have shown that students with sufficient rest perform better in testing situations.

The day of ...

> **Eat a hearty breakfast high in protein.** As with the rest of your body, your brain needs ample energy to perform well.

> **Arrive 30 minutes early to the testing center.** Arriving early will allow sufficient time in the event of a classroom change.

> **Pack a sizeable lunch.** A hearty lunch is especially important if you plan to be at the testing center most of the day.

> **Remember to relax.** You've come this far and spent weeks preparing and studying for the GED® Test. Now it's your time to shine!

GED® JOURNEYS

Richard Carmona

Richard Carmona used his GED® certificate as a springboard to many career successes, including his service as the U.S. Surgeon General.

"It's my sense of having to make up for lost time."

It takes about an hour to travel by air from New York City to Washington, D.C. For Richard Carmona, however, the journey to our nation's capital took considerably longer. Carmona, the U.S. Surgeon General from 2002 to 2006, went from one of our country's toughest neighborhoods to one of its highest positions.

As a teenager in Harlem, New York, Carmona left school without his high school diploma. At age 17, he enlisted in the U.S. Army. In the military, Carmona earned his GED® credential and joined the Special Forces, winning two Purple Hearts during the Vietnam War.

After leaving active duty, he earned an associate's degree from Bronx (N.Y.) Community College. Carmona later received his undergraduate degree (1977) and M.D. (1979) from the University of California at San Francisco, where he also was named the school's top graduate. Carmona explained his desire to achieve: "It's my sense of having to make up for lost time."

In 1985, Carmona moved to Arizona, where he started the region's first trauma care program. He also worked as a paramedic, a registered nurse, a physician, and a SWAT team member. Carmona's extensive experience led to his appointment as the 17th U.S. Surgeon General, the country's chief health educator, in August 2002. Among other achievements, Carmona worked to inform Americans about the dangers of tobacco, smoking, and secondhand smoke.

CAREER HIGHLIGHTS: *Richard Carmona*

- Became the first member of his family to earn a college degree
- Taught as a clinical professor at the University of Arizona
- Served as U.S. Surgeon General from 2002 to 2006

- Serves as president of a health and wellness nonprofit group
- Serves as chairperson to health-related groups, such as the STOP Obesity Alliance and the Partnership to Fight Chronic Disease

Life Science

Unit 1:
Life Science

Whenever you eat lunch, go to the gym, or even take a nap, you are using pieces of information from life science to guide and enrich your well-being. On a much larger scale, life science enables us all to understand ourselves and our environment.

Similarly, life science plays an important part in the GED® Science Test, comprising 40 percent of all questions. As with other areas of the GED® Science Test, life science questions will test your ability to interpret text or graphics and to answer questions about them by using thinking skills such as identifying cause and effect, generalizing, and drawing conclusions. In Unit 1, the introduction of core skills for understanding text and graphics combined with essential science content will help you prepare for the GED® Science Test.

Table of Contents

Scientists working in the field and in laboratories use life science concepts to study our environment and the living things that inhabit it.

Interpret Illustrations

SCIENCE CONTENT TOPICS: L.b.1, L.d.1, L.d.2, L.d.3
SCIENCE PRACTICES: SP.1.a, SP.1.b, SP.1.c, SP.7.a

UNIT 1

1 Learn the Skill

An **illustration** provides information in a visual way. An illustration can show objects that are too small to see normally. Some illustrations show how the parts of a whole fit together. Other illustrations show what occurs at each stage of a process. When you **interpret an illustration**, you look at the figures and labels in the illustration to understand how the parts of what is being shown fit together.

2 Practice the Skill

By practicing the skill of interpreting illustrations, you will improve your study and test-taking abilities, especially as they relate to the GED® Science Test. Study the information and illustration below. Then answer the question that follows.

CELLS

Cells are the smallest units of living things. Some organisms, such as the bacterium shown here, are unicellular. They are made of only one cell. Other organisms, such as humans, are multicellular. Humans are made up of millions of different types of cells.

a A cutaway illustration shows part of the outside of an object cut away to provide a view of the inside of the object. This cutaway illustration shows the tiny structures inside the bacterium cell.

b To interpret the illustration, read a label, such as the cell wall label. Then follow the line that points to the structure. Look at its shape to help you understand what you read about the structure.

Cell membrane
Pliable structure that encloses the cell and allows waste and nutrients to move in and out

Ribosome
Structure that makes proteins

b **Cell wall**
Rigid structure outside the cell membrane that keeps the cell's shape

Flagellum
Structure that helps move the cell

Nucleoid
Material that is passed on in reproduction

TEST-TAKING TIPS

A test question may ask you to identify part of an illustration or how parts of an illustration relate to one another. Read the labels and study the illustration to determine the answer to such a question.

1. Which structure of the bacterium cell makes proteins?

   A. cell wall
   B. flagellum
   C. ribosome
   D. cell membrane

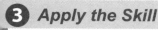

DIRECTIONS: Study the information and illustration, read each question, and choose the **best** answer.

MITOSIS

Cell theory is a scientific theory stating that the cell is the smallest unit of living things and that all cells come from cells. To form new cells, a cell divides. For most cells, mitosis is the part of the cell division process by which the cell nucleus divides. Before a cell reproduces, it goes through a period called interphase. During interphase, the cell grows and material in its nucleus replicates, or duplicates itself. After interphase, mitosis begins. The four major phases of mitosis—prophase, metaphase, anaphase, and telophase—are shown in the illustration.

Parent cell has chromosomes that will replicate in interphase.

Prophase
Replicated chromosomes condense. Each chromosome has two identical sister parts. Nucleus membrane breaks down.

Metaphase
Chromosomes align in middle of cell.

Anaphase
Sister parts separate, become independent chromosomes, and move to opposite ends of cell.

Telophase
Nucleus membranes form around new sets of chromosomes. Cytoplasm separates, and two daughter cells form.

2. Based on the illustration, during which phase of mitosis does the parent cell begin to separate into two cells?

   A. prophase
   B. metaphase
   C. anaphase
   D. telophase

3. If a parent cell has four chromosomes, how many chromosomes will each daughter cell have?

   A. two
   B. four
   C. eight
   D. sixteen

DIRECTIONS: Study the information and illustration, read the question, and choose the **best** answer.

ANIMAL CELL STRUCTURE

Animal cells all contain the same basic organelles, or structures, for making energy, digesting food, packaging proteins, and reproducing. Mitochondria make energy for life functions, lysosomes digest food, and the Golgi complex packages proteins. The nucleus controls the functions of the cell and contains material that is passed on in reproduction.

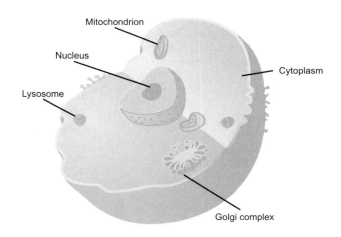

4. In the illustration, what are the unlabeled organelles shown near the Golgi complex?

   A. a lysosome and a nucleus
   B. a lysosome and cytoplasm
   C. a nucleus and a mitochondrion
   D. a mitochondrion and a lysosome

Identify Main Idea and Details

SCIENCE CONTENT TOPICS: L.a.1, L.d.2
SCIENCE PRACTICES: SP.1.a, SP.1.b, SP.1.c, SP.7.a

UNIT 1

① Learn the Skill

The **main idea** is the most important point of an informational passage, an article, a paragraph, or a visual element. Other points that provide additional information about the main idea are **supporting details**. Supporting details include facts, statistics, data, explanations, and descriptions. A main idea may be easily identified, or it may be implied. If a main idea is implied, you must use supporting details to determine the main idea.

② Practice the Skill

By practicing the skill of identifying main idea and details, you will improve your study and test-taking abilities, especially as they relate to the GED® Science Test. Read the passage below. Then answer the question that follows.

ⓐ One sentence in a passage may state the main idea. Think about whether the rest of the passage gives more information about the idea in the sentence. If so, the sentence is most likely the main idea.

ⓑ Supporting details typically follow the main idea. Here, the supporting details are examples of how cells are specialized and organized to perform specific functions.

ORGANIZATION OF CELLS IN A MULTICELLULAR ORGANISM

An organism may be made up of millions of cells of many different types. The cells in an organism are not all alike, nor do they have the same jobs. Cells specialize to perform specific functions and are organized to perform these functions. For example, bone cells serve very different functions from skin cells.

Organized groups of cells work together to carry out a specific function by forming tissues. In the human body, for example, muscle tissue attached to bones contracts and relaxes to make the body move.

Tissues may combine to form organs. The heart is made up of muscle tissues working together to provide the power to pump blood throughout the body.

Groups of organs working together form larger systems with specific functions. The heart, blood vessels, and arteries work together to move blood throughout the body. The blood carries nutrients to and waste away from parts of the body. The systems of an organism work together to perform life functions such as circulation, digestion, respiration, movement, and reproduction.

TEST-TAKING TIPS

Emphasis on the words *most clearly* in the question tells you that more than one answer choice might make sense. To answer correctly, determine which answer choice is best supported by the rest of the passage.

1. Which sentence from the passage **most clearly** states the main idea?

   A. An organism may be made up of millions of cells of many different types.
   B. The cells in an organism are not all alike, nor do they have the same jobs.
   C. Cells specialize to perform specific functions and are organized to perform these functions.
   D. Organized groups of cells work together to carry out a specific function by forming tissues.

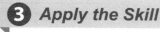

DIRECTIONS: Study the information and illustration, read the question, and choose the **best** answer.

NERVOUS SYSTEM

Cells in the human body are organized into systems, such as the nervous system. The nervous system includes the brain, the spinal cord, and about 100 billion nerve cells, or neurons. Neurons carry signals through the body that allow a person to move, sense things, think, and learn. The illustration shows a neuron.

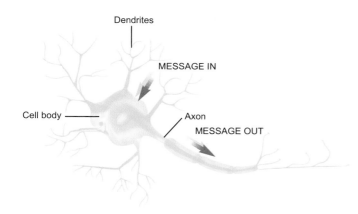

2. Which detail from the illustration supports the main idea that neurons carry signals to allow a person to move, sense things, think, and learn?

   A. Axons send messages out from neurons.
   B. The cell body of a neuron is irregular in shape.
   C. Dendrites have many branches.
   D. Axons are thicker than dendrites.

DIRECTIONS: Read the passage and the question, and choose the **best** answer.

WHAT BONES DO

Bones operate with muscles to move the body. They also safeguard internal organs such as the heart and lungs. Bones store calcium and other minerals for the body to use. Additionally, the marrow inside bones produces blood cells.

3. Which sentence would **best** fit in this passage to state the main idea?

   A. Some bone cells release calcium into the blood.
   B. Bone can be compact or spongy.
   C. Bones are reshaped throughout a person's life.
   D. The skeletal system has numerous functions.

DIRECTIONS: Study the illustration, read each question, and choose the **best** answer.

DIGESTIVE SYSTEM AND DIGESTION

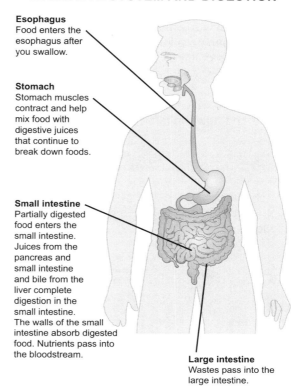

Esophagus
Food enters the esophagus after you swallow.

Stomach
Stomach muscles contract and help mix food with digestive juices that continue to break down foods.

Small intestine
Partially digested food enters the small intestine. Juices from the pancreas and small intestine and bile from the liver complete digestion in the small intestine. The walls of the small intestine absorb digested food. Nutrients pass into the bloodstream.

Large intestine
Wastes pass into the large intestine.

4. Which statement expresses the main idea of the illustration?

   A. Digestion begins even before a person swallows.
   B. Digestion is mostly complete when the food leaves the small intestine.
   C. Digestion is a complex process involving several organs.
   D. Digestion takes place mostly in the stomach.

5. Which detail explains that secretions from organs aid with digestion in the small intestine?

   A. Partially digested food moves from the stomach to the small intestine.
   B. Pancreatic juice, intestinal juice, and bile complete digestion in the small intestine.
   C. The walls of the small intestine absorb digested food.
   D. Nutrients pass from the small intestine into the bloodstream.

UNIT 1

Interpret Tables

SCIENCE CONTENT TOPIC: L.a.3
SCIENCE PRACTICES: SP.1.a, SP.1.b, SP.1.c, SP.3.b

UNIT 1

1 Learn the Skill

A **table** is a tool used to organize and present information in columns and rows. A table generally includes only main points, not extra details. **Interpreting tables** can help you identify information quickly without reading a long paragraph.

Besides columns and rows, a table may contain other parts. A title tells the topic of the table. Column headings and row headings tell what type of information is provided in each column and row. A key provides the meanings of symbols, abbreviations, or language used in the table. Source information tells the origin of the information presented in the table. Understanding a table involves paying attention to all parts of the table and how the information in those parts fits together.

2 Practice the Skill

By practicing the skill of interpreting tables, you will improve your study and test-taking abilities, especially as they relate to the GED® Science Test. Study the table below. Then answer the question that follows.

a First, look at a table's title and column and row headings. Here, they tell you the table is about foods that naturally contain B vitamins.

b A column in a table contains information of a single type. The entries under the heading "B Vitamin" are names of different B vitamins.

FOODS CONTAINING B VITAMINS **a**

B Vitamin **b**	Found Naturally In...
Thiamin (vitamin B1)	Brown rice, grits, whole-wheat bread, baked beans, black beans, black-eyed peas, peanuts
Riboflavin (vitamin B2)	Milk, cheese, yogurt, beef, poultry, broccoli, turnip greens
Niacin (vitamin B3)	Meat, poultry, fish, whole-grain breads
Vitamin B6	Pork, liver, kidney, poultry, fish, eggs, whole-wheat bread, brown rice, oatmeal, soybeans, peanuts, walnuts
Vitamin B12	Beef liver, clams, fish, eggs, milk, cheese

c Most tables present information from left to right. The entries in a row contain related information. For example, the first row has information about thiamin, which also is known as vitamin B1.

1. According to the table, which food contains vitamin B12?

   A. black-eyed peas
   B. eggs
   C. broccoli
   D. peanuts

TEST-TAKING TIPS

To answer this question, you need look only at one row. For other questions based on tables, you might need to look only at one column, look in several parts of the table, or skim all the information in the table.

DIRECTIONS: Study the information and table, read each question, and choose the **best** answer.

THE HUMAN BODY AND NUTRIENTS

The human body needs nutrients to carry out complex life processes, such as cell growth and division. Nearly all the nutrients our bodies need come from the foods we ingest. It is important to consume a balanced diet to ensure that your body receives the nutrients it needs to function. Nutrients are organized into classes, and the body needs nutrients from each class. Understanding where different nutrients can be found and how nutrients work in your body can help you make informed decisions about what you eat. The table provides more information about nutrients.

Class	Example Sources	Uses
Carbohydrates	Breads, cereals, pasta, corn, peas, potatoes, sugar, honey, fruit	Provide energy for muscles, nerves, brain
Fats	Salmon, swordfish, nuts, meat, butter, olive oil, corn oil, whole milk	Provide energy; aid in absorption of vitamins; insulate and cushion organs
Proteins	Fish, meat, soy, eggs, milk, yogurt, cheese, beans, lentils, nuts, seeds, grains	Build muscles and immune system; fight infection; repair cells
Vitamins	Eggs, dairy products, vegetables, fruits, nuts, meats	Regulate body processes
Minerals	Dairy products, vegetables, meats, eggs	Build bones, teeth, blood; help the body use energy
Water	Water, juice, fruits, vegetables	Gives cells shape; transports other nutrients; eliminates waste; regulates temperature
Dietary fiber	Beans, peas, oats, apples, wheat bran, nuts, vegetables, fruits	Controls blood sugar; reduces risk of diabetes and heart disease; keeps digestive tract regular

2. Which title **best** conveys the topic of the table?

    A. Vitamins and Minerals
    B. Major Nutrient Classes
    C. Healthful Eating
    D. Nutrient Uses

3. Based on the table, a lack of which nutrient type would most affect the skeletal system?

    A. minerals
    B. proteins
    C. water
    D. carbohydrates

4. Based on the table, which action provides a person with nutrients from the greatest number of nutrient classes?

    A. eating beans
    B. drinking water
    C. taking vitamins
    D. eating vegetables

DIRECTIONS: Study the information and table, read the question, and choose the **best** answer.

BACTERIA: NOT ALWAYS THE BAD GUYS

Because they are linked to illness, we often think of bacteria in negative terms. However, not all bacteria cause disease. Many helpful bacteria are decomposers, which break down and recycle nutrients in the bodies of dead plants and animals. Other helpful bacteria live inside the human body, where they aid digestion and produce vitamins the body needs. Also, bacteria play a role in the production of many popular foods, such as cheeses. Scientists have even discovered how to put bacteria to work to clean up contaminated water and soil.

Large Intestine Bacterium	How It Is Helpful
Lactobacillus acidophillus	Crowds out harmful microbes, preventing them from growing
Escherichia coli	Provides vitamin K and some B vitamins
Klebsiella	Benefits people with diets that are too low in protein
Methanobacterium smithii	Digests carbohydrates that cannot be digested by humans

5. Which idea is supported by both the passage and the table?

    A. Some bacteria that live in the digestive tract of humans are beneficial.
    B. Bacteria break down and recycle nutrients.
    C. The production of some foods relies on the help of bacteria.
    D. Many millions of bacteria live inside the human body.

Identify Cause and Effect

SCIENCE CONTENT TOPIC: L.a.2
SCIENCE PRACTICES: SP.1.a, SP.1.b, SP.1.c, SP.7.a

UNIT 1

❶ Learn the Skill

A **cause** is an action or object that makes an event happen. The **effect** is the event that results from the cause. A cause may result in more than one effect, and an effect may result from more than one cause. Also, causes and effects can make up chains of events.

Text related to science often discusses causes and effects. Illustrations and other nontextual presentations of scientific material can show causes and effects. In many cases, causes and effects are directly stated. Sometimes they are implied. Being able to **identify cause and effect** is integral to understanding science content.

❷ Practice the Skill

By practicing the skill of identifying cause and effect, you will improve your study and test-taking abilities, especially as they relate to the GED® Science Test. Study the illustration below. Then answer the question that follows.

RESPONSE TO INJURY

ⓐ The illustration shows events that occur when an object cuts the skin. The initial effect is that bacteria enter the body. The presence of bacteria then causes the body to release histamine.

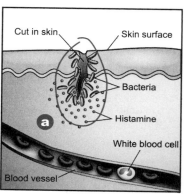
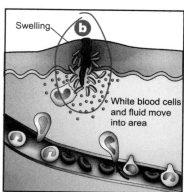

ⓑ The presence of histamine becomes the cause of another effect—swelling and redness around the wound.

When a sharp object breaks the skin, bacteria can enter the body. Bacteria trigger a part of the body's immune system. As a first step in fighting infection, the body releases a chemical called histamine.

INSIDE THE ITEMS

Each item on the GED® Test is given a level of complexity from 1 to 3. This item is Level 2. You can expect about 80 percent of the items on the test to be Level 2 or 3.

1. Based on the illustration, what is the effect of the body's release of histamine?

   A. Blood and fluids drain from the injured area, carrying bacteria to other body parts.
   B. The body's own bacteria attack the foreign bacteria.
   C. The flow of blood and other fluids to the area increases, producing swelling.
   D. The blood vessels in the area around the wound narrow.

Spotlighted Item: DROP-DOWN

DIRECTIONS: Read the passage titled "Sweating and Body Odor." Then read the incomplete passage that follows. Use information from the first passage to complete the second passage. For each drop-down item, choose the option that **best** completes the sentence.

SWEATING AND BODY ODOR

The cause of sweating and body odor stems from your body's temperature regulation system, specifically your sweat glands. Sweating helps maintain your body temperature, hydrates your skin and balances your body fluids and electrolytes, chemicals in your body such as sodium and calcium.

Your skin has two types of sweat glands: eccrine glands and apocrine glands. Eccrine glands occur over most of your body and open directly onto the surface of the skin. Apocrine glands develop in areas abundant in hair follicles, such as on your scalp, armpits and groin and open into the hair follicle just before it opens onto the skin surface.

When your body temperature rises, your autonomic nervous system stimulates the eccrine glands to secrete fluid onto the surface of your skin, where it cools your body as it evaporates. This fluid (perspiration) is composed mainly of water and salt (sodium chloride) and contains trace amounts of other electrolytes—substances that help regulate the balance of fluids in your body—as well as substances such as urea.

Apocrine glands, on the other hand, secrete a fatty sweat directly into the tubule of the gland. When you're under emotional stress, the wall of the tubule contracts and the sweat is pushed to the surface of your skin where bacteria begin breaking it down. Most often, it's the bacterial breakdown of apocrine sweat that causes an odor.

Reprinted from MayoClinic.com article SWEATING AND BODY ODOR, www.MayoClinic.com; accessed 2013

2. When you get hot, you likely take action to cool yourself. This might mean shedding a sweatshirt, putting on shorts, or jumping in a pool. These actions are helpful, but more important is what occurs inside your body to help cool you.

As the temperature of the body rises, signals are sent to the eccrine glands. These signals cause [2. Drop-down 1] . Evaporation causes the body to [2. Drop-down 2] . In addition to helping the body maintain its temperature, this process also regulates fluids in the body.

Sometimes, sweat has an odor. This odor is caused by [2. Drop-down 3] when they break down the sweat pushed to the skin's surface by the [2. Drop-down 4] .

Drop-Down Answer Options

2.1 A. the heart rate to increase
B. sweat to appear on the skin
C. salt to be absorbed
D. bacteria to cause odor

2.2 A. break down bacteria
B. secrete fluids
C. cool
D. sweat

2.3 A. eccrine glands
B. temperature regulators
C. body fluids
D. bacteria

2.4 A. apocrine glands
B. adrenal gland
C. pituitary gland
D. eccrine glands

Interpret Graphs and Maps

SCIENCE CONTENT TOPIC: L.a.4
SCIENCE PRACTICES: SP.1.a, SP.1.b, SP.1.c, SP.3.b, SP.3.d

UNIT 1

1 Learn the Skill

Graphs and thematic **maps** are tools used to show data visually. Types of graphs include bar graphs, circle graphs, and line graphs. A thematic map focuses on a particular topic and shows relevant data for an area, a country, or even the world.

You can find, compare, and analyze data and identify trends quickly and easily by **interpreting graphs and maps**. Many graphs have an *x*-axis and a *y*-axis that identify variables related to the data. Titles, keys, and labels often are included on graphs and maps. All these features help you understand the data.

2 Practice the Skill

By practicing the skill of interpreting graphs and maps, you will improve your study and test-taking abilities, especially as they relate to the GED® Science Test. Study the information and graph below. Then answer the question that follows.

LYME DISEASE

Lyme disease is a bacterial infection that is spread through the bite of a tick. The tick picks up the infection from feeding on mice or deer that have the infection. The tick can then spread the infection to a person through a bite.

a A bar graph may be stacked, having bars that are divided to show subcategories. In this graph, the two subcategories are confirmed cases and probable cases.

b A bar graph compares data. This graph compares the number of cases of Lyme disease reported each year over a 10-year period.

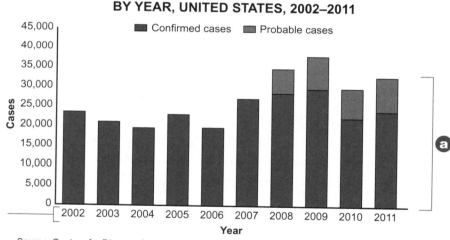

REPORTED CASES OF LYME DISEASE
BY YEAR, UNITED STATES, 2002–2011

Source: Centers for Disease Control and Prevention

TEST-TAKING TIPS

Always read the title and labels on a graph carefully. They give important information about the data. If the graph has a key, or legend, study it carefully too.

1. According to the graph, in which year were the most confirmed and probable cases of Lyme disease reported?

   A. 2007
   B. 2008
   C. 2009
   D. 2010

DIRECTIONS: Study the information and map, read the question, and choose the **best** answer.

INFLUENZA

Fever, cough, sore throat, headache, muscle aches, and vomiting—chances are you have had these symptoms at some point. They are symptoms of influenza, or the flu.

The flu is a respiratory illness caused by viruses. Every year, scientists predict which flu viruses will wreak the most havoc during the next flu season. Then they make vaccines against those strains and hope they have predicted correctly. Not everyone gets the flu vaccine, and not everyone who gets it avoids the flu.

The Centers for Disease Control and Prevention tracks estimated flu cases across the country each week to determine how the numbers of infected people are changing. The map shows the results from one week.

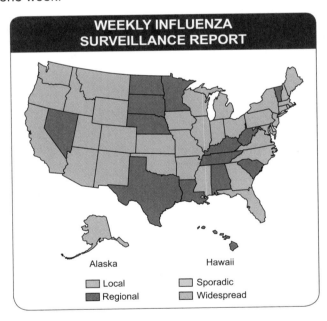

2. Which category of geographic spread of the flu applied to the most states during the week addressed by the map?

   A. sporadic
   B. local
   C. regional
   D. widespread

DIRECTIONS: Study the information and graph, read each question, and choose the **best** answer.

HEPATITIS

Hepatitis is a contagious liver disease caused by viruses. The three forms generally seen in the United States are hepatitis A, B, and C. The three types vary in how they are spread. Hepatitis A is spread when a person ingests fecal matter of an infected person. For example, if an infected person uses a public restroom but does not wash his or her hands, that person can pass on the infection to others in the public through even microscopic amounts of fecal matter. The fact that the spread of hepatitis A is easily prevented through proper hygiene is becoming more widely known.

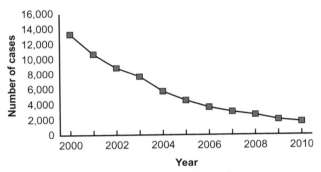

ACUTE HEPATITIS A CASES, UNITED STATES, 2000–2010

Source: Centers for Disease Control and Prevention

3. Based on the graph, which statement describes the trend in the occurrence of hepatitis A cases in the United States between 2000 and 2010?

   A. The number of cases decreased.
   B. The number of cases stayed the same.
   C. The number of cases increased.
   D. The number of cases doubled.

4. Which assumption could be supported by the passage and the trend shown in the graph?

   A. The number of viral infections is increasing due to fewer prevention options.
   B. The hepatitis A virus is becoming weaker and less contagious.
   C. Greater knowledge about control of the spread of hepatitis A has led to fewer infections.
   D. Fewer people are going to the doctor when they have symptoms of hepatitis A.

Interpret Diagrams

SCIENCE CONTENT TOPICS: L.c.1, L.c.2
SCIENCE PRACTICES: SP.1.a, SP.1.b, SP.1.c, SP.7.a

UNIT 1

① Learn the Skill

Diagrams show relationships between ideas, objects, or events in a visual way. Diagrams also can show the order in which events occur. When you **interpret diagrams**, you find out how objects or events relate to one another.

② Practice the Skill

By practicing the skill of interpreting diagrams, you will improve your study and test-taking abilities, especially as they relate to the GED® Science Test. Study the information and diagram below. Then answer the question that follows.

ECOSYSTEMS

An ecosystem includes all the living things in an area, along with their nonliving environment. Energy flows through the living parts of an ecosystem. In most ecosystems, the energy originates from the sun. Plants use energy from sunlight and nutrients from air, water, and soil to make food. Animals eat the plants, other animals eat the plant eaters, and so on. Each organism gets energy from its food and passes on energy to any organism that feeds on it. A food chain shows a single path of feeding relationships among certain organisms in an ecosystem. The diagram shows a food chain in a grassland ecosystem.

ⓐ Diagrams can take many forms. Flowcharts use boxes and arrows to show steps in a process or order of events. Some flowcharts are circles or ovals. They show events that occur in cycles.

ⓑ The parts of this diagram are arranged in a line, with arrows pointing from one part to the next. The arrows show the direction in which food moves from one organism to the next.

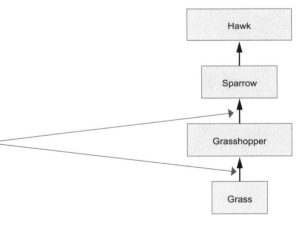

1. Which statement describes a feeding relationship shown in the diagram?

    A. Hawks eat grass.
    B. Grasshoppers eat sparrows.
    C. Sparrows eat grasshoppers.
    D. Hawks eat grasshoppers.

TEST-TAKING TIPS

Review the answer choices. How would the diagram have to look for each answer choice to be true? Compare the imagined diagram with the actual diagram to determine the correct answer.

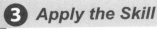

DIRECTIONS: Study the diagram and information, read each question, and choose the **best** answer.

MOVEMENT OF NUTRIENTS IN AN ECOSYSTEM

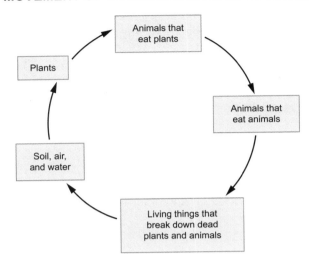

Matter, or the material that makes up everything around us, is continuously recycled in an ecosystem. Organisms get materials they need to live from the environment. They then release waste matter back into the environment. Nutrients are one form of matter that cycles through an ecosystem. The diagram shows the movement of nutrients in a land-based ecosystem.

2. Based on the diagram, which statement describes a flow of nutrients in a land-based ecosystem?

A. Most animals obtain nutrients by eating other animals.
B. Plants obtain nutrients from soil, air, and water.
C. Animals that eat animals are a source of nutrients for animals that eat plants.
D. Living things that break down dead plants and animals contribute no nutrients to the ecosystem.

3. What would happen to the movement of nutrients shown in the diagram if all the plants in the ecosystem died?

A. Nutrients would continue to cycle through the ecosystem, skipping the missing step.
B. Plant-eating animals would start eating other animals.
C. The nutrients cycle would end.
D. Soil, air, and water supplies would decrease and eventually end.

DIRECTIONS: Study the information and diagram, read each question, and choose the **best** answer.

MOVEMENT OF ENERGY IN AN ECOSYSTEM

As energy flows through an ecosystem, it is conserved. That is, the amount of energy neither increases nor decreases. Plants get energy by making food. Animals get energy by eating food in the form of plants and other animals. Living things convert the energy stored in food into energy for movement, growth, and repair. A small amount of energy that a living thing takes in is stored in the cells of its body. Most of the energy is lost to the environment as heat, sound, motion, and—in some cases—light. Energy pyramids show how energy flows through ecosystems. The diagram shows an energy pyramid for a forest ecosystem.

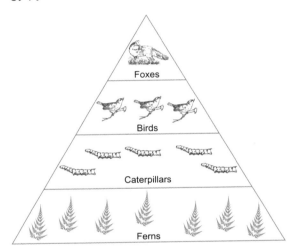

4. What is one way in which energy flows through the forest ecosystem represented by the diagram?

A. from ferns to caterpillars
B. from foxes to ferns
C. from birds to ferns
D. from birds to caterpillars

5. What idea does the shape of an energy pyramid **most likely** reinforce?

A. In general, larger animals in an ecosystem eat smaller animals in the ecosystem.
B. Plants use sunlight to obtain energy and form the basis for all food chains in an ecosystem.
C. Organisms at higher levels of a food chain live at higher levels in an environment.
D. The amount of available energy decreases as energy passes from organism to organism.

UNIT 1

LESSON 7

Categorize and Classify

SCIENCE CONTENT TOPIC: L.c.4
SCIENCE PRACTICES: SP.1.a, SP.1.b, SP.1.c, SP.6.a, SP.6.c

❶ Learn the Skill

When you **categorize**, you choose the criteria for placing organisms, objects, processes, or other items in groups. Such groups are based on shared characteristics or relationships. When you **classify**, you put things into groups that already exist.

Presentations of scientific material often involve categorization and classification because many things in science are organized in groups. In life science, for example, cells are categorized and classified according to their functions. Living things in an ecosystem are categorized and classified by roles they play in the ecosystem. Ecosystems are categorized and classified based on their physical traits.

❷ Practice the Skill

By practicing the skill of categorizing and classifying, you will improve your study and test-taking abilities, especially as they relate to the GED® Science Test. Study the information and diagram below. Then answer the question that follows.

PREDATOR-PREY RELATIONSHIPS

a The passage and diagram give information about one type of relationship between organisms—the predator-prey relationship. Relationships can be organized in categories. Predator-prey is a category.

b Once categories have been created, you can classify something specific, such as a specific relationship, into the appropriate category. The question asks you to classify.

a All organisms have relationships with other organisms. These relationships are known as symbiotic relationships. One such relationship is that of <u>predator and prey</u>. This relationship is called a predator-prey relationship, or predation. A predator is an organism that kills and eats another organism. Its prey is the organism it eats. The arrow in the diagram shows that the rabbit is eaten by the cougar. The rabbit is prey, and the cougar is a predator. Predators and prey live together in the same environment, and their numbers affect each other.

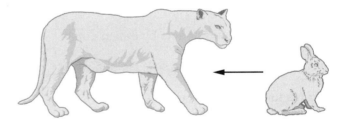

TEST-TAKING TIPS

Organisms, objects, and processes often can be categorized and classified in more than one way. Look for the best fit when categorizing and classifying on a test.

1. Based on the information, which relationship between organisms **most likely** can be classified as a predator-prey relationship?

   A. bear-fish
   B. goat-pig
   C. bee-flower
   D. barnacle-whale

DIRECTIONS: Read the passage. Then read the item, and fill in your responses in the boxes.

PARASITISM

Symbiosis is a situation in which two organisms from different species live close together. There are different types of symbiotic relationships. One type is parasitism. In a parasitic relationship, one organism, the parasite, benefits from and harms another organism, the host. For example, a tapeworm lives in the intestines of an animal, getting food by eating the animal's partly digested food. The animal then is unable to obtain all the nutrients available in the food it ingests.

2. Based on the passage, label each organism to classify it as a parasite or a host.

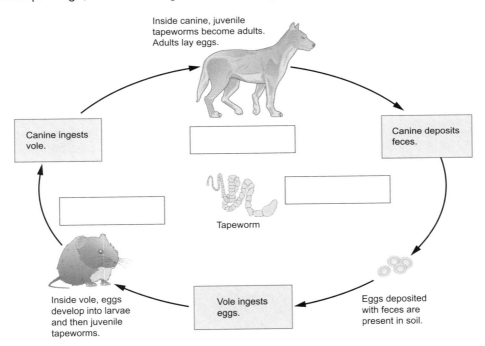

Inside canine, juvenile
tapeworms become adults.
Adults lay eggs.

Canine ingests
vole.

Canine deposits
feces.

Tapeworm

Inside vole, eggs
develop into larvae
and then juvenile
tapeworms.

Vole ingests
eggs.

Eggs deposited
with feces are
present in soil.

DIRECTIONS: Read the passage. Then read the question, and fill in your answer in the box.

HARMLESS SYMBIOTIC RELATIONSHIPS

Several types of symbiotic relationships exist. Commensalism is a relationship in which one organism benefits and the other does not benefit but is not harmed. For example, certain orchids use the branches of large trees in tropical forests as places to grow and live. The trees receive no benefit, but the orchids do not harm the trees. Another type of symbiotic relationship is mutualism. In a mutualistic relationship, both organisms benefit, and neither is harmed.

3. What are the categories of symbiotic relationships discussed in the passage?

Generalize

SCIENCE CONTENT TOPICS: L.c.3, L.c.4
SCIENCE PRACTICES: SP.1.a, SP.1.b, SP.1.c, SP.3.b, SP.6.c

UNIT 1

1 Learn the Skill

When you **generalize**, you use specific information to make a broad statement that applies to an entire group of objects, organisms, places, or events. A **generalization** can be valid or invalid. Valid generalizations are supported by facts and examples. Invalid generalizations are not.

2 Practice the Skill

By practicing the skill of generalizing, you will improve your study and test-taking abilities, especially as they relate to the GED® Science Test. Study the information and illustration below. Then answer the question that follows.

a To make a generalization, first gather and compare information about a topic. Then use the information to make a statement that is usually true. This statement is your generalization.

b Even if a statement describes all the members of a particular group, it is not necessarily a generalization. For instance, the statement that a community is all the populations in an area is a fact, not a generalization.

LEVELS OF ORGANIZATION IN AN ECOSYSTEM

An ecosystem is made up of different kinds of living things. Scientists often think of the living things in an ecosystem as being organized in levels. The lowest level of organization is the individual organism. Individual organisms are arranged into populations. A population is a group of organisms that are all the same species and that all live in the same area. For example, all the blue jays in a forest make up a population. Populations are organized into communities. A community is all the populations in an area. Most communities contain many populations, and these populations affect each other in various ways. Groups of communities make up the ecosystem.

Organism   Population   Community   Ecosystem

1. Based on the information, which statement is a valid generalization about the living things in an ecosystem?

   A. There are different kinds of living things in an ecosystem.
   B. The communities in most ecosystems are made up of many different species.
   C. Populations in an ecosystem are made up of individual organisms.
   D. All organisms in a population are of the same species.

★ Spotlighted Item: **FILL-IN-THE-BLANK**

DIRECTIONS: Study the information and graph. Then complete each statement by filling in the box.

CARRYING CAPACITY

Carrying capacity is the maximum number of individuals of a given species that an area's resources can sustain. Competition for resources and many other factors can affect carrying capacities. The graph shows a pattern of change over time for one population in one ecosystem.

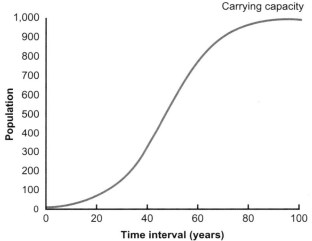

2. Based on the graph, a population generally

until it reaches its carrying capacity.

3. The graph represents one population in one ecosystem. A generalization can be made that similar populations in similar ecosystems are

between years 40 and 60.

4. Suppose that a new competitor of the population represented in the graph is introduced in the ecosystem. The graph would change by showing a generally lower

.

DIRECTIONS: Read the passage and question, and choose the **best** answer.

INVASIVE SPECIES

Invasive species, or species not native to the ecosystem in which they are living, cause ecological and economic harm. An invasive species competes with native species for resources and often does not have any predators in the ecosystem. An invasive species population can thrive to the extent that it makes up a large percentage of the biomass, or mass of living organisms in an ecosystem.

5. Based on the passage, a valid generalization is that competition from invasive species

A. usually leads to decreased carrying capacity for other organisms in an ecosystem.
B. typically ensures that only the healthiest species survive.
C. always negatively affects both the invasive species and other species.
D. generally leads to an increase in the carrying capacity for the organism that is out-competed.

Compare and Contrast

SCIENCE CONTENT TOPICS: L.c.2, L.c.5
SCIENCE PRACTICES: SP.1.a, SP.1.b, SP.1.c, SP.3.a, SP.6.a, SP.6.c

UNIT 1

1 Learn the Skill

When you **compare**, you identify the ways in which organisms, objects, data, behaviors, events, or processes are similar. When you **contrast**, you identify ways in which such things are different.

You may need to compare and contrast while studying scientific subject matter presented in text, illustrations, or diagrams or while examining data in tables or graphs. Comparing and contrasting as you learn deepens and clarifies your understanding. You can use tools such as tables and diagrams to organize information in ways that help you compare and contrast aspects of scientific presentations.

2 Practice the Skill

By practicing the skill of comparing and contrasting, you will improve your study and test-taking abilities, especially as they relate to the GED® Science Test. Study the information and table below. Then answer the question that follows.

MONITORING BIODIVERSITY

Throughout the world, animal and plant species face possible elimination. Some issues that threaten organisms are habitat change, climate change, and disease. Even the loss of a species in just one ecosystem contributes to decreased biodiversity, or variety in species. Biodiversity is a characteristic of vigorous ecosystems.

The International Union for Conservation of Nature (IUCN) tracks and seeks solutions to the problem of decreasing biodiversity. As part of its efforts, the IUCN maintains the Red List, a document identifying the known status of thousands of species around the world. The table below provides a portion of the extensive data found in the IUCN Red List.

a When comparing, look for ways things are alike. Scan the parts of the table to determine what the groups of vertebrates listed in the table have in common. They all include threatened species.

b When contrasting, look for ways things are different. In the table, the threatened species figures differ among the groups. Also, the figures for each group differ from 2006 to 2012.

Vertebrate Group	Number of Threatened Species in 2006	Number of Threatened Species in 2012
Mammals	1,093	1,139
Birds	1,206	1,313
Reptiles	341	807
Amphibians	1,770	1,933
Fishes	800	2,068

Source: IUCN Red List

1. What do the data in the table suggest is a similarity among all the groups of vertebrates?

A. The issue of threatened species in each group is no longer a problem.
B. More than 1,000 species in each group are threatened.
C. The number of known threatened species in each group has increased.
D. The 2012 figures for threatened species in each group are almost the same as the 2006 figures.

CONTENT TOPICS

You can think of an ecosystem like a city. Parts of a city work together to keep the city functioning. Likewise, parts of an ecosystem work together to maintain the ecosystem's health.

★ Spotlighted Item: **DRAG-AND-DROP**

DIRECTIONS: Read the passage and question. Then use the drag-and-drop options to complete the diagram.

FACTORS OF HEALTHY AND UNHEALTHY ECOSYSTEMS

An ecosystem consists of living and nonliving components that interact to form a stable system. Living and nonliving components include more than plants, animals, soil, and rocks. Soil chemistry, nutrient and water supplies, temperature, and amount of sunlight are all factors in the workings of an ecosystem. A healthy ecosystem is balanced. All these elements are present in the right amounts to ensure the success of all the ecosystem's parts.

All healthy ecosystems have a high degree of biodiversity. Biodiversity is variety in the species living in an ecosystem and, therefore, doing their parts to make the ecosystem work. Why does biodiversity contribute to the health of an ecosystem? Organisms in an ecosystem rely on each other. Each group gets nutrients and energy from another group, and the cycle is continuous. Imagine an ecosystem that has only one or two main plants to produce food. What would happen if one of these plants were to contract a disease and stop producing? This event would bring about changes in the entire ecosystem. In an ecosystem with greater biodiversity, the loss of one producer would have less impact because many other producers would be available. Biodiversity helps maintain the balance that is vital to a healthy ecosystem.

Even though an ecosystem with a high level of biodiversity is more resilient than one with less biodiversity, any ecosystem can become unhealthy. Many external factors can disrupt an ecosystem and affect its balance. Some are natural events, such as flooding or fire. Others are disturbances caused by humans, such as pollution, habitat destruction, and introduction of invasive, or nonnative, species.

2. Compare and contrast healthy and unhealthy ecosystems. Based on the passage, determine whether each drag-and-drop option is a characteristic of a healthy ecosystem, an unhealthy ecosystem, or both. Then record each characteristic in the appropriate part of the diagram.

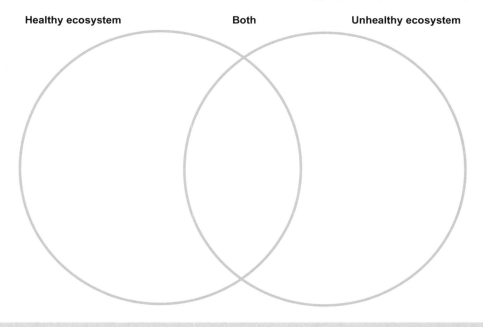

Healthy ecosystem   **Both**   **Unhealthy ecosystem**

Drag-and-Drop Options

living and nonliving parts
correct proportions of nutrients and sunlight
loss of habitat
nonnative species
high level of biodiversity
polluted water

UNIT 1

UNIT 1

SCIENCE CONTENT TOPICS: L.d.3, L.e.1
SCIENCE PRACTICES: SP.1.a, SP.1.b, SP.1.c, SP.7.a

1 Learn the Skill

Illustrations, tables, graphs, maps, and diagrams present information visually. They help you understand text they accompany by providing additional information or by providing information in a different way. Alternatively, text can help you interpret accompanying visuals. In this way, text and visuals support one another. **Relating text and visuals** allows you to fully understand the information being presented.

2 Practice the Skill

By practicing the skill of relating text and visuals, you will improve your study and test-taking abilities, especially as they relate to the GED® Science Test. Study the illustration and information below. Then answer the question that follows.

a The illustration presents information that is not included in the passage. It depicts each of the 23 pairs of chromosomes found in human cells. This information will help you answer the question.

HUMAN CHROMOSOMES

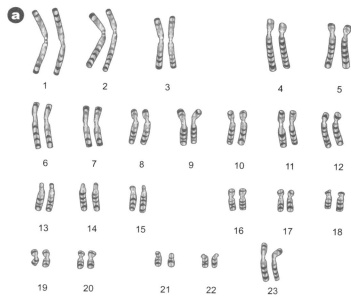

b Text often tells you about a visual and may include information that is not in the visual. In this case, very little information is included in both the illustration and the passage.

It is possible to identify a human as a human because organisms of the same kind are similar. Also, individuals are especially like their parents. All these similarities are due to heredity, or the passing of traits from one generation to the next. Hereditary material is carried on chromosomes, which are tiny structures in cells. Each species has a certain number of chromosomes in its cells. In humans and other organisms, chromosomes that are homologous—similar in size and structure—form pairs. When cells divide to form new cells, chromosomes copy themselves. This replication allows each new cell to have a complete copy of the organism's hereditary material. During sexual reproduction, cells from two parent organisms join so that hereditary material from both parents is passed on.

TEST-TAKING TIPS

When you answer a multiple-choice question, you can eliminate wrong choices. When a question is about text and a visual, first use one element to eliminate choices. Then use the other to eliminate more choices.

1. The illustration and passage suggest that

    A. all human chromosomes are identical.
    B. humans have 23 pairs of chromosomes in their cells.
    C. human chromosomes double in size when a cell divides.
    D. humans have fewer chromosome pairs than other species.

DIRECTIONS: Study the information and illustration, read the question, and choose the **best** answer.

DNA

The basis of heredity is deoxyribonucleic acid, or DNA. The chromosomes in an organism's cells contain tightly coiled DNA molecules, with nearly every cell containing the same DNA. The thin, ladder-shaped DNA molecules are made of millions of tiny units called nucleotides. Each nucleotide contains one of four different bases—adenine (A), guanine (G), thymine (T), or cytosine (C); a sugar; and a phosphate. The bases form pairs, always A with T and C with G, and make up the rungs of the ladder. Sugars and phosphates form the ladder's sides.

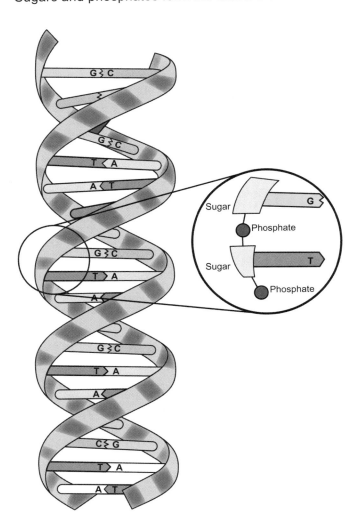

2. Based on the passage and illustration, which statement describes DNA structure?

   A. Sugars are located along the sides and in the middle of a DNA molecule.
   B. Sugars and phosphates form the rungs of the ladder shape of a DNA molecule.
   C. One side of a DNA molecule is longer than the other side.
   D. Nucleotide bases combine to form different patterns in different parts of a DNA molecule.

DIRECTIONS: Study the information and illustration, read the question, and choose the **best** answer.

GENES

Proteins make the body develop and function as it does, from producing the substance that makes eyes a certain color to causing hair and nails to grow. The instructions for building these proteins come from genes. The DNA carried on an organism's chromosomes has many genes. Each gene consists of a unique sequence of nucleotide bases. According to the arrangement of these bases, genes give instructions for building proteins that determine the functions particular cells will perform.

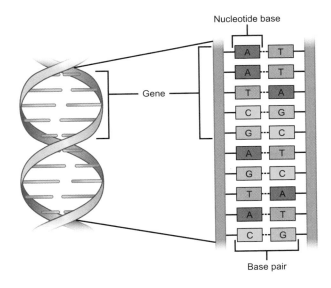

3. Based on the passage and illustration, which sentence is a correct statement about genes?

   A. Genes are segments of DNA.
   B. All genes have five pairs of bases.
   C. One DNA strand may have millions of genes.
   D. The nucleotide bases in genes are proteins.

Understand Content-Based Tools

SCIENCE CONTENT TOPIC: L.e.2
SCIENCE PRACTICES: SP.1.a, SP.1.b, SP.1.c, SP.3.d, SP.8.b, SP.8.c

UNIT 1

1 Learn the Skill

A **content-based tool** is a symbol, an equation, a visual element, or another aid used with certain types of subject matter. Sometimes in science, you need to **understand content-based tools** to comprehend explanations, make determinations, or calculate answers. Knowing how to use and obtain information from content-based tools will enable you to answer questions about specific topics accurately and efficiently.

2 Practice the Skill

By practicing the skill of understanding content-based tools, you will improve your study and test-taking abilities, especially as they relate to the GED® Science Test. Study the information and diagram below. Then answer the question that follows.

GENETICS OF PEA PLANTS

Through sexual reproduction, parent organisms contribute genes to their offspring. Genes produce traits, and certain traits are passed from one generation to the next through heredity. Genetics is the study of patterns of heredity. Gregor Mendel's experiments with pea plants in the mid-1800s laid the foundation for the science of genetics. Mendel wanted to learn how offspring inherit traits from their parents. The diagram shows the results of an investigation in which Mendel bred pea plants having purple flowers with pea plants having white flowers.

a Different tools serve different purposes. Genetics diagrams are useful for understanding how a trait is passed from parents to offspring across generations. In this case, the trait is flower color.

Parent generation

Purple flowers   X   White flowers

First generation of offspring

All plants have purple flowers

Second generation of offspring

$\frac{3}{4}$ of plants have purple flowers $\frac{1}{4}$ of plants have white flowers

1. What do the investigation results suggest about the trait of flower color in pea plants?

   A. Plants with purple flowers cannot produce plants with white flowers.
   B. A trait may reoccur even after it does not occur in a generation.
   C. Plants with purple flowers are more likely to survive than plants with white flowers.
   D. A single offspring shows a blending of the traits of both parents.

TEST-TAKING TECH

For multiple-choice and hot spot items on the GED® Test, you click a part of the computer screen to answer. As needed, practice moving a mouse and clicking to prepare for the test.

Spotlighted Item: HOT SPOT

DIRECTIONS: Study the information and diagram. Then read the question, and answer by marking the appropriate hot spot.

GENOTYPE AND PHENOTYPE

Differing traits, such as different flower colors in pea plants, are related to alleles. Alleles are the two forms of a gene in a gene pair. An organism receives one allele from each parent for each gene. A gene's alleles can be identical or different. Also, alleles can be dominant or recessive. Scientists use symbols such as *PP*, *Pp*, or *pp* to represent the alleles of a gene. A capital letter indicates the dominant allele. If the dominant allele is present, the organism demonstrates the trait associated with that allele. The term *genotype* refers to the makeup of the alleles in a gene pair. The term *phenotype* refers to the observable expression of a particular genotype.

When the genotypes of parents are known, scientists can use Punnett squares to show the potential genotypes of their offspring. On a Punnett square, the genotype of one parent forms column headings, and the genotype of the other parent forms row headings. Each box is filled in with the letters from the corresponding row heading and column heading. The Punnett square below represents the breeding of two pea plants, with *P* representing the allele for purple flower color and *p* representing the allele for white flower color. Scientists can determine the likelihood that two parents will produce offspring with a certain genotype based on the frequency with which that genotype appears in a Punnett square.

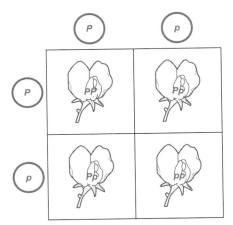

2. Based on the Punnett square, which phenotype is likely to occur in offspring 75 percent of the time? Mark an *X* on the correct phenotype.

Purple flower color   White flower color

DIRECTIONS: Read the passage and question. Then answer by marking the appropriate hot spot or hot spots.

PEDIGREE CHARTS

Scientists use various tools to show genetic inheritance. One tool is a Punnett square. Another tool is a pedigree chart. A pedigree chart is useful for tracking traits through multiple generations.

3. In the pedigree chart, *A* represents the allele for long eyelashes, and *a* represents the allele for short eyelashes. Genotypes for the grandchildren of Fred and Ann are not shown. Mark an *X* on the box for any grandchild who could have short eyelashes.

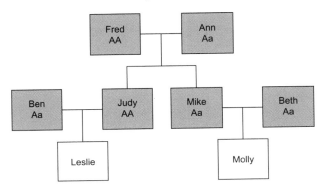

Use Context Clues

SCIENCE CONTENT TOPICS: L.d.3, L.e.3
SCIENCE PRACTICES: SP.1.a, SP.1.b, SP.1.c, SP.3.b, SP.7.a

UNIT 1

1 Learn the Skill

Using context clues helps you understand what you are reading. **Context clues** are hints in surrounding text or visuals about the meaning of a particular word, phrase, or idea. Context clues include restatements of words or phrases and additional details about ideas. You can use context clues to grasp information in scientific material without having to look elsewhere for clarification.

2 Practice the Skill

By practicing the skill of using context clues, you will improve your study and test-taking abilities, especially as they relate to the GED® Science Test. Read the passage below. Then answer the question that follows.

GENETIC VARIATION

a To grasp unfamiliar parts of a text, begin by scanning for words you know that help you identify the topic of the text. The words *chromosomes* and *genes* tell you that the passage relates to inheritance.

Organisms that reproduce sexually differ from one another. Factors causing organisms to develop uniquely include events that occur during meiosis, the cell division process that produces gametes (sex cells).

Because the chromosomes that carry genes occur in pairs, a gene has two forms, or alleles. During meiosis, the chromosomes making up a chromosome pair come together, and their parts may cross over each other. When this happens, DNA strands are broken and rejoined to form new combinations of genes. This process of genetic recombination mixes paternal and maternal genes, contributing to genetic variation.

b Look for clues in the same sentence as a term you do not know. Then look at the sentences around it. Try to determine the meaning of *genetic variation* by examining sentences in the second paragraph.

After paired chromosomes come together, they separate. Each gamete resulting from meiosis contains only one chromosome from each pair and, therefore, only one allele for each gene. This segregation of alleles helps further ensure that an organism produces gametes containing varied genes. Moreover, genes located on different chromosomes act independently from one another. That is, the distribution of one gene's alleles to one gamete or another does not affect the distribution of another gene's alleles. Because of this independent assortment of alleles, the inheritance of one trait typically is not related to the inheritance of another trait. However, two genes located close to each other on a chromosome may stay together during meiosis and be inherited together.

USING LOGIC

Using context clues to determine the meaning of unfamiliar language involves making a logical interpretation based on what you know about a topic. For example, you know that genes produce traits.

1. Based on context clues in the passage, what does **genetic variation** mean?

   A. segregation of alleles to different gametes
   B. differences in traits among individuals
   C. an event that occurs during meiosis
   D. distance between genes on a chromosome

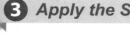

⭐ Spotlighted Item: **HOT SPOT**

DIRECTIONS: Read the passage and question. Then answer by marking the appropriate hot spot or hot spots.

MUTATIONS

Over time, organisms show traits that were not present in previous generations. These new traits occur because of mutations, or changes that result when errors occur during DNA replication. In DNA replication, the two strands of a DNA molecule unwind from their double helix and then unzip from each other. Each single strand becomes a template for a new strand of DNA. Nucleotides move into place to form a new strand of DNA that is complementary to the template DNA. The positioning of nucleotides depends on their bases. For example, where the template DNA has bases CATG, the new DNA will have complementary bases GTAC because C pairs with G and A pairs with T. Sometimes a mistake happens, creating a mutation. Mutations can result from mitosis or meiosis. A mutation formed during meiosis is passed to offspring, creating a new allele for a gene that can be inherited by future offspring.

2. The illustrations represent results of DNA replication. Use context clues from the passage to determine the meaning of **mutation**. Then mark an *X* on any illustration that shows a mutation.

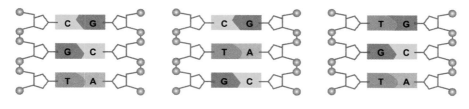

DIRECTIONS: Read the passage. Then read each question, and choose the **best** answer.

EPIGENOME

An organism's genome, or complete set of genetic material, can be influenced by its epigenome, or the set of chemical compounds that affect DNA. These chemical compounds do not change DNA; rather, they regulate the activity of genes. That is, epigenetic marks can turn genes on or off to make a cell function in a certain way. For example, an epigenetic mark in a bone cell may turn off a gene that promotes muscle growth. Unlike a genome, an organism's epigenome can change due to influences such as environmental factors. Specifically, what an organism eats or drinks and what pollutants it encounters can change its epigenome. These changes may be harmless or may have consequences and be passed to offspring.

3. Based on context clues from the passage, what is an **epigenetic mark**?

    A. an environmental factor
    B. an organism's DNA
    C. a genetic mutation
    D. a chemical compound

4. One example of an **environmental factor** is

    A. a chemical compound on DNA.
    B. a gene for blue eyes.
    C. secondhand smoke.
    D. the trait of being double-jointed.

UNIT 1

Understand Scientific Evidence

SCIENCE CONTENT TOPIC: L.f.1
SCIENCE PRACTICES: SP.1.a, SP.1.b, SP.1.c, SP.3.a, SP.3.b, SP.7.a

UNIT 1

1 Learn the Skill

A scientific idea can result from an observation, a series of observations, or a question about the natural world. The idea must be verified through scientific investigation. The idea also must be shown to fit logically with or to refute what is already known. **Scientific evidence** is the set of test results and recorded observations that supports a scientific idea.

Scientific ideas that are supported by evidence are accepted as reliable. When you take steps to **understand scientific evidence**, you increase your knowledge about scientific ideas.

2 Practice the Skill

By practicing the skill of understanding scientific evidence, you will improve your study and test-taking abilities, especially as they relate to the GED® Science Test. Study the information and illustration below. Then answer the question that follows.

COMMON ANCESTRY

a Since Charles Darwin's time, scientists have continued to collect evidence to support the idea of evolution. Keep in mind that you may be reading about only one aspect of the evidence that supports a scientific idea.

b Scientific evidence might involve unfamiliar terms. Look for definitions or context clues in the text to determine the meanings of such terms.

Organisms have developed over many generations through the process of biological evolution. Because organisms have shared ancestors, they have characteristics similar to each other. In his book *On the Origin of Species by Natural Selection*, Charles Darwin noted that the skeletal structures of human, bat, porpoise, and horse forelimbs are similar. As shown in the illustration below, each includes a humerus, a radius, an ulna, carpals, and phalanges. These similar **a** parts are called homologous structures. Homologous structures are one type of evidence used to support the idea of common ancestry. The human, bat, porpoise, and horse forelimbs have different functions, according to the requirements of each organism's lifestyle. Humans lift and grasp, bats fly, porpoises swim, and horses run. However, their **b** homologous structures are evidence of a common ancestor.

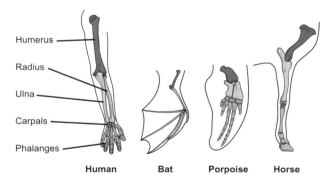

Humerus
Radius
Ulna
Carpals
Phalanges

Human   **Bat**   **Porpoise**   **Horse**

CONTENT TOPICS

Evolutionary theory suggests that all life came from a common ancestor and that, over time, modifications have occurred and are occurring that result in a wide variety of organisms.

1. According to the information, what is one type of evidence scientists use to support the idea that the living things mentioned have a common ancestor?

   A. similar functions of forelimbs
   B. similar lifestyles
   C. similar bone structures
   D. similar habitats

DIRECTIONS: Study the information and illustration, read the question, and choose the **best** answer.

EMBRYONIC DEVELOPMENT

Homologous structures are physical characteristics that are similar in different organisms. In addition to exhibiting homologous structures, organisms may show similarities in their embryonic development. An embryo is an unborn or unhatched animal in its earliest stages. Early on, embryos of different animals can develop almost identically. Human embryos have gill-like structures and tails, which disappear before birth. Embryos of apes, chickens, snakes, and other vertebrates also have structures that are not present when the animal is born or hatches. The illustration shows examples of embryonic development. Similar embryonic development provides evidence that the diverse animals that exist today evolved from a common ancestor.

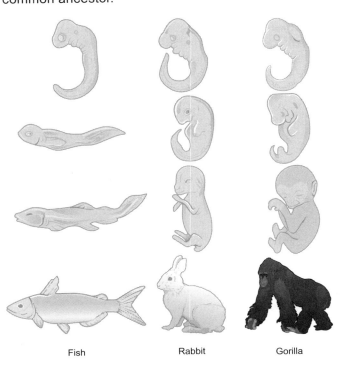

| Fish | Rabbit | Gorilla |

2. According to the passage and illustration, what evidence leads scientists to believe that fish, rabbits, and gorillas have a common ancestor?

   A. They have limbs that perform similar functions.
   B. Their developing embryos have similar structures.
   C. Their bone structures are almost identical.
   D. They each go through four stages of development.

DIRECTIONS: Study the information and diagram, read each question, and choose the **best** answer.

HOW SCIENTISTS USE CLADOGRAMS

To support the idea of evolution, scientists use evidence to determine which traits in living things were present in a common ancestor and which developed later. They use cladograms to organize their findings. On a cladogram, organisms with similar traits are grouped, and the groups are ordered. A common trait represents a characteristic of a common ancestor. The original characteristic is the common trait shared by all the organisms. The first group of organisms on the cladogram has this trait. The next group has not only the original characteristic but also a derived characteristic, or a new trait. Each subsequent group has all the previous traits plus a new derived characteristic. A cladogram has a trunk and branches. The original and derived characteristics are listed along the trunk, and the groups of organisms are listed at the ends of the branches. The cladogram below shows evolutionary relationships among groups of plants.

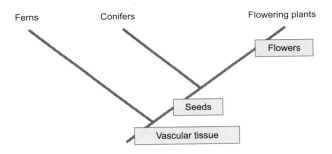

3. Based on the evidence represented by the cladogram, how do conifers differ from ferns?

   A. Conifers do not have vascular tissue.
   B. Conifers are flowering plants.
   C. Conifers have seeds.
   D. Conifers and ferns have no common traits.

4. The cladogram shows that flowering plants have a derived characteristic that developed after conifers came into existence. What does this evidence suggest?

   A. Flowering plants and conifers cannot have a common ancestor.
   B. Flowering plants and conifers probably share no derived characteristics.
   C. Flowering plants may have many derived characteristics that conifers do not have.
   D. Flowering plants must have come into existence after conifers.

Make and Identify Inferences

SCIENCE CONTENT TOPIC: L.f.2
SCIENCE PRACTICES: SP.1.a, SP.1.b, SP.1.c, SP.3.b, SP.3.c, SP.6.c, SP.7.a

UNIT 1

1 Learn the Skill

An **inference** is a logical guess based on facts, evidence, experience, observation, or reasoning. You **make inferences** by thinking critically about the details of material being presented to understand any implied meanings.

It is important not only to make your own inferences but also to **identify inferences** being made in scientific materials. Scientists use facts, evidence, experience, observation, or reasoning to make inferences about natural objects, events, and processes. To gain a full understanding of scientific presentations, you must be able to identify inferences and the details that support those inferences.

2 Practice the Skill

By practicing the skill of making and identifying inferences, you will improve your study and test-taking abilities, especially as they relate to the GED® Science Test. Study the information and illustration below. Then answer the question that follows.

NATURAL SELECTION

a Skills such as comparing and contrasting and identifying cause and effect can help you make inferences. If a helpful trait occurs more often in a population, what might happen to a harmful trait?

b People often make incorrect inferences. To make accurate inferences, avoid over-generalizing.

Individuals within a species have differing traits. In any environment, certain traits are advantageous, whereas others are neutral or detrimental. Individuals having advantageous traits are better able to survive and, therefore, more likely to reproduce. Likewise, individuals having detrimental traits do not survive to reproduce. <u>An advantageous trait that is heritable, or able to be inherited, is passed on to future generations and becomes more common in the population.</u> Natural selection is the process by which individuals best adjusted to an environment survive and reproduce, thereby perpetuating traits best suited to the environment.

Most deer mice are dark brown. However, deer mice living in Nebraska's Sandhills have lighter coats. This feature allows them to hide from predators more easily in the area's light-colored terrain.

USING LOGIC

An inference is an idea that follows logically from information you already have. When making an inference, say to yourself, "If a is true, then b is probably true."

1. Which statement is an inference that can be supported by the information?

   A. Factors in an organism's environment have little effect on its survival.
   B. Heritable detrimental traits occur less often in a population over time.
   C. Natural selection is unrelated to evolutionary change in a species.
   D. All traits that help members of a species are passed on to future generations.

⭐ Spotlighted Item: **DRAG-AND-DROP**

DIRECTIONS: Study the information. Then use the drag-and-drop options to complete the diagram.

DARWIN'S OBSERVATIONS OF POPULATION SIZE

Charles Darwin traveled around the world, observing plants and animals in many different places. He used his observations to make inferences as he developed his theory of evolution.

Observation 1: Resources such as food and shelter are limited in a given ecosystem.
Observation 2: If all individuals in a population reproduce, the population quickly grows out of control.
Observation 3: In most cases, the size of a population stays basically stable over time.

2. Determine which two drag-and-drop options are appropriate inferences based on the observations. Then record those inferences in order in the boxes below.

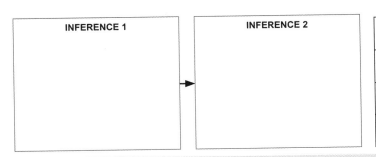

Drag-and-Drop Options

Traits that help individuals acquire and use resources are important to survival.
No two members of a population have identical traits.
An increase in population size must lead to an increase in available resources.
Competition for resources keeps many individuals from surviving to reproduce.

DIRECTIONS: Read the passage and question, and choose the **best** answer.

REQUIREMENTS FOR NATURAL SELECTION

Three factors are needed for natural selection to occur. (1) Organisms within a population must have variation in traits. (2) Differential survivability must exist. That is, certain individuals must have a trait that helps them survive and reproduce in their environment. (3) The beneficial trait must be heritable. Given the criteria, if a certain species of beetle can have a green shell or a brown shell and the beetle's main predator usually eats green beetles, then the heritable trait of a brown shell will become predominant in the population over time.

3. Which statement **best** expresses the information used to support the inference made in the last sentence of the passage?

A. Natural selection can occur only when variation in traits, differential survivability, and heritable advantageous traits exist.
B. The color of an organism's exterior and the preferences of its predator are factors needed for natural selection to occur.
C. Whenever organisms within a population have varying traits, natural selection can occur.
D. When members of a population have a trait that helps them survive in their environment, differential survivability occurs.

UNIT 1

Draw Conclusions

SCIENCE CONTENT TOPIC: L.f.3
SCIENCE PRACTICES: SP.1.a, SP.1.b, SP.1.c, SP.3.a, SP.3.b, SP.6.c, SP.7.a

UNIT 1

1 Learn the Skill

A **conclusion** is a reasoned understanding of something. Often, a conclusion is based on a collection of inferences. Remember that an inference is a logical guess based on facts, evidence, experience, or observations. When you **draw a conclusion**, you make a statement that explains the overall meaning of various pieces of information and inferences you have made.

A valid conclusion conveys an idea that is supported by all available information and accurate inferences. Conclusions can be supported by information presented in text or information presented visually.

2 Practice the Skill

By practicing the skill of drawing conclusions, you will improve your study and test-taking abilities, especially as they relate to the GED® Science Test. Read the passage below. Then answer the question that follows.

SELECTION PRESSURE, ADAPTATION, AND SPECIATION

a To draw a conclusion, make inferences. From this information and what you know, you can infer that selection pressures cause natural selection.

Selection pressures are features of an environment that affect an organism's ability to survive and reproduce in the environment over time. Changes in these pressures, such as climate changes, enable animals having traits suitable to the new environment to flourish and cause others to struggle and possibly even die off.

b From this information, you can infer that adaptations are passed from generation to generation.

Over time, selection pressures and natural selection lead to adaptation. Through adaptation, species develop traits that allow them to respond to certain features of their environment. These traits, or adaptations, can be physical or behavioral.

c From this information, you can infer that adaptation is related to evolution.

Biological evolution is a process of constant change over generations. Because adaptation is ongoing, species change over time. Sometimes populations of a species develop different adaptations in response to different selection pressures. These differences can be substantial enough that the populations eventually become separate species. Formation of a new species is called speciation.

USING LOGIC

Think carefully about what the question is asking. In this case, the question asks for a conclusion. Therefore, the correct answer will not be directly stated in the passage.

1. Which statement is a valid conclusion supported by the passage?

   A. Over time, changing selection pressures affect a species' ability to survive and reproduce in its environment.
   B. Species can develop adaptations that allow them to respond to features of their environments.
   C. Evolution is the result of selection pressures, natural selection, and adaptation.
   D. If populations of a species develop different adaptations, they always become separate species.

Apply the Skill

⭐ Spotlighted Item: **SHORT ANSWER**

DIRECTIONS: Read the passage, and study the table. Then read the question, and write your response on the lines. This task may take approximately 10 minutes to complete.

SIGNIFICANCE OF ADAPTATIONS IN REPTILES

Almost all amphibians must spend part of their lives in an aquatic habitat to survive. One reason is that they must be able to replenish water they lose through their thin, porous skin. Also, their eggs are laid in water and will dry out and die if they do not remain submerged. Reptiles do not lose much water through their skin, and they lay their eggs on land, sometimes in holes they dig. Despite these differences, scientists think that reptiles share a common amphibian ancestor. This ancestor probably lived more than 300 million years ago. Various adaptations arose in generations of reptile ancestors, allowing them to move to drier environments over time. The table contrasts the traits of amphibians and reptiles.

Group	Characteristics
Amphibians	Eggs lacking shells
	Development of lungs and legs following birth
	Moist skin
	Toes lacking claws
Reptiles	Eggs having fluid contained by leathery shells
	Born with lungs and legs
	Scaly skin
	Toes with claws

2. Draw a conclusion about how adaptation has resulted in the ability of reptiles to live in different environments than amphibians. Include support from the passage and table in your response.

_____

_____

_____

_____

_____

_____

_____

_____

_____

_____

_____

_____

_____

DIRECTIONS: Study the graph, read each question, and choose the **best** answer.

The graph shows the growth of one population of living things in a grassland ecosystem.

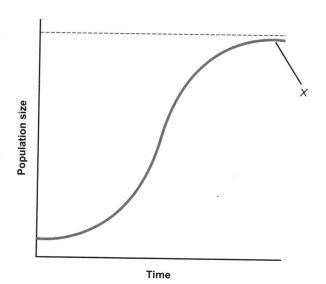

1. What happened to the population at point *X*?

   A. It began to grow more quickly.
   B. It suddenly decreased.
   C. It stopped growing.
   D. It disappeared from the ecosystem.

2. Which statement explains the **most likely** cause for what happened to the population at point *X*?

   A. The ecosystem reached carrying capacity for the population.
   B. A predator of the population was introduced in the ecosystem.
   C. Resources needed by the population became unlimited in the ecosystem.
   D. Adult members of the population were unable to find mates.

3. Suppose that the growth of the population followed the same curve as shown in the graph but the population size at point *X* was smaller. Which factor would be the **most likely** cause?

   A. introduction of a disease
   B. an increase in number of offspring
   C. an unlimited food supply
   D. fewer available resources

DIRECTIONS: Study the information and illustration, read each question, and choose the **best** answer.

The digestive system does the important job of extracting nutrients from food to be absorbed into the blood and carried to cells in the body. The process of digestion breaks down food into its smallest parts so that the body can use them for energy. The illustration shows body parts involved in digestion.

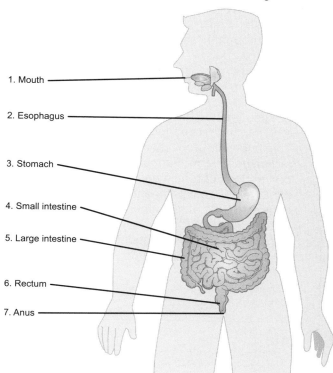

1. Mouth
2. Esophagus
3. Stomach
4. Small intestine
5. Large intestine
6. Rectum
7. Anus

4. Based on the information, what must happen before food mixes with digestive juices in the stomach?

   A. The body must absorb nutrients from the food.
   B. Waste must accumulate in the large intestine.
   C. Waste must pass out of the rectum.
   D. The food must travel through the esophagus.

5. In which part of the digestive system does the absorption of nutrients into the blood occur?

   A. mouth
   B. esophagus
   C. small intestine
   D. rectum

DIRECTIONS: Study the table, read each question, and choose the **best** answer.

ORGANISMS IN A TIDAL ECOSYSTEM

Species	Primary Diet
Clam worm	Zooplankton
Cordgrass	N/A
Herring gull	Soft-shelled clam, smelt
Marsh periwinkle	Cordgrass
Peregrine falcon	Herring gull, snowy egret, short-billed dowitcher
Phytoplankton	N/A
Short-billed dowitcher	Clam worm, marsh periwinkle
Snowy egret	Smelt
Soft-shelled clam	Phytoplankton
Smelt	Zooplankton
Zooplankton	Phytoplankton

6. Based on the information in the table, which simple food chain is **most likely** to occur in the ecosystem?

   A. herring gull → soft-shelled clam → phytoplankton
   B. cordgrass → marsh periwinkle → short-billed dowitcher
   C. peregrine falcon → herring gull → smelt
   D. cordgrass → zooplankton → clam worm

7. What is a likely effect of removing cordgrass from the ecosystem represented by the table?

   A. The populations of marsh periwinkles and short-billed dowitchers would decrease.
   B. All consumers would be eliminated from the ecosystem.
   C. Phytoplankton populations would increase.
   D. Peregrine falcons would have greater food resources.

DIRECTIONS: Read the passage and question, and then answer by marking the appropriate hot spot.

Mitosis is one way in which the cell nucleus divides during the cell division process. The phases of mitosis are prophase, metaphase, anaphase, and telophase. Cytokinesis is the part of the cell division process by which the cytoplasm of the parent cell divides.

8. Cytokinesis occurs concurrently with mitosis over two phases of mitosis. Mark an *X* on the phase of mitosis during which cytokinesis completes.

MITOSIS

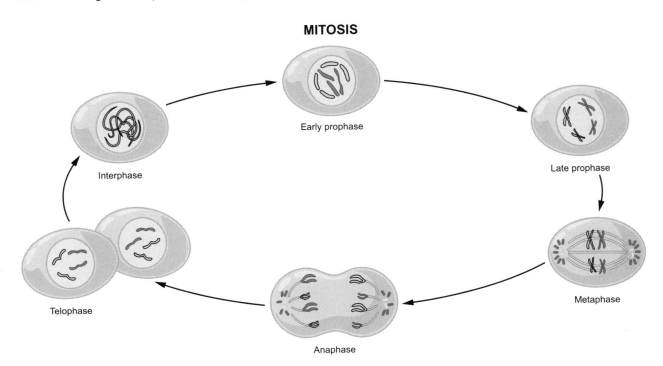

Interphase

Early prophase

Late prophase

Metaphase

Anaphase

Telophase

UNIT 1

DIRECTIONS: Read the passage and question, and choose the **best** answer.

Symbiotic relationships exist between many species in an ecosystem. Three categories of symbiotic relationships are mutualism, commensalism, and parasitism. An example of mutualism is the relationship between bees and flowers. From flowers, bees obtain nectar for food. Bees also carry pollen from flower to flower, allowing the plants to reproduce. Viceroy butterflies and monarch butterflies have a commensalistic relationship. The viceroy mimics the color pattern of the monarch because monarchs contain cardiac glycosides that make them distasteful to birds. Birds avoid monarchs and, by default, viceroys. Fleas are considered parasites of dogs, cats, and other animals. Fleas bite the skin of the animals and suck their blood for nourishment.

9. Which statement accurately contrasts mutualism and commensalism?

   A. Both species benefit in mutualism, whereas only one species benefits in commensalism.
   B. Neither species benefits in mutualism, whereas one species benefits in commensalism.
   C. One species benefits in mutualism, whereas both species benefit in commensalism.
   D. Both species benefit in mutualism, whereas one species benefits while harming the other species in commensalism.

DIRECTIONS: Read the passage. Then read the question, and fill in your answer in the box.

Cystic fibrosis is a genetic disease in humans that causes large amounts of mucous to be secreted in the lungs. People who have two normal alleles of the gene for cystic fibrosis do not have cystic fibrosis. Nor do people who have one normal allele and one mutant allele of the gene. However, people having two mutant alleles of the gene have cystic fibrosis.

10. Which allele of the gene for cystic fibrosis is recessive?

   [   ]

DIRECTIONS: Study the information and table, read each question, and choose the **best** answer.

The main sources of Calories in a person's diet are carbohydrates, proteins, and fats. These nutrients are considered to be macronutrients. Carbohydrates and proteins each provide four Calories per gram. Fats provide nine Calories per gram. The table shows the recommended macronutrient proportions by age based on the percentage of total Calorie intake.

Age Group	Carbohydrate	Protein	Fat
Young children (1–3 years)	45–65%	5–20%	30–40%
Older children and adolescents (4–18 years)	45–65%	10–30%	25–35%
Adults (19 years and older)	45–65%	10–35%	20–35%

Source: United States Department of Agriculture's Center for Nutrition Policy and Promotion

11. What percentage of an adult's Calorie intake should be proteins?

   A. 10 percent to 30 percent
   B. 10 percent to 35 percent
   C. 20 percent to 35 percent
   D. 45 percent to 65 percent

12. Which statement describes a recommendation suggested by the information in the table?

   A. A young child should consume a higher percentage of Calories from fats than from carbohydrates.
   B. An older child or adolescent should consume a higher percentage of Calories from proteins than from carbohydrates.
   C. People in all age groups should consume as few Calories from fats as possible.
   D. Carbohydrates should account for a higher percentage of an adult's total Calorie intake than fats.

13. What conclusion can be drawn based on the information in the table?

   A. Adults burn fat faster than children.
   B. The human body needs fat for growth.
   C. A person should eat the same number of Calories of carbohydrates throughout life.
   D. Fats provide more nutrients than carbohydrates or proteins.

DIRECTIONS: Study the information and table, read each question, and choose the **best** answer.

Different plants and animals live in different ecological communities. In general, the plants and animals in a specific ecological community have adaptations that allow them to survive in that area's climate. As an alternative, an animal might migrate in and out of an area, depending on the range of conditions the animal can withstand. Temperature and amount of rainfall are two of the most important climate factors to which living things must adapt. The table gives information about plants and animals in two types of climate regions.

	Boreal Forest	Tundra
Average yearly temperature range	−40°C to 20°C	−40°C to 18°C
Average yearly precipitation in centimeters (cm)	30 cm to 90 cm	15 cm to 25 cm
General climate description	Long, cold winters and short, cool summers	Very long, cold winters and short, cool summers
Common animals	Moose, coyote, bobcat, elk, porcupine, snowshoe hare	Caribou, lemming, musk ox, ptarmigan, arctic fox, wolf, polar bear
Common plants	Evergreen trees, mosses	Mosses, various flowers and shrubs

14. What inference can be made about how the animals living in boreal forests and tundras are similar?

   A. They have adaptations that allow them to survive in cold weather.
   B. They all require the same amount of water to survive.
   C. They all use tall trees for food and shelter.
   D. None can survive without long periods of warm weather.

15. Which statement describes the use of migration as an adaptation?

   A. Musk oxen have dense, waterproof undercoats and long, coarse outercoats.
   B. Ptarmigans have plumage that is brown in the summer and white in the winter.
   C. Small shrubs preserve warmth by growing low to the ground.
   D. Caribou live in the tundra during the growing season and in the boreal forest during winter.

DIRECTIONS: Study the information, read each question, and choose the **best** answer.

In pea plants, yellow seed color is a dominant trait, and green seed color is a recessive trait. This means that green seed color occurs only if an offspring receives the allele for the recessive trait from both parents. The Punnett square shows the potential genotypes for seed color in the offspring of a cross between two particular pea plants.

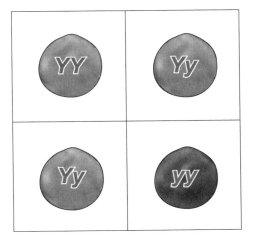

Y = yellow-seed allele
y = green-seed allele

16. What must be true about the genotypes of the parent plants for the trait of seed color?

   A. Neither parent carries the recessive allele.
   B. Both parents carry the recessive allele.
   C. Only one parent carries the dominant allele.
   D. Only one parent carries the recessive allele.

17. What must be true about the phenotypes of the parent plants for the trait of seed color?

   A. Both produce yellow seeds.
   B. Both produce green seeds.
   C. One produces green seeds, and the other produces yellow seeds.
   D. Each produces both green and yellow seeds.

18. What is the probability that the parent plants will produce an offspring with green seeds?

   A. $\frac{1}{8}$

   B. $\frac{1}{4}$

   C. $\frac{1}{2}$

   D. $\frac{3}{4}$

DIRECTIONS: Read the passage and question, and choose the **best** answer.

Once a top predator throughout the southeastern United States, the red wolf nearly vanished due to loss of habitat and human persecution. As a result, a managed breeding program was established in 1973 at Point Defiance Zoo & Aquarium to conserve the remaining red wolves and increase their numbers. The success of the breeding program led to the reintroduction of red wolves in 1987 in the Alligator River National Wildlife Refuge, North Carolina. Red wolves now inhabit a five-county area in northeastern North Carolina, and although their numbers have grown, human caused mortalities, such as gunshot and vehicle strikes, can threaten their survival. The red wolf is one of our planet's most endangered species.

Credit: U.S. Fish and Wildlife Service; RED WOLVES brochure, fws.gov, accessed 2013

19. Which detail from the passage supports the conclusion that the drastic decrease in red wolf numbers resulted from the actions of people?

   A. Red wolves are one of the world's most endangered species.
   B. A program for breeding red wolves was established.
   C. Red wolves were nearly eliminated due to loss of habitat and persecution by humans.
   D. Human-caused deaths, such as vehicle strikes, pose a current threat to red wolves.

DIRECTIONS: Read the passage and question, and choose the **best** answer.

To stay healthy, the human body works to maintain homeostasis. Feedback systems in the body cause it to respond to fluctuating internal conditions by changing in various ways. The purpose for these changes is to ensure that conditions in the body remain stable.

20. Which phrase is **most similar** in meaning to **homeostasis**?

   A. ability to react quickly
   B. tendency toward a balanced state
   C. capacity for fluctuation
   D. condition of being healthy

DIRECTIONS: Read the passage and question, and choose the **best** answer.

For natural selection to occur, three factors are necessary: genetic variability, differential survivability, and inheritability. Consider an example of a population of insects in which some are brown, matching the tree bark on which they live, and others are green. Each successive generation of insects has more brown insects than green insects. The brown insects are more likely to survive because they are camouflaged; therefore, the trait of brown color is naturally selected.

21. Why is inheritability necessary for natural selection to occur?

   A. Differences must exist in the traits of a population of individuals.
   B. Offspring must receive a different allele for the trait of color from each parent.
   C. Individuals must have a trait that helps them survive and reproduce in their environment.
   D. Organisms must be able to pass on a beneficial trait to future generations.

DIRECTIONS: Study the illustration, read the question, and choose the **best** answer.

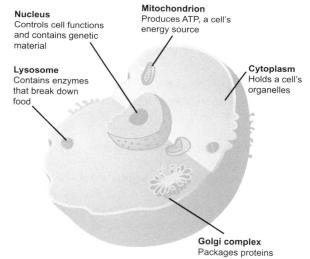

Nucleus Controls cell functions and contains genetic material

Mitochondrion Produces ATP, a cell's energy source

Lysosome Contains enzymes that break down food

Cytoplasm Holds a cell's organelles

Golgi complex Packages proteins

Processes cells must perform are digesting food, making energy, and reproducing.

22. Which part of a cell is involved in the cellular process of making energy?

   A. nucleus
   B. cytoplasm
   C. Golgi complex
   D. mitochondrion

DIRECTIONS: Read the passage and question. Then use the drag-and-drop options to complete the diagram.

A cladogram organizes organisms with similar traits. It is a useful tool for understanding how organisms are related through common ancestors. Cladograms may focus on a very small amount of time and only minor differences or on a period of millions of years and major changes.

23. The cladogram shows how animals diverged at some major turning points in evolution. Determine whether each drag-and-drop option represents a derived characteristic on the cladogram. Then record each animal name in the appropriate part of the cladogram.

Drag-and-Drop Options

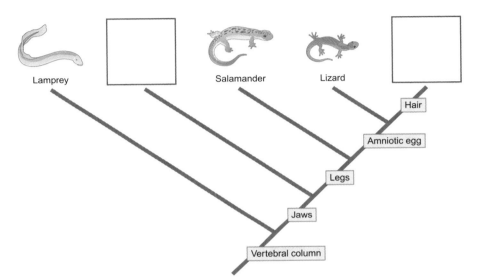

DIRECTIONS: Read the passage and question, and choose the **best** answer.

Dengue fever is an illness caused by one of four related bloodborne viruses. It is spread to humans through the bites of mosquitoes. This form of transmission is known as indirect contact because there is no direct human-to-human contact. Dengue fever is most prevalent in tropic and subtropic regions having warm weather and adequate rainfall—ideal conditions for mosquitoes to thrive. A person with dengue fever experiences a high fever and may experience fatigue, aches, nausea, and vomiting. Using mosquito repellent, wearing protective clothing, and reducing mosquito habitat are precautions that help people avoid contracting dengue fever.

24. Which statement is a valid generalization based on the information in the passage?

A. Recommendations for controlling the spread of dengue fever involve reducing the risk of mosquito bites.
B. Illnesses caused by bloodborne viruses are more likely to occur in tropic or subtropic regions.
C. Someone who has dengue fever must seek medical attention.
D. Diseases transmitted through indirect contact are more dangerous than those transmitted through direct contact.

DIRECTIONS: Read the passage, and study the illustration. Then read the incomplete passage that follows. Use information from the first passage and the illustration to complete the second passage. For each drop-down item, choose the option that **best** completes the sentence.

New traits can occur in a population over time due to mutations. A mutation is caused by an error that occurs during DNA replication and changes a gene. When a cell divides to form new cells, the DNA contained in the cell's chromosomes replicates. In DNA replication, a new strand of DNA is made by new nucleotides that have bases that pair with the bases on the existing strand of DNA. The process of DNA replication is shown in the illustration.

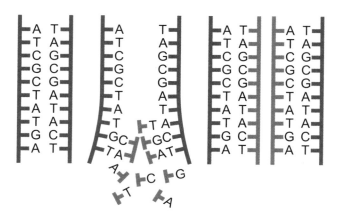

25. The process of DNA replication begins with the unwinding of the double helix and the unzipping of the two strands of DNA. Next, individual [25. Drop-down 1] bind to the nucleotides on an existing strand of DNA. This binding is very specific. Adenine (A) binds only with thymine (T), and cytosine (C) binds only with guanine (G). Sometimes an error occurs during DNA replication, causing [25. Drop-down 2]. An example of this would be the nucleotide base pairing [25. Drop-down 3]. Mutations can result from mitosis or meiosis. A mutation formed during meiosis could create a gene with a new [25. Drop-down 4] that can be passed on to offspring.

Drop-Down Answer Options

25.1 A. double helixes
B. strands
C. nucleotides
D. adenines

25.2 A. a gene
B. a replication
C. a mutation
D. a base pairing

25.3 A. C-A
B. C-G
C. A-T
D. T-A

25.4 A. nucleotide
B. trait
C. cell
D. allele

DIRECTIONS: Read the passage and question, and choose the **best** answer.

Desertification is the degradation of dryland ecosystems due to human activities and climate change. Over time, tree and plant cover is removed through overgrazing and nonsustainable farming practices. Wind and water erosion carry away topsoil, leaving dust and sand behind. Desertification drastically changes ecosystems, and many animals and plants are unable to survive in the new environment.

26. An inference supported by the passage is that desertification results in

A. an increase in production of crops.
B. a loss of biodiversity.
C. an influx of invasive species.
D. an increase in flooding.

DIRECTIONS: Read the passage, and study the illustration. Then read the question, and write your response on the lines. This task may take approximately 10 minutes to complete.

Evolutionary theory suggests that the wide variety of species in existence today came from a common ancestor. Every organism carries evidence of evolutionary change. Some evidence is most visible when an organism is a developing embryo. During their development, the embryos of many organisms pass through stages that look similar to embryonic stages of their ancestors. Scientists study these similarities to determine how species may be related. The illustration shows a chicken embryo and a gorilla embryo.

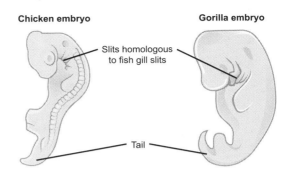

27. Based on the passage and illustration, what evidence exists to support the idea that chickens and gorillas have a common ancestor?

_____

_____

_____

_____

_____

_____

_____

_____

_____

_____

_____

_____

_____

DIRECTIONS: Read the passage and question, and choose the **best** answer.

In multicellular organisms, cells differentiate during reproduction to produce specialized cells. Specialized cells work together to form tissues. Tissues work together to form organs. Organs work together to form body systems. In this way, levels of organization in a multicellular organism become increasingly complex.

28. Which statement explains how an organ and a body system are similar?

A. Their organization is less complex than tissues but more complex than cells.
B. Both are made up of tissues that are made up of cells.
C. They represent the least complex levels of organization in an organism.
D. Both are made up of cells that did not differentiate.

GED® JOURNEYS

Danica Patrick

After obtaining her GED® certificate, winning an Indy Car event, and claiming the pole position at the Daytona 500, Danica Patrick's career is in high gear.

From an early age, Danica Patrick had a need for speed. Patrick, today one of racing's most popular drivers, first developed an interest in auto racing while driving go-karts as a girl. At age 16, Patrick wanted to pursue a career in racing. She left high school, obtained her GED® certificate, and moved to England, where she raced in several open-wheel series. Patrick signed with Rahal Letterman Racing in 2002 and finished third in the Toyota Atlantic Championship two years later.

In May 2005, Patrick became only the fourth woman to drive in the Indianapolis 500 and was named the Indy Racing League's Rookie of the Year. In 2008, Patrick became the first female race winner in IndyCar history with a victory in the Indy Japan 300. The next year, Patrick finished third at the Indianapolis 500, the race's highest ever finish by a woman driver. Patrick notes that science and technology, ranging from fuel strategies to wind drafts, play large roles in her racing success: "Technology provides our pit crews and race strategists with the data they need to make split-second decisions that can make the difference between winning and losing a race."

In 2012, Patrick began competing in the NASCAR Nationwide and Sprint Cup series. In 2013, she became the first female driver to claim the pole position at NASCAR's biggest race, the Daytona 500. She has been featured in national magazines, has appeared in various commercials, and has hosted several television shows.

"Technology provides our pit crews and race strategists with the data they need to make split-second decisions that can make the difference between winning and losing a race."

CAREER HIGHLIGHTS: *Danica Patrick*

- Published her autobiography *Danica: Crossing the Line* in 2006
- Became the first female driver to win an IndyCar event with a victory at the Indy Japan 300 in 2008
- Became the first female driver to claim the pole position at the Daytona 500 in 2013, recording a lap of over 196 miles per hour

Physical Science

Unit 2: Physical Science

From cooking and baking to developing new technologies and on through unlocking the secrets of the universe, physical science literally guides our every move. Physical science is often divided into chemistry (the study of matter) and physics (the study of the relationship between matter and energy).

Physical science is prominent in the GED® Science Test, where it makes up 40 percent of the questions. As with the rest of the GED® Science Test, physical science questions will assess your ability to successfully interpret passages and visuals. In Unit 2, the introduction of certain skills and the reinforcement of others in combination with essential science content will help you prepare for the GED® Science Test.

Table of Contents

A variety of workers, from chemists to physicists to engineers, use physical science at their jobs each day.

Understand Scientific Models

SCIENCE CONTENT TOPIC: P.c.1
SCIENCE PRACTICES: SP.1.a, SP.1.b, SP.1.c, SP.7.a

1 Learn the Skill

Scientific models help clarify complex topics. They can represent objects that are too large or too small to be seen at actual size. Also, they can represent processes that occur too slowly or too quickly to be observed directly. **Understanding scientific models** helps you visualize structures of objects or interpret events in processes to better comprehend a variety of science topics.

Some scientific models are illustrated models, which can be two-dimensional or three-dimensional. Like other graphical representations, an illustrated model may have parts such as a title, a key, and labels. Scientific models also can be expressed as groupings of symbols or as mathematical equations.

2 Practice the Skill

By practicing the skill of understanding scientific models, you will improve your study and test-taking abilities, especially as they relate to the GED® Science Test. Study the information and model below. Then answer the question that follows.

STRUCTURE OF MATTER

Matter is what makes up the observable universe. The elements, such as hydrogen, helium, and iron, are matter. Air, water, and soil are matter. Living things are matter. Manufactured objects are matter.

a To understand a scientific model, first read any text that relates to the model. Then analyze the model to understand what it represents.

Matter is composed of atoms, which are made up of protons, neutrons, and electrons. Protons and neutrons form the nucleus, or small central region, of an atom. The nucleus is surrounded by a larger region where electrons are located.

An element is matter made up of only one type of atom. Each element has a unique number of protons in its atoms. Hydrogen is the simplest element. The nucleus of a hydrogen atom has one proton. The illustrated model shows a hydrogen atom and a helium atom.

b Illustrated models do not show things as they really are. For simplicity, the locations of electrons are represented in the model by rings. However, electrons actually occur in a cloud around an atom's nucleus.

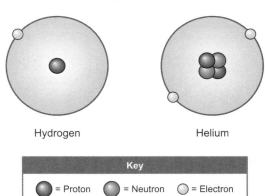

Hydrogen   Helium

Key		
● = Proton	● = Neutron	○ = Electron

CONTENT TOPICS

Every element has a symbol. For example, the symbol for hydrogen is H. The symbol for helium is He. A chemical formula uses these symbols to represent the ways atoms combine to form a type of matter.

1. Based on the model, which statement describes a helium atom?

   A. A helium atom has more protons than electrons.
   B. The nucleus of a helium atom contains protons, neutrons, and electrons.
   C. The number of protons in a helium atom is four.
   D. A helium atom has one more proton than a hydrogen atom.

DIRECTIONS: Study the information and model, read each question, and choose the **best** answer.

MOLECULES

Most matter is a collection of atoms joined through the process of chemical bonding. One way atoms bond is by sharing electrons. A bond formed by sharing electrons is a covalent bond. When two or more atoms share their electrons in covalent bonds, they form a molecule. The illustrated model shows the process of two hydrogen atoms bonding to form a hydrogen molecule.

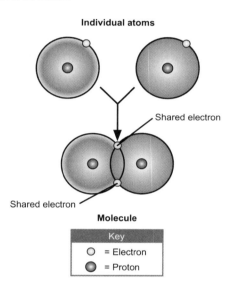

Individual atoms

Shared electron

Shared electron

Molecule

Key	
○	= Electron
●	= Proton

2. Based on the illustrated model, what happens to electrons when two atoms form a covalent bond?

    A. The number of electrons remains the same.
    B. The total number of electrons doubles.
    C. Half the electrons become protons.
    D. The electrons are destroyed.

3. Why is it clear that the atoms represented in the model are hydrogen atoms?

    A. A nucleus is located in the center of each atom.
    B. Each atom has only one proton.
    C. In each atom, the electron moves around the nucleus.
    D. Only hydrogen atoms join to form molecules.

DIRECTIONS: Study the information and model, read the question, and choose the **best** answer.

CHEMICAL COMPOUNDS

An element is composed of only one type of atom. A compound is composed of different types of atoms. Compounds containing covalent bonds are covalent compounds. Ammonia is a covalent compound made up of nitrogen and hydrogen atoms. The model represents an ammonia molecule.

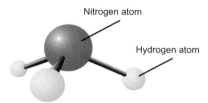

Nitrogen atom

Hydrogen atom

4. What atoms make up the ammonia molecule?

    A. one nitrogen atom and one hydrogen atom
    B. three hydrogen atoms
    C. four ammonia atoms
    D. one nitrogen atom and three hydrogen atoms

DIRECTIONS: Study the information and model, read the question, and choose the **best** answer.

CHEMICAL AND STRUCTURAL FORMULAS

A chemical formula tells the number of atoms of each type in a molecule. The chemical formula for the hydrogen molecule is H_2. H is the symbol for hydrogen; 2 represents the two hydrogen atoms that make up the molecule. A structural formula is a model of a chemical formula. Structural formulas help show the structures of molecules. The structural formula below is for ethane, a compound found in natural gas and made up of hydrogen (H) and carbon (C).

$$\begin{array}{ccc} H & & H \\ | & & | \\ H - C & - C & - H \\ | & & | \\ H & & H \end{array}$$

5. Based on the structural formula, what is the chemical formula of ethane?

    A. CH_3
    B. C_2H_6
    C. H_2C_6
    D. C_2H_4

UNIT 2

Interpret Complex Visuals

SCIENCE CONTENT TOPIC: P.c.2
SCIENCE PRACTICES: SP.1.a, SP.1.b, SP.1.c, SP.3.b, SP.6.c, SP.7.a

UNIT 2

1 Learn the Skill

Illustrations, graphs, and diagrams are visual aids that show relationships between data, ideas, objects, or events. **Complex visuals** show more details than simple illustrations, graphs, or diagrams do. When **interpreting complex visuals**, keep in mind that they may show more than one idea or type of information.

2 Practice the Skill

By practicing the skill of interpreting complex visuals, you will improve your study and test-taking abilities, especially as they relate to the GED® Science Test. Study the complex visual and information below. Then answer the question that follows.

a When studying a complex visual, first read the title and headings to find out the main idea. In this example, the title and headings indicate that molecular spacing is important in defining states of matter.

b Pullout illustrations in this visual represent magnified views of water molecules. Use them to learn the relationship between a state of matter and the arrangement of particles in the matter.

STATES OF MATTER AND MOLECULAR SPACING

Solid	Liquid	Gas
Ice	Liquid water	Water vapor

Molecules packed tightly together in orderly arrangement

Molecules close together in random arrangement

Molecules very far apart in random arrangement

Matter occurs in different states. The basic states of matter are solid, liquid, and gas. The amount of space between particles in a substance and the movements of those particles relate to the substance's state. The visual provides information about the spacing of molecules in different states of matter.

1. Based on the visual, how does the spacing of molecules compare in solids, liquids, and gases?

   A. Gases have the least space between molecules.
   B. Liquids have the most space between molecules.
   C. Solids have the least space between molecules.
   D. The molecules are spaced equally in all states of matter.

USING LOGIC

Use logic to infer relationships represented in a complex visual, based on the arrangement of information. Here, states of matter are shown in order of least to greatest spacing between molecules.

Spotlighted Item: FILL-IN-THE-BLANK

DIRECTIONS: Read the passage, and study the diagram. Then read each question, and fill in your answer in the box.

CHANGES IN STATE

The moving particles in matter cause matter to have energy. When the energy of matter changes, the matter can undergo a change in state. A familiar example of matter changing state is water (a liquid) changing to ice (a solid) or water vapor (a gas). The diagram shows how changes in the amount of energy in a system of matter affect the state of the matter.

RELATIONSHIP BETWEEN ENERGY AND STATE

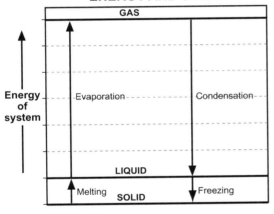

2. According to the diagram, to melt a solid into a liquid or to evaporate a liquid into a gas, must energy be added or released?

3. If enough energy is removed from a liquid, what change of state occurs?

4. The more energy in matter, the faster the particles within the matter move. Based on the diagram, in which state of matter do molecules move the fastest?

UNIT 2

DIRECTIONS: Study the information and graph, read the question, and choose the **best** answer.

HEATING CURVES

In general, when heat is added to a solid, the solid can melt, becoming a liquid. When heat is added to a liquid, the liquid can boil, vaporizing into a gas.

A heating curve provides information about how the temperature of a substance changes as heat is added to it. The heating curve at the right indicates how the temperature of water, in degrees Celsius (°C), changes as energy is added to the water. A heating curve can be used to identify a substance's melting point or boiling point. Melting point is the temperature at which a substance melts. Boiling point is the temperature at which a substance boils.

HEATING CURVE FOR WATER

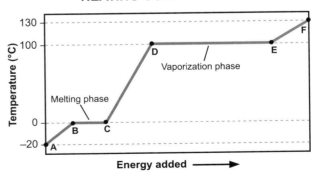

5. Melting and freezing points occur at the same temperature, so liquid water freezes to become ice at

A. −20°C.
B. 0°C.
C. 100°C.
D. 130°C.

Interpret Complex Tables

SCIENCE CONTENT TOPIC: P.c.2
SCIENCE PRACTICES: SP.1.a, SP.1.b, SP.1.c, SP.3.a, SP.3.b, SP.6.a, SP.7.a

1 Learn the Skill

A table is a graphic tool used to display information in an organized and concentrated way. A table that includes several parts or parts organized in a unique way is a **complex table**. For example, a table that has several columns and rows is complex, providing a much greater amount of information than a simple table with two columns and a few rows.

To **interpret a complex table**, you must carefully read the column headings to make sure you know exactly the type of information contained in the table. Also, you might need to examine information outside the columns and rows, such as a key or footnotes that provide additional details.

2 Practice the Skill

By practicing the skill of intepreting complex tables, you will improve your study and test-taking abilities, especially as they relate to the GED® Science Test. Study the information and complex table below. Then answer the question that follows.

PROPERTIES OF MATTER

Each element has unique properties, or traits. Because each element has certain properties, the compounds made up of elements have certain properties. For example, melting point and boiling point are properties. Each compound has its own melting point and boiling point.

a The title indicates that the purpose of this table is to identify boiling points of compounds. However, the column headings tell you that the table provides other information as well.

BOILING POINTS OF SELECT COMPOUNDS

Compound	Formula	Type of Compound	Boiling Point (°C)
Sodium chloride	NaCl	Ionic	1,413
Hydrogen fluoride	HF	Covalent	20
Hydrogen sulfide	H_2S	Covalent	−61
Calcium iodide	CaI_2	Ionic	1,100
Magnesium fluoride	MgF_2	Ionic	2,239

b Typically, all entries in one column of a table give a certain kind of information. Individual entries in each row are related to the entry in the far left column.

c A complex table might use common abbreviations without identifying those abbreviations in a key. This table uses an abbreviation to indicate that boiling point is in degrees Celsius (°C).

TEST-TAKING TIPS

You may need to use different parts of a table to answer a question. Here, you need to look at two columns of data to find the highest boiling point and the chemical formula of the associated compound.

1. Based on the information in the table, which compound boils at the highest temperature?

A. NaCl
B. HF
C. CaI_2
D. MgF_2

Spotlighted Item: **HOT SPOT**

DIRECTIONS: Read the passage and question, and answer by marking the appropriate hot spot or hot spots.

PHYSICAL PROPERTIES

Properties of matter can be physical properties or chemical properties. A physical property can be observed or measured without changing the chemical makeup of the matter. Examples are color, boiling point, and ability to conduct heat. Elements can be grouped according to shared physical properties. For example, certain properties distinguish metals from other elements. Most metals can be pulled into a wire or flattened into a sheet, and most conduct electricity and heat as solids or liquids.

2. A scientist investigates the properties of substances to determine which are metals and records observations in a table. As the scientist would, mark an *X* in the appropriate place on the table to identify any substance that is a metal.

INVESTIGATION OF FOUR SUBSTANCES

Substance	Properties	Metal? Yes	Metal? No
A	Clear; does not conduct electricity or heat well		
B	Gray; conducts electricity and heat		
C	Gray; conducts electricity and heat		
D	Yellow; breaks easily; does not conduct electricity		

DIRECTIONS: Study the information and table, read the question, and choose the **best** answer.

EXTENSIVE AND INTENSIVE PROPERTIES

Physical properties can be extensive or intensive, and many physical properties are measurable. Mass and volume are extensive properties. Mass is a measurement of the amount of matter an object has. Volume is a measurement of how much space a quantity of matter occupies. Density is an intensive property. It is a measurement of how much matter is in a certain volume. The table lists examples of extensive and intensive properties.

TYPES OF PHYSICAL PROPERTIES

Extensive Properties*	Intensive Properties**
Mass, volume, length	Color, taste, melting point, boiling point, density, luster, hardness

*Properties that change depending on sample size
**Properties that do not change depending on sample size

3. Which property changes with sample size?

A. hardness
B. melting point
C. length
D. taste

DIRECTIONS: Study the information and table, read the question, and choose the **best** answer.

CHEMICAL PROPERTIES

A chemical property is observed only when a chemical change to matter occurs. Chemical change requires a chemical reaction. In chemical reactions, the particles of substances are rearranged to form new substances. In contrast, a physical change is a change that does not result in a new substance being formed.

CHEMICAL AND PHYSICAL CHANGES

Material	Change	Observation
Candle	Melted Burned	Solid candle became liquid wax. Candle seemed to disappear.
Silver	Melted Tarnished	Solid silver became liquid silver. Silver developed a dark-colored coating on it.
Paper	Torn Burned	A large piece of paper became smaller pieces. Paper became ashes and smoke.

4. Based on information from the passage and table, which statement supports the conclusion that a chemical reaction occurs when silver tarnishes?

A. Solid silver can become liquid silver.
B. The dark coating is a new substance.
C. Silver can be melted or tarnished.
D. No new substances are formed.

UNIT 2

Understand Chemical Equations

SCIENCE CONTENT TOPICS: P.a.2, P.c.3
SCIENCE PRACTICES: SP.1.a, SP.1.b, SP.1.c, SP.7.a

1 Learn the Skill

Chemical equations use words, symbols, or other components to represent chemical reactions. The parts of a chemical equation identify the elements or compounds involved in a particular reaction.

When you **understand chemical equations**, you can identify the substances involved in chemical reactions. You can distinguish different types of chemical reactions as well. An understanding of chemical equations also reinforces your grasp of an important scientific concept—conservation of mass.

2 Practice the Skill

By practicing the skill of understanding chemical equations, you will improve your study and test-taking abilities, especially as they relate to the GED® Science Test. Read the passage below. Then answer the question that follows.

CHEMICAL REACTIONS

In chemical reactions, substances combine to form new substances. The substances that combine are reactants. The substances formed are products. Also, energy may be absorbed (endothermic reaction) or released (exothermic reaction). New substances are produced during chemical reactions because the atoms making up the reactants bond in new ways. This change in the ways the atoms bond changes the chemical makeup of the matter involved.

Many substances react chemically with each other to form new substances. For example, many elements react to produce compounds. Many compounds react to produce other compounds. A chemical reaction can be represented in the following ways:

Magnesium	+	Oxygen	→	Magnesium oxide
2Mg	+	O_2	→	2MgO

a Here, the same chemical equation is represented with words, symbols, and models. Always, the reactants are on the left, the product is on the right, and an arrow meaning "yields" separates the two sides.

b The version using symbols shows the chemical formulas of the reactants and the product. The version using models is explained by a key.

Key	
●	Magnesium atom (Mg)
○	Oxygen atom (O)
○─○	Oxygen molecule (O_2)
●─○	Magnesium oxide molecule (MgO)

TEST-TAKING TIPS

If a test item uses language that is new to you, review the information in any associated passage or visual element to ensure that you understand exactly what the item is asking.

1. Which statement describes the chemical reaction represented by the three versions of the chemical equation?

    A. Magnesium oxide is a reactant in the reaction.
    B. Magnesium is a product of the reaction.
    C. Oxygen is a product of the reaction.
    D. Magnesium oxide is the product of the reaction.

UNIT 2

DIRECTIONS: Study the information and diagram, read the question, and choose the **best** answer.

LAW OF CONSERVATION OF MASS AND BALANCED CHEMICAL EQUATIONS

During a chemical reaction, the arrangement of atoms in the matter involved changes. However, the total number of each type of atom does not change. This scientific concept is the law of conservation of mass.

A balanced chemical equation reflects the law of conservation of mass and provides accurate quantitative information about a chemical reaction. It tells not only the way that atoms are rearranged during the reaction but also the relative amounts of the substances that make up the reactants and products.

An equation is balanced when the number of atoms of each type on one side equals the number of atoms of each type on the other side. The diagram identifies the parts of a balanced chemical equation. The equation represents the reaction of methane (CH_4) and oxygen (O_2) to produce carbon dioxide (CO_2) and water (H_2O).

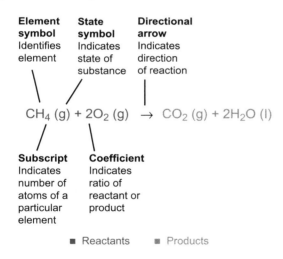

2. Which statement conveys information provided by the equation?

   A. The reactants are a gas and a liquid.
   B. The proportion of carbon dioxide molecules to water molecules produced is 1:2.
   C. The products contain fewer atoms of hydrogen than the reactants.
   D. The products represented can react with each other to form the reactants represented.

DIRECTIONS: Read the passage and question, and choose the **best** answer.

TYPES OF REACTANTS

Different types of chemical reactions occur. In synthesis, two or more reactants combine to form a single product. The general form equation for this reaction type is A + B → AB. In decomposition, a single reactant forms two or more products (AB → A + B). In single displacement, one element replaces another in a compound (AB + C → AC + B). In double displacement, two reactants form two new products (AB + CD → AD + CB).

3. In the general form equation for a single displacement reaction, what does AC represent?

   A. an atom
   B. an element
   C. a reactant
   D. a product

DIRECTIONS: Read the passage and question, and choose the **best** answer.

LIMITING REACTANTS

Depending on the amount of each reactant involved in a chemical reaction, a limiting reactant can exist. A limiting reactant limits the amount of product that can be formed because the reaction stops when all the limiting reactant is consumed. Consider the equation that represents the reaction of benzene (C_6H_6) and oxygen (O_2) to produce carbon dioxide (CO_2) and water (H_2O):

$$2C_6H_6 + 15O_2 \rightarrow 12CO_2 + 6H_2O$$

As with any reaction, depending on the amounts of certain substances involved, the reaction represented by the equation can be limited.

4. Which statement describes the potential role of a limiting reactant in the reaction represented by the equation?

   A. The amount of carbon dioxide may limit the amount of benzene that can be formed.
   B. Either carbon dioxide or water may limit the amount of product that can be formed.
   C. Either benzene or oxygen may limit the amount of product that can be formed.
   D. Whenever benzene and oxygen combine, the reaction will have a limiting factor.

Predict Outcomes

SCIENCE CONTENT TOPIC: P.c.4
SCIENCE PRACTICES: SP.1.a, SP.1.b, SP.1.c, SP.3.b, SP.3.c, SP.3.d, SP.7.a

① Learn the Skill

An **outcome** is the result that occurs when someone manipulates factors in a scientific investigation. In other words, the investigator asks, "What will happen if I do this?" The answer is the outcome. An outcome also can be the effect that is observed when certain factors apply to a situation.

Scientists use their knowledge base to predict what will happen when they mix materials or cause certain events to occur. By learning about science topics, such as the chemical properties of substances and variables that affect those properties, you can **predict outcomes**, too.

② Practice the Skill

By practicing the skill of predicting outcomes, you will improve your study and test-taking abilities, especially as they relate to the GED® Science Test. Read the passage below. Then answer the question that follows.

SOLUTIONS

A solution is formed when at least one substance dissolves in another substance. A substance that dissolves is a solute. A substance in which a solute dissolves is a solvent.

a Scientists analyze patterns in observations and data to make generalizations. You can predict outcomes by using established generalizations or by analyzing patterns yourself.

For a mixture of substances to be a solution, it must be homogeneous. A mixture is homogeneous if the molecules of the substances making up the mixture are distributed evenly within it. Because a solution is a homogeneous mixture, all samples of a solution contain the same percentages of solute and solvent and, therefore, have the same properties. Air is a familiar example of a solution. Oxygen and other gases dissolve in nitrogen to form air. Any sample of air contains the same percentages of oxygen, nitrogen, and the other gases involved as any other sample of air.

b The rules of solubility are generalizations that can be used to predict outcomes. →

Some chemical compounds are more soluble, or susceptible to being dissolved, than others. <u>The rules of solubility provide information about which compounds are soluble or insoluble in water.</u> For example, compounds formed from the alkali metals, such as lithium, sodium, and potassium, are soluble. A substance is classified as soluble if more than 0.1 gram (g) of the substance dissolves in 100 milliliters (ml) of solvent.

CONTENT PRACTICES

Making predictions based on data is an important science practice addressed by the GED® Test. Mastering the skill will improve your chances for success.

1. Sodium chloride is a compound formed from the ionic bonding of sodium and chlorine. What outcome can be predicted when 0.5 g sodium chloride is mixed with 100 ml water?

   A. The substance that is produced will not be a solution.
   B. A new chemical compound will be formed.
   C. The sodium chloride will dissolve in the water to form a solution.
   D. Different parts of the substance formed will have different properties.

UNIT 2

DIRECTIONS: Read the passage and question, and choose the **best** answer.

CONCENTRATION AND SATURATION

A solution can be described by its concentration, or relative amount of solute. A dilute solution contains a relatively smaller ratio of solute to solvent. A concentrated solution contains a relatively larger ratio of solute to solvent. As more solute is dissolved in a solvent, a solution becomes more concentrated. Eventually, no more solute will dissolve. Solubility is the amount of solute that can be dissolved in a given amount of solvent at a specific temperature. Saturation is the point at which no more solute can be dissolved at the current temperature.

2. A student dissolves 32 g sucrose (table sugar) in 750 ml water. He then adds 250 ml water to the solution. What outcome can be predicted?

   A. The solution will be more concentrated.
   B. The solution will be more dilute.
   C. The solution will be saturated.
   D. The concentration will remain unchanged.

DIRECTIONS: Study the graph, read the question, and choose the **best** answer.

EFFECT OF TEMPERATURE ON SALT SOLUBILITIES

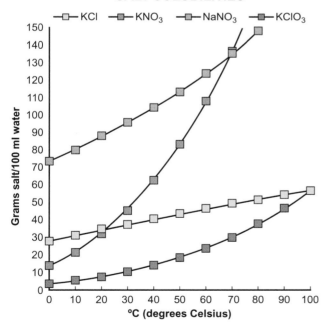

3. A saturated solution of potassium chlorate ($KClO_3$) dissolved in water is heated from 0°C to 100°C. What outcome can be predicted?

   A. The solution will no longer be saturated.
   B. The solubility will remain unchanged.
   C. The ratio of solute to solvent will change.
   D. The solution will become more concentrated.

DIRECTIONS: Read the passage. Then read each question, and choose the **best** answer.

CATEGORIES OF SOLUTIONS

Solutions form in different ways, depending on the solutes and solvents involved. Solutions can be categorized based on what occurs when the solute dissolves.

Some solutes retain their molecular structure when they dissolve in aqueous solutions (solutions for which the solvent is water). For example, when sucrose dissolves in water, the relatively weak bonds between the sucrose molecules are broken, and the individual sucrose molecules bond with water molecules.

Other solutes dissociate into ions, or ionize, in aqueous solutions. For example, when the salt sodium chloride (NaCl) is dissolved in water, the ionic bonds of the compound are broken, and the individual ions (Na^+ and Cl^-) are released into solution. Acids, bases, and salts are compounds that ionize when dissolved in water. Acids ionize to form H^+ (hydrogen ions), and bases ionize to form particles that bond with H^+. A strong acid or base ionizes completely; a weak acid or base ionizes only partially.

4. Hydrochloric acid is a strong acid. It would be expected

   A. to be insoluble in water.
   B. to ionize completely in solution.
   C. to retain its molecular structure in solution.
   D. to dissociate partially into ions in solution.

5. Which equation represents the outcome that occurs when an acid is dissolved in water?

   A. $LiBr \rightarrow Li^+ + Br^-$
   B. $NaOH \rightarrow Na^+ + OH^-$
   C. $KI \rightarrow K^+ + I^-$
   D. $HBr \rightarrow H^+ + Br^-$

Calculate to Interpret Outcomes

SCIENCE CONTENT TOPIC: P.b.1
SCIENCE PRACTICES: SP.1.a, SP.1.b, SP.1.c, SP.7.b, SP.8.b

1 Learn the Skill

Scientific texts often include graphic elements (or visuals) with numerical values on them. These numerical values can be used to find other values. For example, a diagram that includes values for the time it takes a person to travel a specific distance can be used to calculate that person's speed.

Based on the information they provide, visuals with numerical values can be used to find values such as speed, velocity, or acceleration. When you use this process, you **calculate to interpret outcomes**.

2 Practice the Skill

By practicing the skill of calculating to interpret outcomes, you will improve your study and test-taking abilities, especially as they relate to the GED® Science Test. Study the information and diagram below. Then answer the question that follows.

DISTANCE, SPEED, AND DISPLACEMENT

a This text provides information about calculation. It states that to calculate average speed, you divide distance by time: $s = \frac{d}{t}$.

Distance, speed, and displacement are quantities used to describe the motion of objects. Distance is a measure of the space between two positions. Speed is a measure of how fast an object moves. Average speed is calculated by dividing the distance that the object moved by the time required for the movement. Displacement describes an object's net change in position in both distance and direction.

A commuter uses a scooter to travel 4 miles to work each day. The commuter's route is a straight route east to her job and then a direct route home. The diagram below can help you determine her average speed during a one-way trip to work.

b The question asks you to calculate to interpret an outcome. To calculate speed, use data from the diagram to find numbers for distance and time.

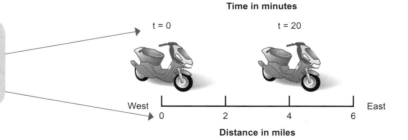

Time in minutes
t = 0   t = 20

West   0   2   4   6   East

Distance in miles

1. What is the commuter's average speed in miles per hour (mi/hr) during her one-way trip to work?

   A. 4 mi/hr
   B. 6 mi/hr
   C. 12 mi/hr
   D. 20 mi/hr

DIRECTIONS: Study the information and diagram, read each question, and choose the **best** answer.

SPEED AND VELOCITY

Average speed can be calculated by dividing distance traveled by the time required to travel that distance. The direction of travel is unimportant in calculating speed. However, direction is important in calculating velocity. An object's velocity is its total displacement divided by the amount of time the object is in motion. Therefore, if an object's motion returns it to its starting point, it has an average velocity of zero, even if it was traveling at high speed the whole time.

Velocity is a measurement of the rate at which an object changes its position. It is not enough to say that an object is traveling at 60 mi/hr. Velocity is expressed in units of speed and direction, such as 60 mi/hr west. The only exception to this is when velocity is zero. In this case, a direction is not specified.

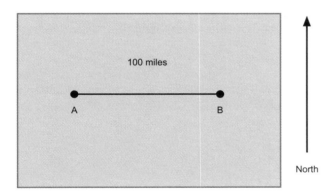

North

2. A bird flies from Point A to Point B in 5 hours. What is its approximate speed and velocity?

   A. speed: 5 mi/hr; velocity: 5 mi/hr north
   B. speed: 10 mi/hr; velocity: 10 mi/hr east
   C. speed: 20 mi/hr; velocity: 20 mi/hr east
   D. speed: 50 mi/hr; velocity: 50 mi/hr north

3. A bird flies from Point A to Point B, and then from Point B back to Point A. The trip takes 10 hours. What is the bird's average velocity for the whole trip?

   A. 0 mi/hr
   B. 10 mi/hr west
   C. 20 mi/hr
   D. 50 mi/hr north

DIRECTIONS: Study the information and graph, read each question, and choose the **best** answer.

ACCELERATION

Acceleration is a value used to describe motion. It is a change in an object's velocity over time. The formula for acceleration, then, is $\frac{d/t}{t}$, where d is distance and t is time. Acceleration might be negative (as when something is slowing down) or positive (as when something is speeding up).

An object's change in velocity over time has been plotted on the graph below. From information in the graph, the object's acceleration during specific intervals can be calculated and expressed in meters per second per second (m/s/s), which is the same as meters per second squared (m/s^2).

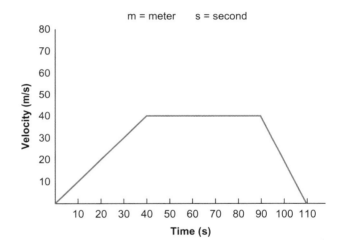

4. Which statement describes the object's acceleration between 0 and 40 seconds?

   A. It is increasing at a steady rate.
   B. It is constant.
   C. It is decreasing at a steady rate.
   D. It is increasing and then decreasing.

5. What happens to the object's motion at 90 seconds?

   A. Constant velocity turns to positive acceleration.
   B. Velocity stops and then increases rapidly.
   C. Increasing velocity turns to acceleration.
   D. Constant velocity turns to negative acceleration.

Understand Vector Diagrams

SCIENCE CONTENT TOPIC: P.b.2
SCIENCE PRACTICES: SP.1.a, SP.1.b, SP.1.c, SP.7.a, SP.7.b

❶ Learn the Skill

Vectors are quantities that have direction and magnitude, such as forces. In **vector diagrams**, arrows show the direction and magnitude, or strength, of such quantities. **Understanding vector diagrams** enables you to represent and analyze the magnitudes and directions of forces.

❷ Practice the Skill

By practicing the skill of understanding vector diagrams, you will improve your study and test-taking abilities, especially as they relate to the GED® Science Test. Study the information and diagram below. Then answer the question that follows.

a The passage explains what forces are and how they are measured. Forces are vectors because they have magnitude and direction.

b The question asks you to make assumptions about the strengths of the forces shown. In vector diagrams, the longer or thicker the arrow, the greater the magnitude of the force.

NEWTON'S FIRST LAW AND VECTORS

A force is a push or a pull on an object that results from its interaction with another object. A force can start, stop, or change the speed or direction of the motion of the object. In the 1600s, Isaac Newton developed three laws of motion that explain how forces affect the motion of objects. Newton's first law of motion states that an object at rest tends to stay at rest and an object in motion tends to stay in motion unless acted on by an unbalanced force. A force can be measured in newtons (N) and is described by both its magnitude and its direction, as in "10 N downward."

Vector diagrams can be used to show the magnitudes and directions of forces. The diagram shows four objects of equal mass at rest and a force that is acting on each of them. One of the forces is a pulling force; the others are pushing forces.

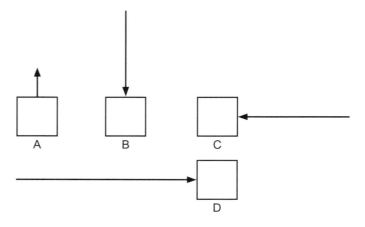

TEST-TAKING TIPS

The arrows in a vector diagram are a visual representation of direction and magnitude; therefore, they do not always include numbers. When in doubt about relative magnitudes, measure the arrows.

1. The magnitudes of the forces shown in the diagram are 2 N, 7 N, 9 N, and 15 N. Which force has a magnitude of 7 N?

   A. Force A
   B. Force B
   C. Force C
   D. Force D

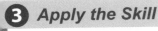

DIRECTIONS: Study the information and diagram, read each question, and choose the **best** answer.

NEWTON'S SECOND LAW AND VECTORS

Newton's second law of motion states that the net force on an object equals the mass of the object multiplied by the object's acceleration. This can be written as $F = ma$, where F represents the net force, m represents the object's mass, and a represents the object's acceleration. The diagram below represents the second law of motion and shows the object's mass in kilograms (kg) and its acceleration in meters per second squared (m/s^2).

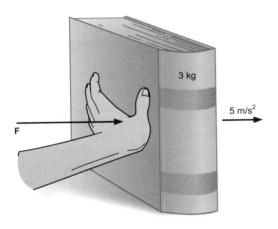

2. The diagram shows a force being applied toward the right. How much force is being applied?

   A. 0.6 N
   B. 3 N
   C. 8 N
   D. 15 N

3. If a person were to apply the same force to move a book having a greater mass, how would the arrows representing the vectors for force and acceleration change in the diagram?

   A. The arrow showing force would be shorter, and the arrow showing acceleration would be longer.
   B. The arrow showing force would not change, and the arrow showing acceleration would be shorter.
   C. The arrow showing force would not change, and the arrow showing acceleration would be longer.
   D. The arrow showing force would be longer, and the arrow showing acceleration would be shorter.

DIRECTIONS: Study the Information and diagram, read each question, and choose the **best** answer.

NEWTON'S THIRD LAW AND VECTORS

Newton's third law of motion states that for every force there is an equal and opposite force. For example, when a person stands on the floor, the person's weight pushes down on the floor. To hold the weight, the floor pushes up on the person's feet with an equal and opposite force.

In the diagram below, the person has a mass of 50 kg. The force he exerts on the floor is equal to his weight. Near Earth's surface, an object's weight is equal to its mass in kilograms times 9.8. Therefore, the force the person exerts is 50 kg x 9.8, or 490 N.

4. What is the value of F_n?

   A. 9.8 N
   B. 19.6 N
   C. 50 N
   D. 490 N

5. What is the value of F_n for a person who has a mass of 65 kg?

   A. 9.8 N
   B. 65 N
   C. 637 N
   D. 1,274 N

Apply Scientific Laws

SCIENCE CONTENT TOPICS: P.b.1, P.b.2
SCIENCE PRACTICES: SP.1.a, SP.1.b, SP.1.c, SP.6.c, SP.7.a, SP.7.b, SP.8.b

1 Learn the Skill

A **scientific law** is a statement that describes how matter and energy behave. In physical science, most laws can be expressed as a mathematical equation. For example, Newton's second law of motion describes the relationship between force, mass, and acceleration. The equation for this law is: $F = ma$.

When you **apply a scientific law**, you identify situations that illustrate the law. You can then use the scientific law to make predictions about such situations.

2 Practice the Skill

By practicing the skill of applying scientific laws, you will improve your study and test-taking abilities, especially as they relate to the GED® Science Test. Study the information and diagram below. Then answer the question that follows.

UNIT 2

LAW OF UNIVERSAL GRAVITATION

a When reading about scientific laws, consider what you already know about those laws.

b The passage provides information needed for answering questions about the relationship between gravity and distance.

The law of universal gravitation states that the force of gravity between two objects is directly proportional to the product of their masses and inversely proportional to the square of the distance between their centers. So the more mass two objects have together, the greater the gravitational force between them is. The greater the distance between two objects, the smaller the gravitational force between them is. The force of gravity is the same as "weight," which is different from mass. An object's mass is the amount of matter contained by the object. In calculations of gravitational force, an object's mass does not change, but its weight does.

The diagram shows the distance in kilometers (km) between a rocket and Earth's center at different points in time—before liftoff and sometime after liftoff. The mass of the rocket remains the same, but its weight—the measure of Earth's gravity acting on the rocket—changes.

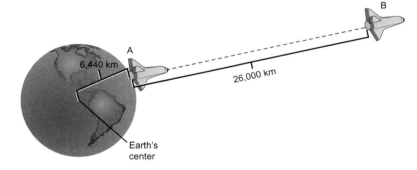

TEST-TAKING TIPS

When using data from diagrams or descriptions, be mindful of whether the value is a plus or a minus value. This is especially important for quantities that have direction as well as magnitude.

1. Which statement describes the force of Earth's gravity on the rocket in the diagram?

   A. It no longer exists at Point B.
   B. It is smaller at Point A than Point B.
   C. It is greater at Point A than Point B.
   D. It is the same at Point A and Point B.

Spotlighted Item: **DRAG-AND-DROP**

DIRECTIONS: Read the passage and question. Then use the drag-and-drop options to match each scenario with the law that applies to it.

APPLYING NEWTON'S LAWS

Newton's law of universal gravitation states that all objects are attracted to one another by a force directly related to their masses and inversely related to their distance from each other. Newton also formulated three universal laws of motion. Newton's first law of motion states that all objects at rest remain at rest unless acted on by an outside force. Conversely, all objects in motion maintain the same motion unless an outside force acts on them. Newton's second law of motion states that the change in momentum of a body depends on the amount and direction of the force acting on it. So the greater the mass of an object, the more force must be applied to alter its speed or direction. Newton's third law states that for every action there is an equal and opposite reaction. Therefore, for any force, there is an equal reaction force acting in the opposite direction.

2. Apply Newton's laws to real-world scenarios. Determine which drag-and-drop option applies to each scenario. Then record the name of each law in the appropriate box.

Scenario A. Astronauts orbiting miles above Earth's surface in the International Space Station can bounce around the cabin in a weightless state that would be impossible on Earth.	
Scenario B. A rocket fires its engines, creating a great force downward against Earth's surface. It eventually lifts off into the atmosphere.	
Scenario C. Two sisters, one 5 years old and the other 14 years old, kick balls of equal size. The 5-year-old's ball rolls about 10 feet. The 14-year-old's ball flies through the air and lands 40 feet away.	
Scenario D. A box sitting on the passenger seat of a car flies forward into the dashboard when the car suddenly stops.	

Drag-and-Drop Options

first law of motion
second law of motion
third law of motion
law of universal gravitation

DIRECTIONS: Read the passage and question, and choose the **best** answer.

LAW OF MOMENTUM CONSERVATION

Momentum can be calculated by using the equation $p = mv$, where p is momentum, m is mass, and v is velocity. The law of momentum conservation states that the momentum of a system is constant if no external force acts on the system. This means that the total momentum stays the same when two bodies collide.

Consider two supermarket carts. A full cart with a mass of 35 kilograms (kg) is shoved toward the east at 2 meters per second (m/s.) An empty cart with a mass of 10 kg is pushed toward the west at 3 m/s.

Based on the formula $p = mv$, the full cart's momentum is (35 kg) • (+2 m/s), or +70 kg • m/s, with the plus sign meaning it is moving east. The empty cart's momentum is (10 kg) • (−3 m/s), or −30 kg • m/s, with the minus sign meaning it is moving west. Adding the quantities gives the total momentum of the system (both carts) as +40 kg • m/s.

3. If the momentum of the full cart after the collision is +26.25 kg • m/s, what is the momentum of the empty cart after the collision?

A. 26.25 kg • m/s moving west
B. 13.75 kg • m/s moving east
C. 26.25 kg • m/s moving east
D. 1.375 kg • m/s moving west

Access Prior Knowledge

SCIENCE CONTENT TOPIC: P.b.3
SCIENCE PRACTICES: SP.1.a, SP.1.b, SP.1.c, SP.7.a, SP.7.b

UNIT 2

1 Learn the Skill

Prior knowledge is the knowledge you already have about a topic. You acquire knowledge about a topic through formal learning and personal experiences. Because everything you see and do involves science, you probably know more about science than you realize. When you **access your prior knowledge** related to a science topic, you learn new information about the topic more easily.

2 Practice the Skill

By practicing the skill of accessing prior knowledge, you will improve your study and test-taking abilities, especially as they relate to the GED® Science Test. Study the information and diagram below. Then answer the question that follows.

a Read the title to identify the topic of the text, and then consider what you know about the topic. What have you learned about forces? How have you used machines to do work?

→ **WORK, FORCES, AND MACHINES**

In science, work is done when a force moves an object. No work is done if an object does not move, even if a force is applied. Machines make work easier by changing the size or direction of the force needed to do work.

A simple machine is a basic tool used to make work easier. When a simple machine is used, the input force is smaller than or moves in a different direction from the output force. The input force is the force exerted on the simple machine. The output force is the force exerted by the simple machine. The six types of simple machines are lever, wedge, inclined plane, pulley, screw, and wheel and axle. The diagram shows how a lever can be used to lift a box.

b Science topics are interrelated. You have learned how vector diagrams use arrows to show the sizes and directions of forces. Use this knowledge to understand the science content presented here.

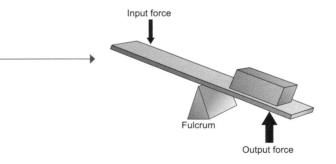

Input force

Fulcrum

Output force

TEST-TAKING TIPS

Your ability to answer any science question correctly increases if you access prior knowledge about science. You also might have to use your knowledge of other areas, such as math.

1. Which statement describes the advantage of using a lever to move an object?

   A. The direction of the force is the same when using your arms or a lever.
   B. The size of the input force equals the size of the output force.
   C. A lever changes the size and direction of the applied force.
   D. No work is needed to move the object on the lever.

★ Spotlighted Item: **HOT SPOT**

DIRECTIONS: Read the information and question. Then answer by marking the appropriate hot spot or hot spots.

USING A WEDGE

A wedge is a type of simple machine. Wedges are commonly used to split objects apart. The head of an ax is a wedge. The input force applied at the base of a wedge is distributed along its angled sides. When a force is applied to an ax, the sides of the ax blade push outward on the wood. The outward force causes the wood to split.

2. Where does output force occur when a wedge is used? In the diagram, mark an *X* on any vector arrow that represents an output force.

UNIT 2

DIRECTIONS: Read the passage and question, and choose the **best** answer.

MEASURING WORK

Work is done when a force moves an object. The amount of work done depends on the size of the force used to move the object and the distance over which the force is applied. The value for amount of work done is expressed in newton-meters, or joules, and is calculated by using the following equation:

$$W = Fd$$
W: work (in newton-meters, or joules)
F: force (in newtons)
d: distance (in meters)

3. Which statement explains a relationship between the amount of work done and the force applied?

A. A larger force results in less work if the distance over which the force is applied remains unchanged.
B. The value for the amount of work done is unrelated to the distance over which the force is applied.
C. The same amount of work is done when forces are used to move boxes weighing different amounts the same distance.
D. If an object does not move any distance when force is applied, the value for work done is zero.

DIRECTIONS: Read the passage. Then read each question, and choose the **best** answer.

MECHANICAL ADVANTAGE AND POWER

Mechanical advantage, or MA, is the amount by which a machine makes work easier. It is a ratio of the size of the output force to the size of the input force. Power describes the rate at which work is done. Expressed in watts, it is a ratio of the amount of work done to the time used to do the work. Mechanical advantage and power are calculated by using the following equations:

$$MA = \frac{output\ force}{input\ force} \qquad power = \frac{work}{time}$$

4. The output force of a particular simple machine is 100 newtons (N). The machine provides a mechanical advantage of 4. What is the input force?

A. 25 N
B. 100 N
C. 104 N
D. 400 N

5. A robotic forklift does 19,600 joules of work to lift a 500-kilogram load 4 meters. The task takes 10 seconds. How much power does the forklift exert?

A. 1,960 watts
B. 2,000 watts
C. 4,900 watts
D. 19,600 watts

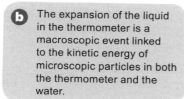

SCIENCE CONTENT TOPICS: P.a.1, P.a.3, P.a.5
SCIENCE PRACTICES: SP.1.a, SP.1.b, SP.1.c, SP.3.b, SP.7.a

UNIT 2

❶ Learn the Skill

In science, events that can be observed directly relate to events that cannot be observed directly. For example, energy and its transfer can be observed as motion, light, sound, heat, and electrical and magnetic fields. However, these observable—macroscopic—events are the result of behaviors and interactions at the unobservable—microscopic—level of particles of matter.

Linking microscopic and observable events allows you to understand how microscopic events are perceived at the observable level.

❷ Practice the Skill

By practicing the skill of linking microscopic and observable events you will improve your study and test-taking abilities, especially as they relate to the GED® Science Test. Study the information and illustration below. Then answer the question that follows.

KINETIC AND THERMAL ENERGY

ⓐ *Microscopic* refers to something so small that it cannot be observed directly. *Macroscopic* refers to something bigger that can be observed directly.

All matter has internal kinetic energy (energy of motion) because the molecules and atoms—and even the subatomic particles—that make it up are constantly moving. Even though this movement is a <u>microscopic</u> event, it can be detected <u>macroscopically</u> as thermal energy, or heat. Also, it can be measured with a thermometer.

A thermometer measures the average kinetic energy of the particles in a sample of matter. The faster the particles are moving, the higher the temperature. Thermal energy is the total kinetic energy of the particles in a sample of matter. Because more matter means more particles, a larger sample of matter has more thermal energy than a smaller sample at the same temperature.

ⓑ The expansion of the liquid in the thermometer is a macroscopic event linked to the kinetic energy of microscopic particles in both the thermometer and the water.

The illustration shows two containers of water. Both thermometers read 80 degrees Celsius (°C).

250 ml

A

500 ml

B

CONTENT TOPICS

Temperature and heat are not the same thing. Heat is thermal energy. Temperature is a measure of the average kinetic energy of the particles in a substance.

1. Which statement describes the energy of the water in the containers?

A. Both containers have the same amount of thermal energy.
B. Container A has more thermal energy than Container B.
C. Container B has a higher temperature than Container A.
D. Container B has more thermal energy than Container A.

★ Spotlighted Item: **HOT SPOT**

DIRECTIONS: Read the passage and question. Then answer by marking the appropriate hot spots.

HEAT TRANSFER

Heat is transferred between objects or systems having different temperatures. Heat moves from hotter to colder matter until both reach the same temperature, that is, establish a thermal equilibrium.

Heat flow occurs by three means: conduction, convection, and radiation. Conduction occurs when objects of different temperatures come in contact with each other and heat flows from the hot object to the cold object. Convection occurs in gases and liquids as groups of hotter particles are free to move, carrying heat to colder areas. Radiation occurs when energy is carried away from a source by waves, called electromagnetic waves, without the need for contact or currents.

2. The diagram of the pot of water on an electric range burner shows the three types of heat transfer. On each set of arrows in the diagram, mark *D* for conduction, *V* for convection, or *R* for radiation.

DIRECTIONS: Read the passage and question, and choose the **best** answer.

CONDUCTION

The transfer of heat, or thermal energy, from objects or substances in contact with each other occurs when the rapidly moving particles of the hotter substance collide with the slower moving particles of the cooler substance, causing the slower particles to speed up. Eventually equilibrium results—that is, the substances are at the same temperature—when the particles in both substances are moving at about the same rate.

The more dense a substance is, the more easily its particles collide with one another. Those dense substances are said to be good heat conductors. Thus, solids are usually better conductors of heat than liquids. Among solids, metals, which have particles that are compact and tightly positioned in crystal structures, are usually better heat conductors than nonmetals. That is, vibrating particles transfer their motion—and thermal energy—more easily through metals than through most other substances.

3. Assume that two objects of the same size and shape, one made of wood and the other of aluminum, have been in a room long enough to come to room temperature, which is about 70 degrees Fahrenheit (°F). A student, having a typical body temperature of about 99°F, picks up both objects. Which statement describes how the objects feel?

A. The wood feels cooler than the metal because wood does not conduct heat as quickly as metal does; therefore, the thermal energy from the wood transfers more slowly to her hand.
B. The wood feels warmer than the metal because metal is a better conductor of heat; therefore, metal transfers heat from her hand more quickly than wood does.
C. Both the wood and the metal feel about the same because they are both at the same temperature.
D. The metal feels warmer than room temperature because it is a good conductor of heat; therefore, it transfers its thermal energy more quickly to her hand than the wood does.

Interpret Observations

SCIENCE CONTENT TOPIC: P.a.3
SCIENCE PRACTICES: SP.1.a, SP.1.b, SP.1.c, SP.3.b, SP.3.c, SP.7.a

1 Learn the Skill

The first step in the scientific method is to observe, or use one's senses to perceive something. The next steps involve attempting to explain the meaning of what is observed. For example, after observing the way objects behave in nature and in scientific investigations, scientists have made several interpretations about energy. As you build your understanding of science topics, you can **interpret observations** you make or those made by others.

2 Practice the Skill

By practicing the skill of interpreting observations, you will improve your study and test-taking abilities, especially as they relate to the GED® Science Test. Study the information and graph below. Then answer the question that follows.

a In a closed system, energy cannot be created or destroyed, but it can change from one form to another. The total amount of energy in a system always remains the same.

b Observations are often recorded in graphs. Generally, the x-axis of a graph such as this one represents time, even if it is not labeled. Therefore, this graph shows how energy changes over time.

POTENTIAL ENERGY AND KINETIC ENERGY

Scientists have observed that all energy is either stored, as potential energy, or in motion, as kinetic energy. Potential energy is often associated with energy of position. For example, a stone on Earth's surface is said to be storing energy. If you raise the stone with respect to Earth's surface, you are increasing its potential energy. If you drop the stone, the potential energy becomes energy of motion, or kinetic energy. Mechanical energy is the sum of a system's potential energy and kinetic energy.

The graph shows how energy changes when a toy car rolls from the top of a steep ramp (Point 25) to the bottom (Point 0). The potential energy and kinetic energy of the toy are shown at various points along the ramp. Potential energy is greatest at Point 25.

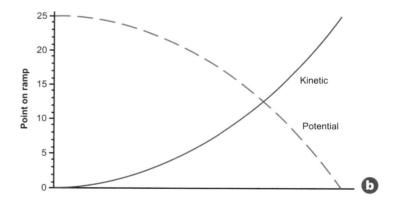

TEST-TAKING TIPS

Although many physical science questions require the use of mathematical calculations, the GED® Test also includes physical science questions that involve interpreting observations without using math.

1. What interpretation is supported by the data in the graph?

   A. As potential energy decreases, kinetic energy increases at the same rate.
   B. An object can have potential energy or kinetic energy, but not both.
   C. An increase in potential energy causes an increase in kinetic energy.
   D. As potential energy decreases, kinetic energy decreases at the same rate.

DIRECTIONS: Study the information and diagram, read the question, and choose the **best** answer.

ENERGY IN A WIND TURBINE

The total amount of energy in a system is the sum of the system's potential energy and kinetic energy. Consider a machine such as a wind turbine. A traditional windmill uses the kinetic energy of the wind to do work, such as pumping water or grinding grain. A wind turbine takes the process one step further, converting kinetic energy into electrical energy, as shown in the diagram.

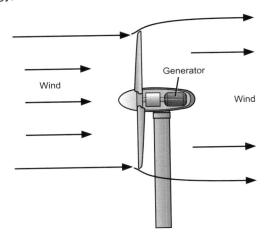

2. The diagram represents an observation of a wind turbine in the presence of wind. What happens to the wind's energy as it passes through the turbine?

   A. The kinetic energy of the wind is greater before it strikes the blades than after it strikes the blades.
   B. The potential energy of the wind is the same before and after it strikes the blades.
   C. The kinetic energy of the wind is greater after it strikes the blades than before it strikes the blades.
   D. The potential energy of the wind is changed to kinetic energy by the wind turbine.

DIRECTIONS: Study the information and diagram, read each question, and choose the **best** answer.

HOW BATTERIES WORK

Potential energy is stored as chemical energy in a non-rechargeable battery. Chemical reactions inside the battery cause electrons to collect on the zinc shell. That potential energy changes to electrical energy once a circuit is completed between the (positive) carbon rod and (negative) zinc shell. The resulting electrical energy can be changed into other forms of energy, as shown in the diagram. As the chemical paste in the battery reacts with the metals in the battery, the metals eventually decompose and the battery "dies."

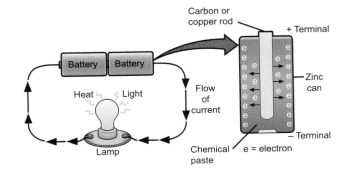

3. Which statement describes what happens to the battery's stored energy in this system?

   A. It changes from electrical, heat, and light energy to chemical energy.
   B. It changes from chemical energy to electrical, light, and heat energy.
   C. It changes from light and heat energy to chemical and electrical energy.
   D. It changes from electrical energy to heat, light, and chemical energy.

4. What would happen to the energy in this system if the wire were disconnected from one terminal of the battery?

   A. The electrical energy would change to potential energy.
   B. The light and heat energy would change to chemical energy.
   C. Energy would stop changing from potential chemical energy into other forms.
   D. Energy would stop changing from kinetic chemical energy into other forms.

UNIT 2

Link Content from Varied Formats

SCIENCE CONTENT TOPIC: P.a.5
SCIENCE PRACTICES: SP.1.a, SP.1.b, SP.1.c, SP.3.b, SP.6.a, SP.6.c, SP.7.a

❶ Learn the Skill

Science topics are more easily understood when they are presented with visual aids such as illustrations, graphs, and tables. Often when different formats are used to present topics, the text and visuals address differing but related content. Knowing how to **link content from varied formats** will help you understand the information being presented.

❷ Practice the Skill

By practicing the skill of linking content from varied formats, you will improve your study and test-taking abilities, especially as they relate to the GED® Science Test. Study the information and diagram below. Then answer the question that follows.

UNIT 2

a Notice that both the text and the diagram address transverse waves only. Other types of waves are not explained.

b When you see labels in a diagram, also look for those words in the text. The text may offer additional explanations that can help clarify the labels.

TRANSVERSE WAVES

When waves travel through substances, they cause the particles in substances to vibrate. In transverse waves, the particles vibrate perpendicular to the direction in which the wave is moving. The diagram shows how particles move away from their resting position when a transverse wave passes through a substance. Crests and troughs are the points where particles are farthest from their resting positions. The distance from any one point to the next identical point is known as the <u>wavelength</u>. **b**

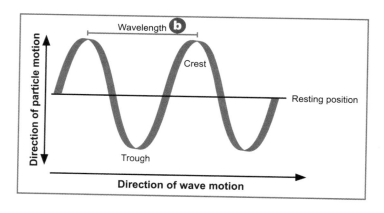

1. Which statement is supported by the information presented?

    A. The wavelength of a transverse wave can be measured only from crest to crest.
    B. The greater the crests and troughs of a transverse wave, the farther the particles move from their resting positions.
    C. Transverse waves cause particles to move in the same direction as the wave motion.
    D. The wavelength of a transverse wave measures how far the particles move from their resting positions.

CONTENT TOPICS

Waves are repeating patterns of motion that transport energy. Certain types of waves must move through a medium (matter).

⭐ Spotlighted Item: **DRAG-AND-DROP**

DIRECTIONS: Read the passage and question. Then use the drag-and-drop options to label the diagram.

TRANSVERSE WAVES AND LONGITUDINAL WAVES

Waves are either transverse, like light waves, or longitudinal, like sound waves. Both types have wavelength, amplitude, and frequency. The wavelength of a transverse wave is the distance between two crests or two troughs. The amplitude of a transverse wave is the height of a crest or the depth of a trough. The frequency of a transverse wave is how many crests or troughs pass a fixed point in a second. Longitudinal waves need a medium through which to travel. Instead of crests and troughs, longitudinal waves have compressions, where the particles in the medium are pressed closer together, and rarefactions, where the particles are spread apart. The wavelength of a longitudinal wave is the distance between two compressions. The amplitude is how much the medium is compressed. The frequency is the number of compressions that pass a fixed point in a second.

2. Identify the types of waves shown in the diagram and the unlabeled part of each wave. Record each label from the drag-and-drop options in the appropriate place on the diagram.

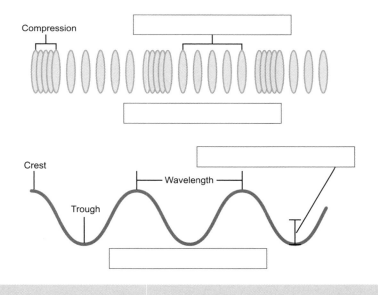

Drag-and-Drop Options

Longitudinal Wave
Transverse Wave
Rarefaction
Amplitude

DIRECTIONS: Study the list and illustration, read the question, and choose the **best** answer.

EM WAVES
- Gamma rays
- X-rays
- Ultraviolet
- Visible Light
- Infrared
- Microwave
- Radio waves

VISIBLE LIGHT

3. Humans can see only one type of electromagnetic (EM) radiation, and we see these waves as colors. What type of EM radiation do we see?

A. gamma rays
B. X-rays
C. ultraviolet radiation
D. visible light

UNIT 2

Draw Conclusions from Mixed Sources

SCIENCE CONTENT TOPIC: P.a.4
SCIENCE PRACTICES: SP.1.a, SP.1.b, SP.1.c, SP.3.b, SP.4.a, SP.5.a

1 Learn the Skill

When you draw conclusions, you come up with explanations or judgments. When you **draw conclusions from mixed sources**, you use the information in illustrations, tables, graphs, and different types of texts to make statements that explain all your observations and the facts that are presented.

2 Practice the Skill

By practicing the skill of drawing conclusions from mixed sources, you will improve your study and test-taking abilities, especially as they relate to the GED® Science Test. Read the passage, and study the diagram. Then answer the question that follows.

ENERGY SOURCES

Plants store energy from the sun when they make food during photosynthesis. To start the process, plants take in carbon dioxide from the air through their leaves and draw water from the soil through their roots. Energy from the sun drives chemical reactions that combine these substances to produce simple sugars, such as glucose, inside plant tissues. The sun's energy is stored in the chemical bonds of the sugars. When energy is used, it is converted from stored energy into other useful forms.

a Remember to use information from all available sources to draw conclusions. For example, here you can use the flowchart to identify the source of coal and then consult the passage to determine the source of the energy in coal.

FORMATION OF COAL

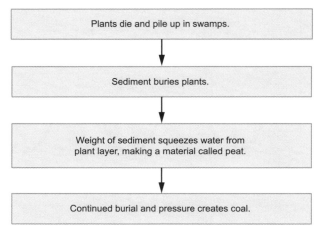

Plants die and pile up in swamps.

↓

Sediment buries plants.

↓

Weight of sediment squeezes water from plant layer, making a material called peat.

↓

Continued burial and pressure creates coal.

USING LOGIC

A flowchart lists major steps in a process. Use logic and information from other sources to determine what might occur before the first step.

1. Based on the passage and the flowchart, what is the source of the energy that exists in coal?

   A. peat
   B. the sun
   C. sediment
   D. pressure

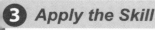

DIRECTIONS: Read the passage, and study the group of graphs. Then read each question, and choose the **best** answer.

THE CLEAN AIR ACT

The burning of fossil fuels to produce energy creates air pollution. This pollution can have harmful effects on the health of people, plants, and animals. To address this problem, the government established the Clean Air Act (CAA) of 1970, which set maximum levels for several pollutants. The CAA also created a national air quality monitoring network to keep track of those levels. When a state's pollutants are above the national standards, the state must submit a plan to bring levels down. The graphs below show the national trend for four major air pollutants, starting in 1980, when air quality monitoring began. In each graph, the black line shows the average level in parts per million (ppm) or micrograms per cubic meter ($\mu g/m^3$). The band of color shows the middle 80 percent of the data distribution.

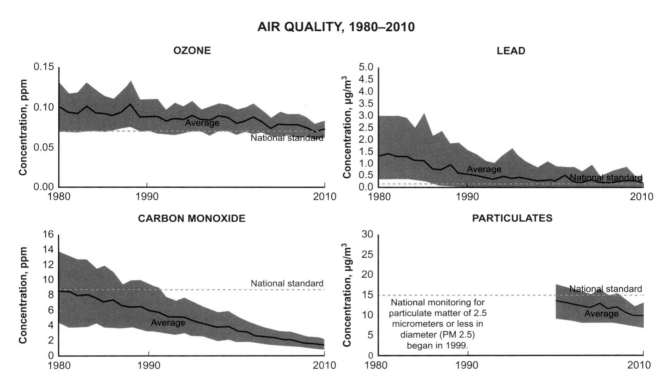

AIR QUALITY, 1980–2010

2. For which air pollutants did some states have to submit pollution reduction plans in 2010, based on average levels?

   A. ozone and particulates
   B. carbon monoxide and particulates
   C. lead and particulates
   D. ozone and lead

3. What conclusion can be drawn based on the passage and the data presented?

   A. The national air quality monitoring program costs more money now than in the past.
   B. Lead is the most important air quality problem in the United States.
   C. The CAA is likely to have led to a reduction in health problems related to air pollution.
   D. The United States no longer will monitor the pollutants identified in the graphs.

SCIENCE CONTENT TOPICS: P.a.4, P.b.2, P.c.1
SCIENCE PRACTICES: SP.2.a, SP.2.b, SP.2.d, SP.2.e, SP.3.b, SP.3.d, SP.7.a, SP.8.a, SP.8.b

UNIT 2

1 Learn the Skill

Scientific experimentation is based on the scientific method and involves established **investigation techniques**. An investigation almost always begins with a question related to an observation. Using previous knowledge, scientists try to answer the question with a hypothesis. The next steps include designing and conducting an investigation that tests the hypothesis and analyzing and interpreting data.

When you **understand investigation techniques**, you can design and conduct scientific investigations. More important practically, you improve your understanding of science in general by being able to identify hypotheses, variables, and sources of error in investigations and understanding ways to interpret data.

2 Practice the Skill

By practicing the skill of understanding investigation techniques, you will improve your study and test-taking abilities, especially as they relate to the GED® Science Test. Read the passage below. Then answer the question that follows.

a A hypothesis is an attempt to explain an observation. A hypothesis never can be proven true, but it can be supported. If a hypothesis is supported repeatedly by investigation, it becomes accepted in the scientific community as valid and eventually may be considered scientific theory or law.

b Data generated from an investigation need to be analyzed and interpreted. If the data validate the hypothesis, they can be used to make predictions.

CONTENT PRACTICES

The scientific method is comprised of a series of logical steps, with each depending on the previous one. For example, you cannot reach conclusions without first analyzing results.

INVESTIGATING ATOMIC STRUCTURE

The goal of a scientific investigation is to test a hypothesis. After conducting an investigation, a researcher analyzes and interprets data from the tests to decide whether the hypothesis is supported. If analysis shows the hypothesis to be incorrect or only partially correct, the researcher looks for errors in the investigation design or modifies the hypothesis and retests it. This process continues until investigations that can be duplicated by others demonstrate support for a hypothesis.

An early investigation into the structure of matter illustrates use of the scientific method and effective investigation techniques. In the early 1900s, scientists did not know that atoms contained most of their mass and all of their positive charge within their nuclei. They believed that positive charge and mass were distributed evenly throughout the atom. Physicist Ernest Rutherford designed an investigation to test this hypothesis. He beamed helium atoms made positively charged by being stripped of their electrons through gold foil. Because he thought based on the hypothesis that positive charges and mass were evenly distributed throughout the gold, he expected that the positively charged particles would pass through it. Instead, some particles bounced back in the opposite direction, as though repelled by a positively charged mass.

1. After analyzing the results of the investigation, which action should Rutherford have taken?

   A. Modify the results to support the original hypothesis.
   B. Modify the hypothesis to state that atoms have positively charged nuclei.
   C. Abandon the investigation because the results did not support the original hypothesis.
   D. Assume that atoms do not have electrical charges.

DIRECTIONS: Read the passage. Then read each question, and choose the **best** answer.

INVESTIGATING FORCE

A researcher designs an investigation that will measure the amount of force needed to move objects of different masses over a specified distance within a specified time interval. In designing the investigation, the researcher takes into account the idea that a valid investigation is controlled; that is, it holds all variables constant except two: an independent variable, which is purposely changed, and a dependent variable, which reacts to those changes.

2. Which hypothesis is the researcher **most likely** testing with this investigation?

   A. Work equals force times displacement.
   B. For every force there is an equal and opposite force.
   C. Force equals mass times acceleration.
   D. The acceleration due to gravity on Earth is 9.8 meters per second squared (m/s^2).

3. In the design of this investigation, which factor is the dependent variable?

   A. the mass of the object
   B. the amount of force applied
   C. the opposing force of friction
   D. the distance the object is displaced

4. Which factor is the independent variable?

   A. the mass of the object
   B. the amount of force applied
   C. the opposing force of friction
   D. the distance the object is displaced

DIRECTIONS: Read the passage and question, and choose the **best** answer.

INVESTIGATING AIR QUALITY

An environmentalist hypothesizes that the air quality in his neighborhood is unhealthful, based on ambient carbon monoxide levels caused by automobile exhaust. He conducts an investigation to find the mean, or average, concentration of carbon monoxide in the air at the intersection near his apartment building. By using a mobile device and available technology, he collects measurements of carbon monoxide concentrations in air at that location every two hours over a twelve-hour period. He records the following figures: 9.1 parts per million (ppm), 15.0 ppm, 11.1 ppm, 11.5 ppm, 12.8 ppm, and 14.2 ppm.

5. What is the mean value of the environmentalist's data set?

   A. 11.1
   B. 12.3
   C. 15.0
   D. 73.7

DIRECTIONS: Read the passage and question, and choose the **best** answer.

INVESTIGATING GRAVITY

A student wants to investigate acceleration due to the force of gravity. She constructs a ramp and uses two jar lids containing metal washers as the objects under the force of gravity. She knows from Newton's laws that the jar lids, if released simultaneously at the top of the ramp, should arrive at the bottom of the ramp at the same time regardless of how many more washers one jar lid may have over the other. However, this is not what she observes in her investigation. Consistently, the jar lid containing the most washers arrives at the bottom of the ramp first.

6. Which statement describes the **most likely** source of error in this investigation?

   A. The force of friction was not adequately controlled.
   B. The mass of the washers was not standardized.
   C. The ramp was too steep, making velocities too great.
   D. The jar lids did not have enough mass.

Evaluate Scientific Information

SCIENCE CONTENT TOPICS: P.c.2, P.c.4
SCIENCE PRACTICES: SP.1.a, SP.1.b, SP.1.c, SP.2.b, SP.2.c, SP.3.b, SP.4.a, SP.7.a

1 Learn the Skill

Scientific information is presented everywhere, not only in scientific journals but also on television, in newspapers, on the Internet, and so on. However, scientific information is only as good as the scientific investigation that produced it. When you **evaluate scientific information**, you analyze the conclusions of an investigation and decide whether they are valid based on how they were obtained.

2 Practice the Skill

By practicing the skill of evaluating scientific information, you will improve your study and test-taking abilities, especially as they relate to the GED® Science Test. Read the passage below. Then answer the question that follows.

VALIDITY OF HYPOTHESES

a Some questions cannot be answered with the scientific method. This is especially true of questions that begin with "why." Science is more about addressing questions beginning with "how."

b A good hypothesis is testable and refutable. That is, it has to be subject to scrutiny. It has to be open to the question: What piece of evidence will falsify the hypothesis?

Scientific investigations often begin with an observation. Then the observation leads to a question. Not all questions can be answered by a scientific investigation. Questions that can be answered by the scientific method are those that can be answered in the form of a testable hypothesis. To formulate a testable hypothesis, scientists make an educated guess about cause-and-effect relationships. The causes and the effects are called variables; the cause is also called the independent variable, and the effect is known as the dependent variable. In a well-designed investigation, data about the independent and dependent variables are collected, recorded, and analyzed. If the hypothesis is validated by the data, the results can be used to make reliable predictions.

c A testable hypothesis identifies something that is measurable. For example, the amount of salt that is added to a sample of water and the temperature at which the water freezes are measurable variables.

TEST-TAKING TIPS

Before answering a question or trying to solve a problem, read the question carefully. Then try to answer the question without reading the answer choices. Finally, find the right match to your answer.

1. Henry noticed that salt water freezes at a lower temperature than freshwater does. This observation led him to the question, "Does increasing the amount of salt in salt water reduce the freezing point of the water?" Which statement is a testable hypothesis that could be formulated from Henry's observation and question?

   A. Adding salt to salt water raises its freezing point.
   B. Adding salt to salt water lowers its freezing point.
   C. Adding salt to salt water has an effect on the freezing point of the water.
   D. Adding salt to salt water does not have a significant effect on the freezing point of the water.

❸ *Apply the Skill*

★ Spotlighted Item: **DROP-DOWN**

DIRECTIONS: Read the passage titled "Effect of pH on Wildlife," and study the diagram. Then read the incomplete passage that follows. Use the information from the first passage and the diagram to complete the second passage. For each drop-down item, choose the option that **best** completes the sentence.

EFFECT OF pH ON WILDLIFE

All matter has chemical properties, including the quality of acidity or basicity (alkalinity). Acids are compounds that release hydrogen ions (H^+) when dissolved in water. Bases are compounds that release hydroxide ions (OH^-) when dissolved in water. The pH scale is used to measure the concentration of hydrogen ions in a solution. A pH of 0 to 6 indicates acidity, 7 indicates neutrality, and 8 to 14 indicates basicity.

A government investigation showed that some common liquids are acidic enough to be toxic to wildlife, even at low concentrations. The results of this investigation are shown in the diagram.

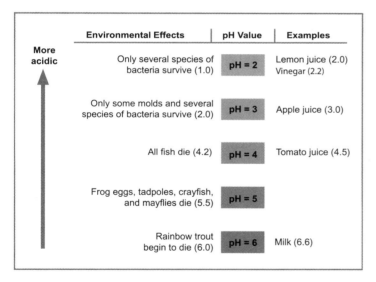

Drop-Down Answer Options

2.1 A. have a pH less than 7 and are, therefore, acids
B. have a pH greater than 7 and are, therefore, bases
C. have a pH near 7 and are, therefore, nearly neutral
D. have released hydroxide ions into the water

2.2 A. identified the pH levels of several substances
B. proved that milk is not a threat to wildlife
C. has been repeated several times
D. measured effects of acidity on several species

2.3 A. bacteria
B. molds
C. mayflies
D. trout

2.4 A. the effects of acid rain on food chains
B. the effects of high acidity on the human digestive system
C. the possible role of tomato juice as a nutrient source for aquatic organisms
D. an analysis of food preferences of tadpoles

2. The scientific information released by the government can be used to understand the effects of pH on wildlife. All the liquids tested in the investigation [2. Drop-down 1]. A logical conclusion from the test data is that most of the tested liquids threaten aquatic life. A strength of the study that helps validate this conclusion is that it [2. Drop-down 2]. Based on the test data, [2. Drop-down 3] are least tolerant of acidity. The test results would be most relevant in a follow-up study on [2. Drop-down 4].

UNIT 2

DIRECTIONS: Study the information and graphic, read each question, and choose the **best** answer.

The periodic table is an organized list of all the elements. Each box of the periodic table presents information about the atoms that comprise an element. For example, each atom of element "X" in the example box below has an atomic number of "A" and an average atomic mass of "Z." The atomic number is the number of protons per atom. The atomic mass is the average number of protons and neutrons of the atoms of the element.

Example

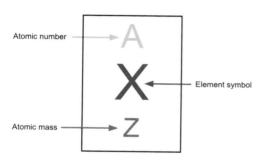

Atomic number → A

X ← Element symbol

Atomic mass → Z

Silicon

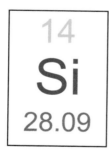

14

Si

28.09

1. What information about silicon is provided by the excerpt from the periodic table?

   A. An atom of silicon has 14 protons.
   B. There is an average of 14 protons in each silicon atom.
   C. There are 28.09 protons in each silicon atom.
   D. Each silicon atom has 28.09 neutrons.

2. Why is atomic mass an average?

   A. The number of neutrons is variable.
   B. The number of protons is variable.
   C. The mass of electrons is variable.
   D. The mass of protons is variable.

DIRECTIONS: Read the passage and question, and choose the **best** answer.

Work is directly proportional to both force and distance, so decreasing force while increasing distance—or vice versa—results in the same amount of work. This is the idea behind simple machines. The amount of work needed to lift an object, for example, would be the same whether it is lifted straight upward or carried up a ramp. Using the ramp requires more distance, but less force. A ramp is a type of simple machine.

Simple machines allow a smaller force to overcome a larger force. That difference in force is called mechanical advantage, or MA. The equation for calculating mechanical advantage is:

$$MA = \frac{output\ force}{input\ force}$$

3. A pulley is a simple machine. A system of pulleys is installed in a factory to allow a worker to lift heavy crates. If the worker exerts a force of 600 newtons (N) on the pulley system to lift a crate that weighs 1,800 N, what is the mechanical advantage of the pulley system?

   A. 18
   B. 6
   C. 3
   D. 0.3

DIRECTIONS: Study the model, read the question, and choose the **best** answer.

Carbon dioxide molecule

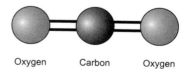

Oxygen   Carbon   Oxygen

4. The model indicates that a carbon dioxide molecule is formed when

   A. one carbon atom loses electrons and two oxygen atoms gain electrons.
   B. two oxygen atoms lose electrons and one carbon atom gains electrons.
   C. one carbon atom and two oxygen atoms share electrons.
   D. a carbon atom is connected to two oxygen atoms by rods.

DIRECTIONS: Study the information and table. Then read the question, and write your response on the lines. This task may take approximately 10 minutes to complete.

Alisha has found two unlabeled powders in the lab. She is certain that one of the powders is copper sulfate and the other is sodium chloride, but she does not know which is which. She knows that when mixed with water, copper sulfate undergoes a chemical reaction but sodium chloride does not. She decides to carry out an investigation to determine the identities of the powders. The table to the right provides information about the investigation.

	A	B
Materials	Beaker 10 milliliters (ml) water 0.5 gram (g) Powder A	Beaker 10 ml water 0.5 g Powder B
Procedure	Place water in beaker. Add powder to water. Stir water 10 times.	Place water in beaker. Add powder to water. Stir water 10 times.
Observations	When the powder is added to the water and stirred, it quickly disappears.	When the powder is added to the water, the water turns blue and the beaker becomes warm.

5. Which powder is copper sulfate, and which is sodium chloride? Include support from the passage and table in your response.

_____

_____

_____

_____

_____

_____

_____

_____

_____

_____

_____

DIRECTIONS: Read the passage and question, and choose the **best** answer.

During a chemical reaction, energy can be released or absorbed. An exothermic chemical reaction produces thermal energy, or heat. During an exothermic reaction, chemical energy changes to thermal energy. An endothermic chemical reaction absorbs thermal energy. During an endothermic reaction, heat is absorbed from the environment to drive the reaction. Thermal energy changes to chemical energy.

6. Which event demonstrates an endothermic reaction?

A. On a family camping trip, a dad and his daughters enjoy a campfire.
B. A student combines citric acid and baking soda in a plastic bag, and the bag feels cooler.
C. A construction worker uses hand warmers while on a break.
D. A student combines sugar, water, and sulfuric acid in a beaker, and the reaction produces heat, steam, and an odor.

DIRECTIONS: Read the passage. Then read each question, and choose the **best** answer.

A student in a science classroom conducts an investigation to test heat flow. She creates equal size dots of candle wax, places the dots of wax equal distances apart on a copper rod, and then inserts one end of the rod into a flame. She observes as the dots of wax melt in order from the dot closest to the heat source to the dot farthest from the heat source. Her observation supports her hypothesis.

7. What hypothesis is the student **most likely** testing?

   A. Heat flows from warmer parts of a solid to cooler parts of a solid.
   B. Heat flows from warmer parts of a metal object to cooler parts of a metal object.
   C. Copper is a better conductor of heat than other metals.
   D. Bringing about heat transfer by radiation is an effective method for melting objects.

8. Another student attempts to repeat the investigation. He also uses wax from a candle and a copper rod, but he observes that one dot of wax appears to begin to melt before a dot of wax that is closer to the flame. What is a likely source of error in his investigation?

   A. The flame produces higher heat later in the investigation.
   B. The copper rod is longer than that used in the first investigation.
   C. The two dots are different types of wax.
   D. The dots are not equal in size.

9. Which investigation design would be best for testing differences in conductivity among metals?

   A. Insert two equal size rods—one copper, one aluminum—into a flame for equal amounts of time, and observe the difference in their temperatures.
   B. Insert two copper rods of different thicknesses into a flame for equal amounts of time, and observe the difference in their temperatures.
   C. Insert two equal size rods—one copper, one glass—into a flame for equal amounts of time, and observe the difference in their temperatures.
   D. Place wax dots on a copper rod and an aluminum rod, insert the rods into a flame, and observe whether the wax dots melt in order on each rod.

DIRECTIONS: Read the passage. Then read each question, and choose the **best** answer.

When dry nitrogen triiodide (NI_3) is touched with a feather, it explodes and gives off a violet cloud of iodine (I_2).

10. Which statement describes evidence that this is a chemical reaction?

    A. Nitrogen triiodide is touched by a feather.
    B. Nitrogen triiodide explodes and gives off a violet cloud.
    C. Nitrogen triiodide is made of two distinct elements.
    D. Nitrogen triiodide maintains its chemical makeup.

11. Which chemical equation represents the reaction described?

    A. $I_2 + N_2 + O_2 \rightarrow 2NI_3$
    B. $N_2 + 3I_2 \rightarrow 2NI_3$
    C. $NI_3 \rightarrow N_2 + I_2 + O_2$
    D. $2NI_3 \rightarrow N_2 + 3I_2$

12. What type of reaction is described?

    A. decomposition
    B. synthesis
    C. single displacement
    D. double displacement

DIRECTIONS: Read the passage and question, and choose the **best** answer.

A student knows that solubility generally increases as temperature increases. He wants to learn more about solubility and saturation and plans the steps for an investigation. He will divide a 100 ml solution of potassium nitrate (KNO_3) dissolved in water evenly between Beaker A and Beaker B. Then he will heat the solution in Beaker A to 20 degrees Celsius (°C) and the solution in Beaker B to 60°C.

13. What prediction can be made about how the solution in Beaker B will differ from the solution in Beaker A at the end of the investigation?

    A. It will have greater solubility.
    B. It will contain more KNO_3.
    C. No more KNO_3 will dissolve in it.
    D. Its temperature will be lower.

DIRECTIONS: Study the information and diagram, read each question, and choose the **best** answer.

Oil shale is sedimentary rock, or shale, that contains a substance called kerogen. Like oil, kerogen is a hydrocarbon, a substance made of carbon and hydrogen. However, kerogen is not as fully cooked in Earth as oil is. Oil shale can be mined and subjected to a process called retorting, which liquifies the kerogen and transforms it into an oil that can be refined into products such as jet fuel and diesel fuel.

FORMATION OF OIL

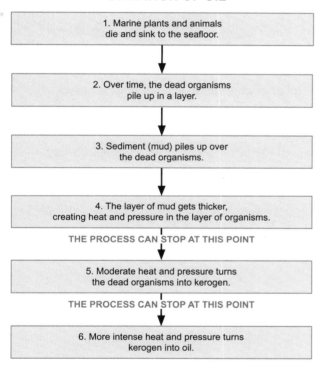

14. The passage says that kerogen is "not as fully cooked" as oil. What does this mean?

A. Kerogen does not have all the ingredients needed to be oil.
B. Kerogen has not been in Earth long enough to be ready for use in a practical application.
C. Kerogen is still in solid form when it is mined.
D. Kerogen has not been subjected to enough heat and pressure to become oil.

15. At what point in the process represented by the flowchart does oil shale form?

A. step 2
B. step 3
C. step 5
D. step 6

16. What does the process of retorting **most likely** involve?

A. heat and pressure
B. additional dead organisms
C. liquifying and refining
D. oil shale and oil

DIRECTIONS: Read the passage. Then read each question, and fill in your answer in the box.

If the velocity of an object is increasing, its acceleration is positive. If its velocity is decreasing, its acceleration is negative. Negative acceleration is also called deceleration. For example, when a car's brakes are applied, the car decelerates. The calculation for deceleration is the same as that for acceleration: Subtract the initial velocity from the final velocity and divide that number by time. If the object's velocity is constant, its acceleration is zero.

17. The velocity of a car changes from 5 meters per second (m/s) to 35 m/s in 5 seconds (s). What is the car's acceleration?

18. A car going 20 m/s takes 10 s to come to a complete stop. What is the car's deceleration?

19. A car is moving at a constant velocity of 20 m/s for 60 s. What is its acceleration over that period of time?

DIRECTIONS: Read the passage. Then read each item, and respond by marking the appropriate hot spot or hot spots.

Waves transfer energy from place to place without transferring matter. A mechanical wave needs a medium, such as air or water, through which to travel. Electromagnetic waves, such as radio waves, do not require a medium. They can travel through empty space. Waves can be further classified into either transverse or longitudinal waves. A transverse wave can be either mechanical, as in ocean waves, or electromagnetic, as in radio waves. When a transverse wave passes through matter, it moves the matter up and down or side to side. The matter moves in a direction perpendicular to the direction in which the wave is traveling. Longitudinal waves are always mechanical waves; that is, they need a medium through which to travel. When a longitudinal wave passes through matter, it causes the matter to expand (at rarefactions) and contract (at compressions). The matter moves in a direction parallel to the direction in which the wave is traveling.

20. Identify movement of matter in a transverse wave. In the diagram, mark X on each arrow that shows how particles move in a transverse wave.

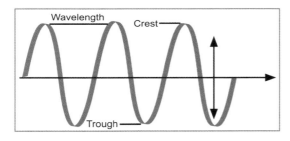

21. Identify movement of matter in a longitudinal wave. In the diagram, mark X at each rarefaction.

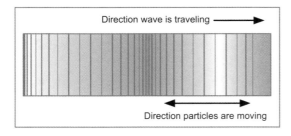

DIRECTIONS: Study the diagram. Then read the incomplete passage that follows. Use the information from the diagram to complete the passage. For each drop-down item, choose the option that **best** completes the sentence.

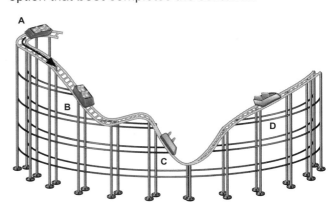

22. Roller-coaster cars, like all moving objects, have ⬚ 22. Drop-down 1 ⬚ energy. The roller-coaster car has the most ⬚ 22. Drop-down 2 ⬚ energy when it is at Point A. As it descends toward Point B, the energy of the car is

⬚ 22. Drop-down 3 ⬚ . The car has the least potential energy and the most kinetic energy at Point ⬚ 22. Drop-down 4 ⬚ .

Drop-Down Answer Options

22.1 A. kinetic
     B. chemical
     C. thermal
     D. electrical

22.2 A. chemical
     B. mechanical
     C. potential
     D. kinetic

22.3 A. being lost to momentum
     B. changing from kinetic to potential
     C. being changed to gravitational energy
     D. changing from potential to kinetic

22.4 A. A
     B. B
     C. C
     D. D

DIRECTIONS: Study the information and diagram, read each question, and choose the **best** answer.

When carbon dioxide (CO_2) is in a solid state, it is called dry ice. Unlike regular ice, which is the solid state of water, dry ice is not melted into a liquid at room temperature and standard atmospheric pressure. Room temperature is 20°C, and standard pressure is 1 atmosphere (atm). Instead, it goes directly to a gaseous phase, as indicated in the phase diagram. The fog that comes from a block of dry ice is actually water vapor that has condensed around the cold CO_2 gas that is being emitted.

CO_2 PHASE DIAGRAM

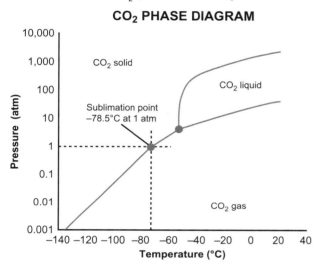

23. Which conclusion is supported by the information presented?

A. Dry ice evaporates into water vapor.
B. Dry ice is sublimated at room temperature and standard pressure.
C. Dry ice undergoes a chemical change to become fog.
D. Dry ice is melted at room temperature and standard pressure.

24. At which combination of atmospheric pressure and temperature is carbon dioxide a liquid?

A. 0.1 atm and −100 °C
B. 1 atm and −80 °C
C. 10 atm and −60 °C
D. 100 atm and −20 °C

DIRECTIONS: Read the passage and question. Then use the drag-and-drop options to complete the table.

Heat, or thermal energy, is a form of kinetic energy that results from events that happen at a scale we cannot see. As heat is transferred from system to system or from object to object, the motion of the particles that make up the object or system speed up or slow down, depending on whether heat is being transferred in or out. The average kinetic energy of all the particles in a substance can be measured as temperature by using a thermometer. The total kinetic energy of an object or system is greater if more particles are present. That is, at the same temperature, a 100 ml sample of water has more kinetic energy than a 50 ml sample of water.

25. Determine whether each drag-and-drop option describes a condition that relates to an increase or a decrease in the kinetic energy of an object or a system. Then record each description in the correct column of the table.

Increase in Kinetic Energy	Decrease in Kinetic Energy

Drag-and-Drop Options

Particles speed up.
Temperature drops.
Heat is transferred in.
Volume is increased.
Particles slow down.
Heat is transferred out.
Volume is reduced.
Temperature is raised.

DIRECTIONS: Study the information and diagram, read the question, and choose the **best** answer.

Two people pulling on ropes are moving a crate across the floor. The force of friction is opposing the motion of the crate. The diagram shows the three forces acting on the crate.

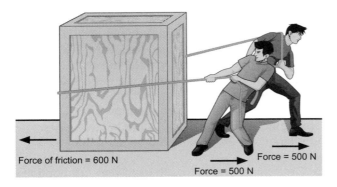

Force of friction = 600 N

Force = 500 N

Force = 500 N

26. What is the magnitude of the net force acting on the crate?

    A. 400 N
    B. 800 N
    C. 1,600 N
    D. 2,000 N

DIRECTIONS: Read the passage. Then read each question, and choose the **best** answer.

A student learning about Newton's laws of motion sets up an investigation to test the relationship between the length of a pendulum's string and the pendulum's frequency of oscillation. Oscillation is back-and-forth motion. She constructs pendulums by tying a metal washer to one end of pieces of string of different lengths. Her hypothesis is that a shorter string will result in a higher frequency of oscillation.

27. What is the dependent variable in the investigation?

    A. length of string
    B. mass of pendulum
    C. frequency of oscillation
    D. angle of oscillation

28. What is the independent variable in the investigation?

    A. length of string
    B. mass of pendulum
    C. frequency of oscillation
    D. angle of oscillation

DIRECTIONS: Study the information and diagram, read each question, and choose the **best** answer.

Energy cannot be created or destroyed; it can only be converted from one kind to another. Electrical energy is generated at a power plant through a series of energy conversions. In a coal-fired plant, the process begins with chemical energy stored in the coal. The coal is burned in a boiler to produce steam. The steam turns the blades of a turbine. The turbine turns the generator that produces electricity.

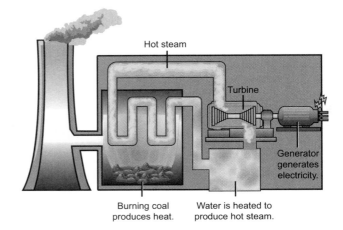

Hot steam

Turbine

Generator generates electricity.

Burning coal produces heat.

Water is heated to produce hot steam.

29. Which type of energy does the action of the turbine represent?

    A. chemical
    B. heat
    C. kinetic
    D. electrical

30. Which sequence describes the chain of energy conversions in a coal-fired power plant?

    A. chemical → heat → mechanical → electrical
    B. heat → chemical → mechanical → electrical
    C. mechanical → chemical → heat → electrical
    D. heat → mechanical → chemical → electrical

DIRECTIONS: Read the passage. Then read each question, and fill in your answer in the box.

The law of momentum conservation states that the total momentum of a closed system is constant if no external force acts on the system. This means that momentum is neither lost nor gained when two bodies collide with each other. Momentum is calculated by using the equation $p = mv$, where p is momentum, m is mass, and v is velocity. Momentum is expressed in units of mass times velocity—such as kilograms (kg) times meters per second—and direction. For example, "10 kg • m/s downward" is an expression of momentum.

31. What is the momentum of a 100 kg object moving at 25 m/s toward the east?

32. The same object catches up with a 20 kg stationary object and collides with it. The collision stops the first object and sets the second object in motion. What is the velocity of the second object after the collision?

DIRECTIONS: Read the passage. Then read each question, and choose the **best** answer.

Average speed is found by dividing total distance by time. Average velocity is found by dividing total displacement by time. If a person walks 300 meters (m) to the east and then returns to the starting point by the same route, the total distance equals 600 m. Total displacement equals 0 m.

33. If the entire trip took 10 minutes, what was the average speed in m/s?

   A. 0 m/s
   B. 1 m/s
   C. 6 m/s
   D. 60 m/s

34. If the entire trip took 10 minutes, what was the average velocity?

   A. 0 m/s
   B. 1 m/s east
   C. 6 m/s west
   D. 60 m/s

DIRECTIONS: Study the information and diagram, read the question, and choose the **best** answer.

According to Newton's first law of motion, an object at rest stays at rest and an object in motion stays in motion with the same speed and in the same direction unless it is acted on by an unbalanced force.

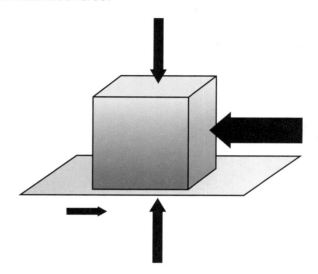

35. Which statement describes the motion of the box when the forces represented in the diagram act on it?

   A. The box will move down.
   B. The box will move to the left.
   C. The box will move to the right.
   D. The box will move up.

DIRECTIONS: Read the passage and question, and choose the **best** answer.

Environmental scientists investigating radiation levels in streams and ponds within a kilometer of a site where nuclear power materials are being stored collected seven water samples. They used equipment to count the number of radioactive particles emitted by each sample in microroentgens per hour (µR/h). They recorded the following measurements for the seven samples: 500.0 µR/h, 520.0 µR/h, 420.0 µR/h, 475.0 µR/h, 410.0 µR/h, 510.0 µR/h, and 445.0 µR/h.

36. What is the mean value of the scientists' data set, rounded to the nearest whole number?

   A. 3,280 µR/h
   B. 520 µR/h
   C. 475 µR/h
   D. 469 µR/h

F. Story Musgrave

F. Story Musgrave's life—and career— took off after he earned his GED® certificate. Among other achievements, Musgrave became the only astronaut to fly missions on all five space shuttles.

F **Story Musgrave wanted to reach for the stars.** So in 1953, Musgrave put his education on hold, leaving St. Mark's School in Massachusetts to join the military. As a member of the U.S. Marine Corps, Musgrave served as an aviation technician and aircraft crew chief and earned his GED® certificate. It served as a springboard for his many successes to come.

After completing his military commitment, Musgrave earned the first of many college degrees, this one in mathematics and statistics from Syracuse (N.Y.) University in 1958. He went on to earn another undergraduate degree and a trio of master's degrees, all in different areas of study. He also earned a doctorate in medicine.

But in many ways, Musgrave's career had only begun to take flight. In 1967, he was selected by NASA as a scientist-astronaut. Over time, Musgrave participated in the design and development of spacesuits and other features related to the shuttle program. Musgrave first reached space in 1983 on the shuttle *Challenger*. He later became the only astronaut to fly missions on all five space shuttles. Musgrave performed numerous mission functions, including several famous spacewalks. He earned the nickname "Dr. Detail" for his disciplined efforts. As he noted, "You want to get the mission done, so you aim at perfection. You aim at perfecting your art of working in space."

All told, Musgrave flew 17,700 hours in 160 different types of civilian and military aircraft. An accomplished parachutist, he made more than 500 jumps. He retired from NASA in 1997 after 30 years of service.

> "You want to get the mission done, so you aim at perfection. You aim at perfecting your art of working in space."

CAREER HIGHLIGHTS: *F. Story Musgrave*

- Served with the U.S. Marines in Korea, Japan, and Hawaii
- Earned a total of six college degrees
- Flew on the maiden voyage of the shuttle *Challenger*
- Performed three spacewalks during the *Endeavour* mission to repair the Hubble Space Telescope

Earth and Space Science

Unit 3:
Earth and Space Science

Every day, whether or not you realize it, you study Earth and space science. Weather forecasts, reports on climate change, stories about renewable energy—all these provide information about the world around us, how the world affects us, and how we affect that world.

Earth and space science also plays an important part in the GED® Science Test, comprising 20 percent of the questions. As with other areas of the GED® Science Test, Earth and space science questions will test your ability to read and analyze different types of text and graphics. Unit 3 spotlights the interpretation of scientific theories, patterns, and other core content that will help you prepare for the GED® Science Test.

Table of Contents

UNIT 3

Knowledge of Earth and space science allows workers to harness new sources of energy that can have a significant impact on the world.

Understand Scientific Theories

SCIENCE CONTENT TOPICS: ES.b.4, ES.c.1
SCIENCE PRACTICES: SP.1.a, SP.1.b, SP.1.c, SP.3.a, SP.3.b, SP.4.a, SP.7.a

❶ Learn the Skill

People often use the word *theory* to mean a guess. However, a **scientific theory** is an explanation that is supported by all the available data. A theory often summarizes a hypothesis or hypotheses that are supported by many observations, knowledge, and repeated investigations. To **understand scientific theories,** examine the evidence that supports them.

A scientific theory is not just a statement describing something that happens in the natural world. A theory also contains an explanation of why or how something happens.

❷ Practice the Skill

By practicing the skill of understanding scientific theories, you will improve your study and test-taking abilities, especially as they relate to the GED® Science Test. Read the passage below. Then answer the question that follows.

ⓐ A scientific theory is supported by evidence. For example, the theory that the Big Bang was the start of the universe is supported by Hubble's observation.

ⓑ A scientific theory is typically a big idea that can explain a number of related occurrences. Here, the idea of the Big Bang provides a common explanation for several scientific phenomena.

BIG BANG THEORY

In 1929, astronomer Edwin Hubble observed that the galaxies in the universe around our galaxy, the Milky Way, are speeding away from us. This model of an expanding universe was important in developing the Big Bang theory.

The Big Bang theory states that all the matter and energy that exists was once inside a hot, dense mass just a few millimeters across. About 14 billion years ago, a huge explosion blasted that material outward in all directions. This blast, known as the Big Bang, was the start of the universe as we know it.

Three major pieces of evidence support the Big Bang theory. First, if the universe began with a tiny mass that exploded, the galaxies that formed after that blast would be moving away from each other. This phenomenon appears to exist. Scientists also calculated that, given the way the first atoms formed, 25 percent of the mass in the universe should be helium. They discovered that this circumstance is also true. Finally, in the 1940s, scientists predicted that the Big Bang should have left behind background radiation throughout the universe. Such cosmic background radiation was detected in the 1960s.

USING LOGIC

Compare the answer choices with what you have learned about the evidence that supports the Big Bang theory. Evaluate which choices are consistent with this evidence and which seem to contradict it.

1. Based on the Big Bang theory, which statement describes an aspect of the universe?

   A. The Milky Way is the center of the universe.
   B. Galaxies will soon begin to move toward each other.
   C. Galaxies are farther apart now than 50 years ago.
   D. A second Big Bang will occur in a few billion years.

DIRECTIONS: Study the information and graph, read each question, and choose the **best** answer.

WORK OF EDWIN HUBBLE

When astronomers looked at distant galaxies 100 years ago, they could not see them in great detail. Still, they could identify the wavelengths of the energy each galaxy emitted. This spectral signature gave astronomers information about the compositions and movements of the galaxies. For example, astronomers determined that if a galaxy were moving toward us, its energy would be shifted toward the blue end of the electromagnetic spectrum. If it were moving away, its energy would be shifted toward the red end. In the 1920s, Edwin Hubble observed that all galaxies seemed to be red-shifted. As a result, he concluded that they were all moving away from Earth.

The graph represents Hubble's findings. It shows the relationship between the distances of other galaxies from ours, in megaparsecs (Mpc), and the velocities at which they move, in kilometers per second (km/s).

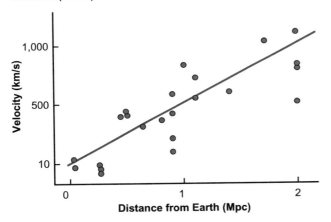

2. Which statement expresses the relationship shown by the graph?

   A. All galaxies in the universe move at the same velocity.
   B. The closer a galaxy is to Earth, the faster it moves.
   C. The farther away a galaxy is from Earth, the faster it moves.
   D. The velocity of a galaxy depends on its mass.

3. How does Hubble's observation of red-shifted galaxies support the Big Bang theory?

   A. The Big Bang would have sent the galaxies flying apart from one another.
   B. The red shift means the galaxies are still hot from the explosion of the Big Bang.
   C. The observation suggests that the galaxies are about 14 billion years old.
   D. The red shift proves that the galaxies are all moving toward each other.

DIRECTIONS: Study the information and map, read the question, and choose the **best** answer.

PLATE TECTONIC THEORY

The theory of plate tectonics explains the structure of Earth's crust and the way that structure affects Earth's landforms. According to this theory, Earth's outer surface, or lithosphere, is composed of several huge slabs of rock called tectonic plates. The tectonic plates fit together like puzzle pieces, as shown in the map. The plates jostle against each other at their boundaries, and move in three different ways. Where they push together at convergent boundaries, plates can form high mountain ranges and deep ocean trenches. Where they pull apart at divergent boundaries, they form deep rift valleys and ridges in the middle of the ocean floor. In places where they slide past each other at transform boundaries, earthquakes are common, and Earth's crust is deformed into hills and torn by faults.

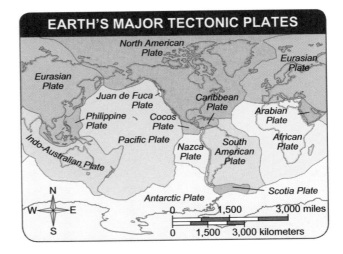

4. What does the plate tectonic theory explain?

   A. the composition of each of Earth's layers
   B. the structure of Earth's surface
   C. the density of Earth's crust
   D. the way Earth's oceans formed

SCIENCE CONTENT TOPICS: ES.c.1, ES.c.2
SCIENCE PRACTICES: SP.1.a, SP.1.b, SP.1.c, SP.7.a

1 Learn the Skill

When you **summarize complex material**, you identify and describe its main points. A summary does not contain the exact words of the original material. Instead, you summarize the information using your own words. A summary of complex material provides a simpler, shorter explanation of what the material conveys.

2 Practice the Skill

By practicing the skill of summarizing complex material, you will improve your study and test-taking abilities, especially as they relate to the GED® Science Test. Study the information and illustration below. Then answer the question that follows.

GALAXIES

When looking up at a clear night sky, people on Earth can see thousands of stars. Yet these are only a tiny fraction of the countless stars in the universe. Astronomers have found that the stars in the universe are organized into huge groups called galaxies. Groups of galaxies form clusters, and groups of clusters form superclusters. A typical galaxy, like our Milky Way, has billions of stars, as well as clouds of gas and dust, all held together by gravity. Scientists think many galaxies are surrounded by dark matter, an entity that we cannot see and that is not yet fully understood. The Milky Way is part of a small cluster called the Local Group. <u>The Local Group contains the Milky Way, Andromeda, Messier 33, and about two dozen smaller dwarf galaxies.</u> The largest clusters contain hundreds of galaxies.

a Summarizing means separating the most relevant information (main idea and supporting details) from less relevant information (extra details). This sentence has interesting details that do not belong in a summary.

b Visual elements often contain information that would be useful in a summary. The fact that there are three types of galaxies does not appear in the text but could be included in a summary.

THREE TYPES OF GALAXIES

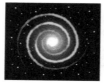  

Spiral	Elliptical	Irregular
Spiral galaxies have a central bulge with curved arms.	Elliptical galaxies have a round or oval shape.	Irregular galaxies have shapes that are not symmetrical.

USING LOGIC

The first sentence of a passage may not always contain its main idea. Here, the main idea appears later in the passage. You must carefully read the entire passage to identify the key information.

1. Which sentence **best** summarizes the information?

    A. Earth is located in the Milky Way galaxy.
    B. There are three types of galaxies: spiral, elliptical, and irregular.
    C. The universe is organized into three types of galaxies composed of stars, gas, dust, and dark matter.
    D. The Local Group contains the Milky Way and several other galaxies of varying sizes.

UNIT 3

DIRECTIONS: Study the illustration and information, read each question, and choose the **best** answer.

CROSS-SECTION OF THE SUN

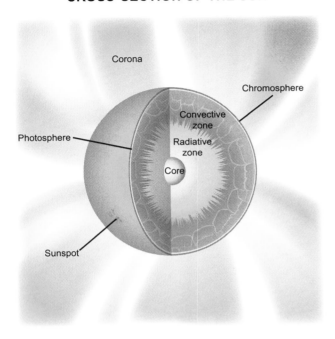

The sun is a star at the center of our solar system. At its core, the sun reaches a temperature of 27 million degrees Fahrenheit, hot enough for nuclear fusion. Fusion is a process in which atoms collide at a high speed and fuse together. In the center of the sun, hydrogen fuses to form helium and release tremendous energy—which we experience on Earth as heat and light. This energy passes from the core to the radiative zone, and then to the convective zone. From there, energy reaches the sun's surface, or photosphere. It is the photosphere that we see from Earth as a bright yellow disk. Energy escapes from the photosphere and travels to Earth at the speed of light—a journey that takes eight minutes. Above the photosphere are the thin chromosphere and corona. The chromosphere and corona are seen from Earth only during a total solar eclipse, as a bright halo around the sun's dark disk.

2. Based on the information, what would be the **best** title for the passage?

   A. Temperature of the Sun
   B. How Nuclear Fusion Works
   C. Our Solar System
   D. Structure of the Sun

3. Which statement **best** summarizes the information in the passage and illustration?

   A. Energy from the sun takes many years to reach Earth.
   B. The sun's energy is produced in its core and passes through several layers before reaching the surface and traveling to Earth.
   C. The sun uses hydrogen atoms as fuel to undergo nuclear fusion.
   D. All solar systems have a star, such as our sun, at their center.

DIRECTIONS: Read the passage. Then read each question, and choose the **best** answer.

Scientists think that stars form within the clouds of gas and dust, or nebulas, scattered within galaxies. A dense portion of a nebula can collapse due to gravity, causing the material at its center to form the hot core of a protostar. Eventually, the core becomes hot enough for nuclear fusion to occur, and the protostar becomes a main sequence star. After millions or sometimes billions of years, the star uses up its hydrogen fuel. When fusion of hydrogen stops, fusion of heavier elements begins. In time, when fusion at its core stops, the star collapses inward. Stars of average mass, such as our sun, shrink to become white dwarfs and eventually burn out. More massive stars heat up to tremendous temperatures and then explode in a fiery supernova that leaves behind a neutron star or a black hole. The remnants of exploded stars mix with surrounding gas and dust in the galaxy. This material is recycled to become new stars and planets.

4. Which point is **most** important to include in a summary of the passage?

   A. Stars are formed from huge clouds of gas and dust.
   B. Nuclear fusion inside stars uses hydrogen as its fuel.
   C. White dwarfs are stars.
   D. Our sun is a main sequence star.

5. Which title **best** summarizes this passage?

   A. Death of a Star
   B. Life Cycle of a Star
   C. Energy of a Star
   D. Birth of a Star

UNIT 3

Understand Patterns in Science

SCIENCE CONTENT TOPICS: ES.c.1, ES.c.2
SCIENCE PRACTICES: SP.1.a, SP.1.b, SP.1.c, SP.3.a, SP.3.b, SP.7.a

1 Learn the Skill

A **pattern** is something that occurs repeatedly. For instance, a pattern can be found in the structure of an object made up of repeated elements. A pattern can be found in an action that happens over and over again. **Understanding patterns in science** is particularly important because it allows you to recognize different types of patterns when they occur and to make predictions and explanations based on them.

2 Practice the Skill

By practicing the skill of understanding patterns in science, you will improve your study and test-taking abilities, especially as they relate to the GED® Science Test. Study the information and diagrams below. Then answer the question that follows.

EARTH'S DAILY PATTERN

One of nature's most recognizable patterns is the daily change from day to night and back again. Earth rotates, or spins, on its axis once every 24 hours. As a result, half of Earth is always facing the sun. This half of the planet has day. Meanwhile, the other half of Earth is facing away. That half of the planet has night. The diagrams illustrate the rotation of Earth from two points of view.

a Day and night is a pattern caused by a type of planetary movement. In the diagrams, that movement is indicated by arrows.

b The diagrams also identify the effect of this movement, an Earth that is half in darkness and half in daylight.

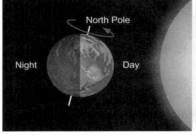
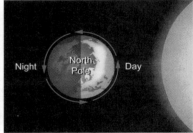

MAKING ASSUMPTIONS

Understanding patterns in science allows you to make assumptions about objects and events and their causes and effects.

1. What pattern creates night and day?

   A. continual nuclear fusion in the sun's core
   B. the rotation of Earth on its axis
   C. the apparent daily movement of the sun across the sky
   D. the revolution of Earth around the sun

DIRECTIONS: Study the illustration and information, read each question, and choose the **best** answer.

INNER AND OUTER PLANETS

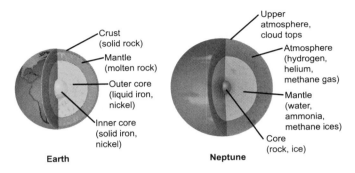

Earth   Neptune

Our solar system has eight planets. The four inner planets—Mercury, Venus, Earth, and Mars—are relatively smaller, rocky bodies. The four outer planets—Jupiter, Saturn, Uranus, and Neptune—are giant bodies made mostly of frozen gases.

The difference in composition in the inner and outer planets is due to how far the planets were from the sun when they formed. The planets formed from the remnants present in each part of the solar system after the sun's formation. These materials differed with distance from the sun. In the warmer areas closer to the sun, dense particles high in substances such as iron and silicate minerals (compounds of oxygen and silicon) coalesced and solidified to form the rocky planets. In the colder outer parts of the solar system, lighter substances such as ammonia and methane solidified into ice to form large parts of the outer planets.

2. What is the **most** important factor in explaining why the inner planets and outer planets formed differently?

    A. the difference in temperature between the inner and outer parts of the solar system
    B. the size of the Milky Way galaxy when the solar system developed
    C. the fact that the inner planets had more time to develop than the outer planets
    D. the decrease in temperature from the outer part of the solar system to the inner part

3. Which statement describes the difference in the structural patterns of the inner and outer planets?

    A. The planet's core makes up a larger percentage of the outer planets.
    B. The inner planets have very little rock.
    C. The outer planets are smaller than the inner planets.
    D. The outer planets are made of less dense material overall than the inner planets.

DIRECTIONS: Study the diagram and information, read the question, and choose the **best** answer.

HOW TIDES FORM

A bulge forms on the other side of Earth due to the centrifugal force created by rotation of the planet.

The moon's gravity pulls the oceans toward it to create one tidal bulge.

Moon's gravitational pull

Moon

The tide is the daily rise and fall of the ocean along Earth's coasts. Tides are caused primarily by the gravitational pull of the moon on Earth's oceans. In most places, two high tides and two low tides occur each day. The highest high tides are called spring tides. The lowest low tides are known as neap tides.

4. Based on the diagram and passage, what accounts for the pattern of two high tides and two low tides across most of Earth each day?

    A. As Earth rotates, lunar gravity causes two bulges of water that bring high tides while lower water levels in between bring low tides.
    B. The amount of water in the ocean increases during high tides and decreases during low tides.
    C. Coastal areas with high elevation have high tides, and coastal areas with low elevation have low tides.
    D. As the sun rises, its gravity creates high tides, and as it sets, there are low tides.

UNIT 3

Interpret Three-Dimensional Diagrams

SCIENCE CONTENT TOPICS: ES.b.4, ES.c.3
SCIENCE PRACTICES: SP.1.a, SP.1.b, SP.1.c, SP.3.b, SP.6.c, SP.7.a

1 Learn the Skill

Like cutaway illustrations, many **three-dimensional diagrams** show part of an object or a structure cut away so that the inside of the object is visible. Typically, these diagrams show layers or relationships among interior parts of a structure or an object. To **interpret three-dimensional diagrams**, pay attention to how the outside of the object relates to the inside features shown in the diagram and how the inside features relate to one another.

2 Practice the Skill

By practicing the skill of interpreting three-dimensional diagrams, you will improve your study and test-taking abilities, especially as they relate to the GED® Science Test. Study the three-dimensional diagram below. Then answer the question that follows.

EARTH'S LAYERS

Scientists think of Earth's structure in terms of layers, based on composition and physical strength. Related to the characteristic of composition, scientists identify three layers of Earth. The crust is made of rock that is not very dense. The mantle is made of denser, hotter solid rock. The core is made of iron and nickel. Related to the characteristic of physical strength, scientists identify Earth's layers differently, as shown in the diagram.

a Brackets are used to show that a label or callout applies to a region of a diagram.

b Diagrams often show an easily recognizable part of an object. This diagram shows continents. This frame of reference can help you figure out how the parts of the diagram are related.

Outer core
The outer core is made of melted iron and nickel.

Lithosphere
The lithosphere consists of the crust and the upper part of the mantle. It is cooler, brittle rock that cannot flow.

Asthenosphere
The asthenosphere is made of hot, soft mantle rock. It is solid, but it can flow under pressure.

Core **a**

Mesosphere
The mesosphere is made of hot, solid rock that is under high pressure.

b

Inner core
The inner core is made of solid iron and nickel.

TEST-TAKING TIPS

When examining a three-dimensional diagram on the GED® Test, first become familiar with its various parts before answering any questions about it.

1. Based on the passage and diagram, which statement describes layers of Earth?

    A. The lithosphere is thicker than the crust.
    B. The inner core is cooler than the crust.
    C. The mantle and outer core are completely liquid.
    D. The lithosphere and asthenosphere have the same composition.

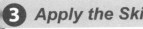

DIRECTIONS: Study the information and diagram, read the question, and choose the **best** answer.

DETERMINING AGES OF ROCKS

Scientists use observations of rock, radiometric dating, and fossils to determine the ages of rock layers. In an undisturbed column of rock, the oldest layer is at the bottom, and the youngest is at the top. The sequence of geological events, therefore, can be seen in the rock. The times in Earth's history when certain plants or animals lived is also known. Therefore, fossils found in rock, as demonstrated in the diagram, can help approximate the rock's age. Radiometric dating can identify the exact age of rock through the use of radioactive isotopes. Isotopes are forms of an element with the same number of protons but different numbers of neutrons. Some isotopes decay, or lose their radioactivity, at a different rate. When scientists know the amount of a radioactive isotope in a rock, the known rate of decay for the isotope, and the amount of the isotope and the product of its decay in a rock, they can pinpoint the age of the rock.

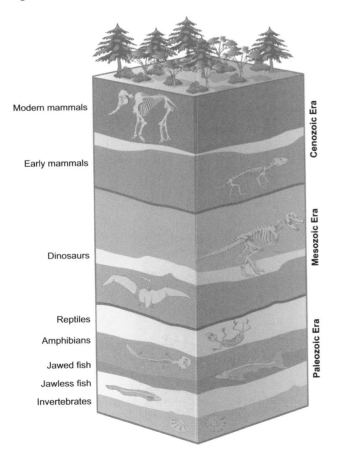

2. Based on the diagram, when in geologic time did jawless fish likely come into existence?

   A. the middle of the Paleozoic Era
   B. the end of the Paleozoic Era
   C. the middle of the Mesozoic Era
   D. the end of the Cenozoic Era

DIRECTIONS: Study the information and diagram, read the question, and choose the **best** answer.

TECTONIC PLATE MOVEMENT

Earth's crust is broken into several large pieces called tectonic plates. The tectonic plates move slowly—about as fast as fingernails grow. As the plates move, they collide, pull apart, or scrape past each other. The movements and interactions of tectonic plates are responsible for the formation of many landforms, such as mountains, and for most earthquakes and volcanic eruptions. The diagram relates tectonic plate movement to Earth's layers and formation of volcanoes.

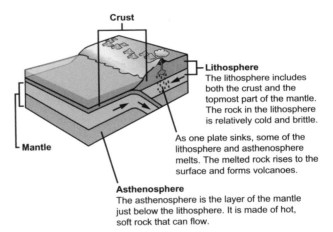

3. Based on the diagram, what conclusion can be drawn about volcanoes?

   A. Formation of volcanoes is unrelated to plate movement.
   B. Volcanoes form when the lithosphere melts.
   C. Most volcanoes are far from the ocean.
   D. The rock in a volcano comes mainly from the lowest part of the mantle.

Apply Science Concepts

SCIENCE CONTENT TOPICS: ES.a.3, ES.b.2
SCIENCE PRACTICES: SP.1.a, SP.1.b, SP.1.c, SP.3.b, SP.7.a

1 Learn the Skill

A **concept** is a fundamental unit of understanding. It can be expressed as a topic, such as "energy transfer among organisms," and represent the body of information associated with the topic. Or it can be a statement about one aspect of a topic. The study of science involves gaining knowledge of new concepts by building on known concepts. In other words, to learn new science information, you **apply science concepts** you have learned already.

2 Practice the Skill

By practicing the skill of applying concepts, you will improve your study and test-taking abilities, especially as they relate to the GED® Science Test. Study the information and diagram below. Then answer the question that follows.

a Earth's waters make up its hydrosphere. As you learn about the hydrosphere, you can apply concepts you have learned about Earth's other systems.

b Like a food chain, a food web represents the concept of energy transfer among organisms. Its arrows show the flow of energy from producers to several levels of consumers.

MARINE FOOD WEBS

Concepts in life science, physical science, and Earth and space science are interrelated because Earth's systems are interrelated. For example, oceans, which are part of Earth's <u>hydrosphere</u>, teem with and have significant impacts on living things, which make up Earth's biosphere. The food web below shows the feeding and energy transfer relationships in a marine, or ocean, ecosystem. Each organism gets energy from the organisms it eats and passes that energy along to any organism that feeds on it.

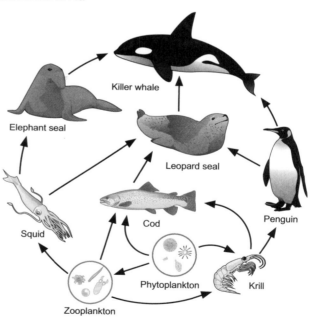

MAKING ASSUMPTIONS

You can assume that all food webs are structured similarly. This allows you to apply the same concepts when you see a food web for any type of ecosystem.

1. Based on the concept of energy transfer among organisms in ecosystems, which organism in this ocean food web is a producer?

   A. cod
   B. killer whale
   C. zooplankton
   D. phytoplankton

DIRECTIONS: Study the diagram and information, read each question, and choose the **best** answer.

ELECTRICITY FROM OCEAN WATERS

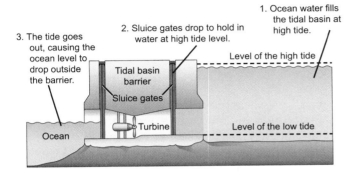

3. The tide goes out, causing the ocean level to drop outside the barrier.

2. Sluice gates drop to hold in water at high tide level.

1. Ocean water fills the tidal basin at high tide.

Level of the high tide

Tidal basin barrier

Sluice gates

Turbine

Level of the low tide

Ocean

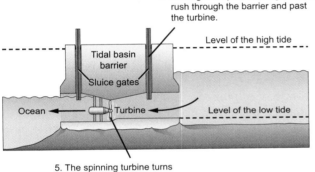

4. Sluice gates open, causing water to rush through the barrier and past the turbine.

Level of the high tide

Tidal basin barrier

Sluice gates

Ocean

Turbine

Level of the low tide

5. The spinning turbine turns a generator that produces electric power.

The movement of ocean waters can be harnessed to produce electricity in several ways. In a barrage system, the difference in water level between high and low tide generates power. Engineers build a barrage, or dam, across a tidal basin, or partially enclosed arm of the sea. At high tide, water fills the basin. A barrier then closes off the tidal basin as low tide approaches. This closure keeps the water level inside the barrage high, even as sea level outside it drops with the approach of low tide. When water level is lowest outside the barrier at low tide, the barrier lifts, and water rushes out of the basin. The rushing water turns a turbine, which spins an electric-current-producing generator.

Ocean waters also drive another type of system, in which underwater turbines are constructed in a narrow channel with a fast-moving current. The rushing water turns the turbines in the way that wind rotates the blades of a windmill. Tidal power has potential along some coasts but is not widely used.

2. Based on the concept of transformation between types of energy, what change occurs when tidal energy becomes electric power?

   A. Potential energy becomes kinetic energy.
   B. Electrical energy becomes kinetic energy.
   C. Kinetic energy becomes electrical energy.
   D. Thermal energy becomes electrical energy.

3. Considering the way that electric power is generated from tidal energy, which statement describes tidal energy?

   A. It is a nonrenewable source of energy.
   B. It is a renewable energy resource.
   C. It releases large amounts of carbon dioxide into the atmosphere.
   D. It can be widely used in every country worldwide.

DIRECTIONS: Read the passage and question, and choose the **best** answer.

EARTH-BASED NUCLEAR FUSION

Two important types of nuclear reactions produce energy: fission and fusion. We use nuclear fission to produce electricity at nuclear power plants. However, scientists cannot yet produce a controlled and continuing nuclear fusion reaction. Scientists are eager to harness fusion—the same type of nuclear reaction that occurs in the sun's core—because of the great amounts of clean energy it could produce. Many elements can produce a fusion reaction, but the first successful fusion reaction likely will involve deuterium and tritium. Both are isotopes of hydrogen. Isotopes are forms of an element that differ because of differing numbers of neutrons in their atomic nuclei. Deuterium occurs naturally in water. Tritium is a radioactive isotope of hydrogen.

4. Based on the concept of nuclear fusion, which statement describes the process scientists hope to accomplish, as discussed in the passage?

   A. It will involve splitting atoms of deuterium to release energy.
   B. It will involve heating deuterium slightly above the boiling point to produce energy.
   C. It will require atoms of deuterium and atoms of tritium to unite with each other to release energy.
   D. It will require using radiation from tritium to make deuterium.

Express Scientific Information

SCIENCE CONTENT TOPICS: ES.b.1, ES.b.3
SCIENCE PRACTICES: SP.1.a, SP.1.b, SP.1.c, SP.3.b, SP.7.a

1 Learn the Skill

You demonstrate your understanding of science concepts by expressing scientific information. You can **express scientific information** verbally, visually, numerically, or symbolically. To effectively express this information, you first have to understand the scientific content that is being presented.

2 Practice the Skill

By practicing the skill of expressing scientific information, you will improve your study and test-taking abilities, especially as they relate to the GED® Science Test. Study the information and graph below. Then answer the question that follows.

THE ATMOSPHERE

a Examining the ways in which scientific concepts are presented can help you express information about those concepts. This paragraph gives information about the gases found in Earth's atmosphere.

The atmosphere is made up of the layers of gases that surround Earth. Without the atmosphere, life would not exist on Earth. The atmosphere provides the oxygen that animals, including people, need to breathe. It also provides the carbon dioxide plants use to make food during photosynthesis. It shields all living things on Earth from the harmful radiation of the sun. Earth's temperature, warm enough to support a diverse range of organisms, is also maintained by the ability of the greenhouse gases, such as carbon dioxide and methane, to trap heat near Earth's surface and warm the planet. The graph below shows the gases that are present in the atmosphere.

b The graph contributes content by providing additional data about these gases. By interpreting all the material presented, you can express the scientific information effectively.

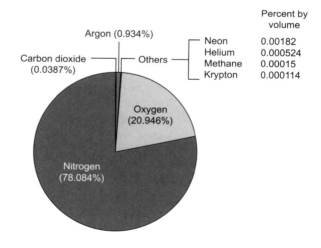

	Percent by volume
Neon	0.00182
Helium	0.000524
Methane	0.00015
Krypton	0.000114

Argon (0.934%)
Carbon dioxide (0.0387%)
Others
Oxygen (20.946%)
Nitrogen (78.084%)

CONTENT PRACTICES

Expressing scientific information is a practice addressed by the GED® Science Test. Knowing how to express such information effectively will help you succeed on the test.

1. The greenhouse gases carbon dioxide and methane are part of Earth's atmosphere. Which phrase expresses numerically the percentage of Earth's atmosphere made up of these gases?

A. about 78 percent
B. more than 20 percent
C. exactly 0.0387 percent
D. less than 1.0 percent

UNIT 3

DIRECTIONS: Study the information and diagram, read each question, and choose the **best** answer.

GREENHOUSE GASES

Earth's average temperature is 14 degrees Celsius, or 57 degrees Fahrenheit. Without the greenhouse gases in Earth's atmosphere, the planet's temperature would be much lower—too cold for the survival of people and most other living organisms. The greenhouse gases—such as carbon dioxide, methane, and nitrous oxide—make up less than 1 percent of Earth's atmosphere. Yet, as the diagram suggests, they are important in warming Earth's surface and atmosphere. After Earth absorbs solar energy, it emits infrared radiation, some of which is kept within the atmosphere by greenhouse gases.

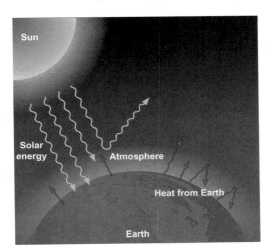

2. Which statement expresses what happens to the energy from the sun?

   A. All of it reaches Earth and is absorbed by Earth's surface.
   B. All of it reaches Earth and is reflected into the atmosphere.
   C. Some is absorbed by Earth's surface, and some is reflected by Earth.
   D. Some is absorbed by Earth's surface, and some is reflected by the atmosphere.

3. Which parts of the diagram express visually the effect of greenhouse gases?

   A. the arrows from Earth that bend back toward Earth
   B. the arrows from the sun to Earth's surface
   C. the arrows from the sun that bend at Earth's atmosphere
   D. the arrows pointing away from Earth

DIRECTIONS: Study the information and map, read each question, and choose the **best** answer.

PRESSURE AND WIND ZONES

Because of its diverse natural environments, Earth's surface absorbs the heat of the sun unevenly. For example, a dark tropical forest absorbs a different amount of solar energy than a white snowfield near the North Pole. Unequal heating causes unequal distribution of air pressure from one place on Earth's surface to another. This condition helps cause wind, which is the movement of air from areas of higher air pressure to areas of lower air pressure. Unequal heating produces huge belts of high and low pressure across Earth. These pressure belts are important in determining global wind zones.

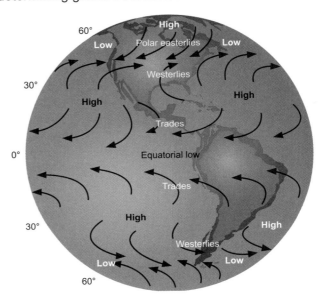

4. To express information about the wind belt that covers most of the United States, you would discuss

   A. the polar easterlies.
   B. the westerlies.
   C. the trades (or trade winds).
   D. the equatorial low.

5. Which statement expresses the relationship between high and low pressure areas as conveyed by the map?

   A. Air moves toward Earth's equatorial low.
   B. Air moves from areas of high pressure to areas of lower pressure.
   C. Air moves in toward high pressure.
   D. Air moves from areas of low pressure to areas of higher pressure.

Identify Problem and Solution

SCIENCE CONTENT TOPICS: ES.a.1, ES.a.2, ES.a.3, ES.b.3
SCIENCE CONTENT PRACTICES: SP.1.a, SP.1.b, SP.1.c, SP.3.a, SP.3.b, SP.3.c, SP.4.a, SP.6.c

1 Learn the Skill

Sometimes, the presentation of scientific material is organized around a **problem** and its **solution**. Authors may state problems and solutions, or you might have to make inferences to recognize them. When you **identify problem and solution**, you determine what problems or solutions an author is presenting.

Identifying problem and solution lays a foundation for thinking more critically about topics. You strengthen your understanding of science concepts and their implications by analyzing problems and evaluating solutions.

2 Practice the Skill

By practicing the skill of identifying problem and solution, you will improve your study and test-taking abilities, especially as they relate to the GED® Science Test. Read the passage below. Then answer the question that follows.

UNIT 3

a It is important to understand why something is a problem. Here, the opening sentences provide background about the problem the author will identify later.

b You may have to read through much of the text before you are able to identify the problem.

SAVING SOIL RESOURCES

Soil might seem like just the dirt beneath our feet, but soil is one of Earth's most important resources. Soil is necessary for plant life and, therefore, is necessary for the survival of all animals, including humans. Because soil takes a long time to form, it is basically a nonrenewable resource. Yet we lose millions of acres of farmland soil each year to erosion. Certain agricultural practices, such as intensive farming on steep slopes, increase erosion. Erosion also increases when forests are cut or fields are cleared of vegetation because of the removal of plant roots that hold soil in place. Still, farmers do have methods to conserve soil. These methods include making terraced fields on steep slopes and limiting the digging up and plowing of fields during planting. Leaving stalks and other crop waste on fields to stabilize the soil also prevents rain from washing soil way. Conservation methods are working in many places, but drought conditions can kill plant cover and again increase soil loss.

CONTENT TOPICS

You might think that soil is abundant and forms easily. But a basic part of soil is weathered or broken rock. It can take hundreds of years for even a thin layer of soil to form.

1. Why should people be concerned about the problem of soil erosion?

   A. Soil is necessary for our survival.
   B. Intensive farming increases erosion.
   C. Drought conditions can kill plant cover.
   D. No methods for conserving soil are available.

Spotlighted Item: **SHORT ANSWER**

DIRECTIONS: Read the passage, and study the map. Then read the question, and write your response on the lines. This task may take approximately 10 minutes to complete.

AFTER KATRINA

Hurricane Katrina struck New Orleans in August 2005, destroying thousands of homes and leaving most of the city under water. A storm surge pushed water up interior canals. It caused flood walls to fail and allowed water to pour into the city's lowest neighborhoods, which sit in a basin as much as 17 feet below sea level.

Each year, 30 square kilometers (12 square miles) of wetlands between New Orleans and the Gulf of Mexico are lost due to subsidence. These wetlands absorb some of the force of storm surges from the Gulf, protecting New Orleans. As they disappear, the city is more vulnerable to storms. A new system of flood protection was erected in and around New Orleans in the years after Katrina. It is meant to protect the city from other storms like Katrina. Such storms have been rare in the past but could be more frequent in the future due to climate change and the warming of tropical waters where they develop.

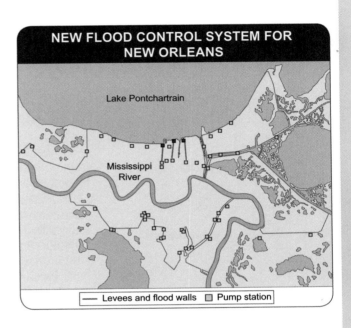

NEW FLOOD CONTROL SYSTEM FOR NEW ORLEANS

Lake Pontchartrain

Mississippi River

—— Levees and flood walls   ☐ Pump station

2. In the aftermath of Katrina, many owners of destroyed businesses have had to decide whether to rebuild in New Orleans or go elsewhere. Consider the information in the passage and map. Then explain why rebuilding in New Orleans might present problems for businesses, and evaluate whether the solution engineers have devised will be effective.

_____

_____

_____

_____

_____

_____

_____

_____

_____

UNIT 3

Analyze and Present Arguments

SCIENCE CONTENT TOPICS: ES.a.1, ES.a.3
SCIENCE PRACTICES: SP.1.a, SP.1.b, SP.1.c, SP.3.a, SP.3.b, SP.4.a, SP.5.a, SP.6.a, SP.6.c

1 Learn the Skill

Scientific facts are not subject to interpretation. They are obtained through observation and experimentation. However, scientists and others use facts to support **arguments**, or certain points of view. When you **analyze an argument**, you identify the point being made and evaluate its support. Also, you can use scientific data to express and defend your own perspectives, or **present arguments**.

2 Practice the Skill

By practicing the skill of analyzing and presenting arguments, you will improve your study and test-taking abilities, especially as they relate to the GED® Science Test. Study the information and graph below. Then answer the question that follows.

UNIT 3

a Information in a reliable source can be used to support a point of view. This information supports an argument for the use of nonrenewable energy resources.

b Some sources contain information that supports more than one point of view. This fact supports an argument for using renewable energy resources.

NONRENEWABLE VERSUS RENEWABLE ENERGY

Almost 90 percent of the energy we use to produce electricity comes from nonrenewable energy sources, such as coal and natural gas. Nonrenewable energy sources are those that are limited in supply. <u>The United States has large reserves of coal and natural gas, so much of the energy we use to light our homes and offices comes from our own mines and wells. This factor is crucial to the movement of the United States toward energy independence.</u> However, nonrenewable energy sources are not a long-term solution for the nation's energy needs. Moreover, the burning of fossil fuels, especially coal, produces carbon dioxide. Most scientists now recognize this gas as a major contributor to climate change. <u>Renewable sources, such as water, the sun's energy, and wind, do not add to atmospheric warming,</u> but today the United States uses these options only sparingly in power plants.

SOURCES OF U.S. ELECTRICITY GENERATION, 2011

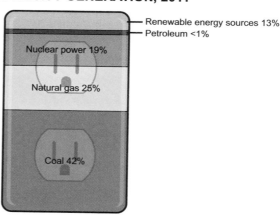

Renewable energy sources 13%
Petroleum <1%
Nuclear power 19%
Natural gas 25%
Coal 42%

TEST-TAKING TIPS

A question may ask you to identify an argument that is based on the material being presented. Read all answer choices carefully, and eliminate any not supported by associated text or graphics.

1. Based on the information, which statement expresses an argument for using renewable energy sources to produce electric power?

   A. They cost much less than other energy souces.
   B. They are available in limited supplies.
   C. The United States already uses them to produce electricity.
   D. Their uses do not release carbon dioxide.

★ Spotlighted Item: **DRAG-AND-DROP**

DIRECTIONS: Study the information and diagram, and read the question. Then use the drag-and-drop options to complete the table.

MOUNTAINTOP-REMOVAL COAL MINING

Mountaintop removal is a very efficient means of strip-mining coal used primarily in Appalachia. Where coal is found deep in mountainous areas, the mountains are blasted away to get at the deposits underneath. The broken rock and dirt is carted away and dumped into nearby valleys. Then huge machines scoop out the coal.

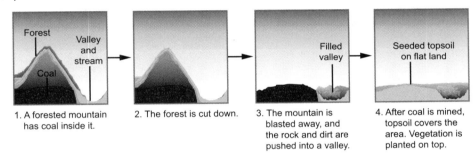

1. A forested mountain has coal inside it.
2. The forest is cut down.
3. The mountain is blasted away, and the rock and dirt are pushed into a valley.
4. After coal is mined, topsoil covers the area. Vegetation is planted on top.

2. People in a community in West Virginia have heard that a company wants to use mountaintop removal to take coal from a nearby mountain. At a town meeting, residents presented arguments for and against mountaintop-removal mining. Determine which drag-and-drop options are pros and which are cons. Then record each argument in the correct column in the table.

Pros	Cons

Drag-and-Drop Options

It provides jobs in an area that badly needs them.	Removal of forests increases erosion on steep slopes, and flooding results.
Diverse forest ecosystems are destroyed and cannot be re-created after mining.	It is safer than mining in deep shafts.
Blasting, mining, and washing the coal can emit unhealthful amounts of coal dust into the air.	It increases domestic supplies of coal, which are preferable to imported oil.

UNIT 3

DIRECTIONS: Study the diagram, read the question, and choose the **best** answer.

1. Which pattern does the diagram show?

   A. the cycle of seasons
   B. the cycle of tides
   C. the cycle of night and day
   D. the cycle of lunar phases

DIRECTIONS: Read the passage and question, and choose the **best** answer.

   In late 2012, the Hubble Space Telescope gave astronomers their deepest view yet into space—of galaxies 13.2 billion light-years away. These galaxies are 10 billion times dimmer than the human eye could ever detect from Earth on its own. To capture the image, the telescope was trained on one area of stars for more than 500 hours over 10 years. The telescope took 2,000 images of the spot. Scientists combined the light and other radiation from the images. This allowed them to build an image that showed the most distant star systems.

2. Which statement **best** summarizes this passage?

   A. Scientists have used the Hubble Telescope to view the most distant galaxies ever seen.
   B. The most distant galaxies are 13.2 billion light-years away.
   C. The Hubble Telescope has taken more than 2,000 images of galaxies.
   D. The most distant galaxies are 10 billion times dimmer than human eyes can see.

DIRECTIONS: Study the diagram. Then read each question, and choose the **best** answer.

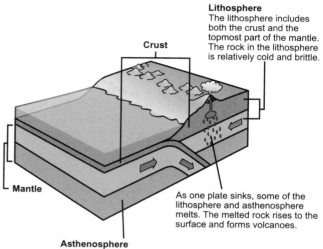

Lithosphere
The lithosphere includes both the crust and the topmost part of the mantle. The rock in the lithosphere is relatively cold and brittle.

Crust

Mantle

As one plate sinks, some of the lithosphere and asthenosphere melts. The melted rock rises to the surface and forms volcanoes.

Asthenosphere
The asthenosphere is the layer of the mantle just below the lithosphere. It is made of hot, soft rock that can flow.

3. Which layer is made of hot, soft rock?

   A. crust
   B. asthenosphere
   C. lithosphere
   D. mantle

4. What does the diagram suggest about the structure of Earth?

   A. The mantle is the thickest layer of rock in Earth's interior.
   B. The uppermost layer of Earth is the crust.
   C. The asthenosphere is part of the lithosphere.
   D. Where plates meet, the crust and the mantle change places.

5. Based on the diagram, where do volcanoes form?

   A. where air is warmed by ocean waters
   B. where two plates meet and one slips under the other
   C. where the asthenosphere is hottest
   D. where two plates pull apart

DIRECTIONS: Study the diagram, and read the question. Then write your response on the lines. This task may take approximately 10 minutes to complete.

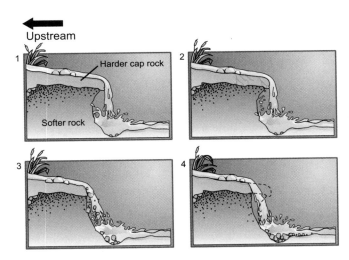

Upstream

Harder cap rock

Softer rock

1 2 3 4

6. The diagram shows the change in a waterfall over time due to weathering and erosion. Interpret the diagram, and then describe the change.

_____

_____

_____

_____

_____

_____

_____

_____

_____

_____

DIRECTIONS: Read the passage and question, and choose the **best** answer.

The Big Bang theory states that all the matter and energy in the universe was once contained inside a tiny, hot, dense mass. A huge explosion blew that tiny mass apart about 14 billion years ago, sending the material that makes up the universe flying outward in all directions. This blast is known as the Big Bang.

7. Which statement is a valid piece of evidence supporting the Big Bang theory?

A. The universe now contains many different galaxies.

B. Huge explosions no longer can occur in the universe.

C. The galaxies in the universe are moving apart rapidly.

D. There is no life anywhere in the universe except on Earth.

DIRECTIONS: Study the map. Then read each item, and fill in your response in the box.

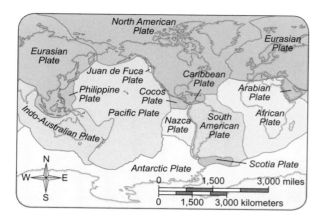

8. The map shows the _____ plates that form Earth's surface.

9. The _____ theory explains the structure of Earth's crust.

10. The movement of plates causes the formation of different _____ on Earth's surface.

DIRECTIONS: Read the passage and question, and choose the **best** answer.

The air pressure of Earth's atmosphere varies from place to place. This uneven distribution of air pressure causes wind and weather patterns. Storms are associated with lower air pressure, whereas fair weather is associated with higher air pressure. Trade winds occur in a wind zone that circles Earth from about 30 degrees latitude North to about 30 degrees latitude South. In a band around Earth's middle, trade winds from the north blowing southeasterly meet trade winds from the south blowing northeasterly. This band of low pressure is the Intertropical Convergence Zone (ITCZ).

11. Based on the information and the concept of wind, which statement describes the trade winds that meet in the ITCZ?

A. They originate in areas of lower air pressure.
B. They originate in areas of higher air pressure.
C. They move to areas of higher pressure.
D. They rarely produce storms.

DIRECTIONS: Read the passage and question, and choose the **best** answer.

Main sequence stars are mostly hydrogen. They use this hydrogen as fuel in nuclear fusion to produce energy. Eventually, stars use up their hydrogen and expand to become huge and relatively cool red giants. Stars of our sun's mass then collapse into small, hot, dense white dwarf stars before becoming cooler, denser black dwarfs. After the red giant stage, more massive stars explode in a supernova. In stars up to four times as massive as our sun, the supernova leaves behind a small, dark, dense body called a neutron star. Even more massive stars become black holes—bodies so dense that no matter or energy can escape them.

12. Which statement **best** identifies a pattern of stars?

A. The universe has many different types of stars.
B. Stars use hydrogen as fuel for nuclear fusion.
C. At the end of their life cycles, stars become relatively small, dense bodies.
D. All stars explode in supernovas at the end of their life cycles.

DIRECTIONS: Read the passage and question, and choose the **best** answer.

Through observation and measurement of certain astronomical events, scientists estimate that Earth is about 4.54 billion years old. Through the process of radiometric dating, scientists can identify the exact age of rock by using radioactive isotopes. The various isotopes decay at specific rates and yield certain products when they decay. Scientists can measure the amounts of a particular isotope and the product of its decay within a rock sample. Then they can calculate the age of the rock sample. Scientists have found a mineral determined to be about 4.4 billion years old in a younger rock. They think it was eroded from an older rock.

13. Which statement expresses a conclusion that can be reached about the dating of rock?

A. Scientists must know the order in which layers of rock were deposited in land formations to know the exact age of rock.
B. Scientists can use radioactive or nonradioactive isotopes for radiometric dating.
C. Knowing the rate of decay of a radioactive isotope is essential in radiometric dating.
D. After a certain amount of time, the radioactive isotopes in rock destroy it, making radiometric dating of the rock impossible.

DIRECTIONS: Study the model, and read the question. Then write your response on the lines. This task may take approximately 10 minutes to complete.

NUCLEAR FUSION IN THE SUN

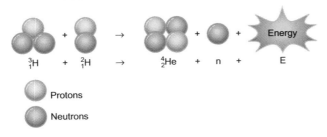

^3_1H + ^2_1H → ^4_2He + n + E

○ Protons

● Neutrons

14. Express scientific information verbally by explaining the fusion reaction that occurs in the sun.

_____

_____

_____

_____

_____

_____

_____

_____

_____

_____

_____

_____

DIRECTIONS: Study the table. Then read each question, and choose the **best** answer.

Inner Planets	Outer Planets
Rocky bodies	Largely gaseous, with relatively small solid cores
Four planets; two of four have one or two moons	Four planets; all have several moons
Hard surfaces of rock	Surfaces are not made of rock
No systems of rings	All have ring systems
Held in orbit by the sun's gravitational pull	Held in orbit by the sun's gravitational pull
Only one has large quantities of liquid surface water	None have large quantities of liquid surface water
Smallest planets	Largest planets

15. What structural pattern exists among the four inner planets?

A. large quantity of surface water
B. system of several thin rings
C. orbited by one or two moons
D. small, with a rocky surface

16. What pattern is displayed among the four outer planets?

A. a body that is completely gaseous
B. hard surfaces
C. a lack of rings
D. several moons

DIRECTIONS: Read the passage and question. Then use the drag-and-drop options to respond.

The ocean affects Earth and Earth's organisms in many ways. One primary way involves the role the ocean plays in the water cycle. Through the process of changing states, water from the ocean becomes water that falls to Earth to become water in the ocean again, and the cycle goes on and on.

17. Based on the concept of states of matter, what happens when water in the ocean is heated by the sun? Determine which drag-and-drop option identifies this change of state, and record the term in the box on the diagram.

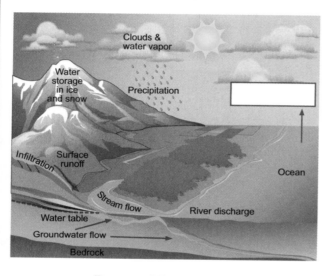

Drag-and-Drop Options

condensation	evaporation
sublimation	melting

DIRECTIONS: Study the diagram, read the question, and choose the **best** answer.

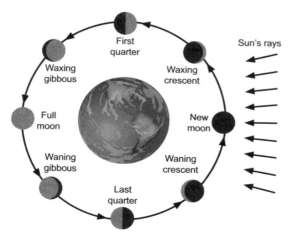

18. Which sequence represents a complete pattern of lunar phases?

A. full moon → last quarter → waning crescent → new moon
B. new moon → first quarter → full moon → last quarter → new moon
C. first quarter → waxing gibbous → full moon → waning gibbous
D. last quarter → waning crescent → new moon → waxing crescent

DIRECTIONS: Study the graph, read each question, and choose the **best** answer.

COMPOSITION OF THE ATMOSPHERE

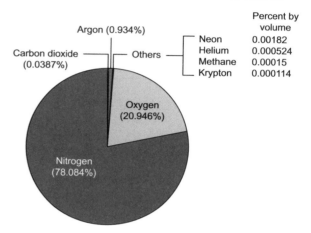

19. Based on the graph, which statement expresses the proportion of oxygen in Earth's atmosphere?

A. Oxygen is the most plentiful gas in Earth's atmosphere.
B. Oxygen makes up less of the atmosphere than any greenhouse gas does.
C. Oxygen and the most plentiful gas make up more than 98 percent of the atmosphere.
D. There is more oxygen than nitrogen but less oxygen than carbon dioxide.

20. Which statement **best** summarizes the information in the graph?

A. Earth's atmosphere is made up mostly of nitrogen and oxygen but contains small percentages of other gases.
B. Nitrogen is the most prevalent gas in Earth's atmosphere.
C. Nitrogen and oxygen are the two primary gases that make up Earth's atmosphere.
D. Gases occurring in less plentiful amounts in Earth's atmosphere include carbon dioxide, argon, and helium.

DIRECTIONS: Study the table. Then read the incomplete passage that follows. Use information from the table to complete the passage. For each drop-down item, choose the option that **best** completes the sentence.

Arguments Supporting Wind Energy	Arguments Opposing Wind Energy
Wind produces electricity without producing pollution.	Wind is an unreliable energy source because there are many times when wind does not blow.
Wind is a free source of energy.	There are a limited number of areas where the wind is strong enough to make installing turbines practical.
Wind is a renewable energy source.	Wind turbines range from 200 feet to 400 feet tall—the size of a 20- to 40-story building. They are often placed on ridges or offshore in scenic areas and, therefore, will always encounter local opposition.
About 67 percent of the wind turbines used in the United States today are made in the United States.	Wind is expensive because of the cost of construction and maintenance of turbines.
When subsidies are stripped away, wind costs $48–$95/megawatt-hour, natural gas costs $61–$231/megawatt-hour, and coal costs $62–$141/megawatt-hour.	Birds and bats are often killed when struck by the blades of huge wind turbines.

21. Many people argue for the growth of wind energy, and others argue against it. One of the main arguments in support of wind energy is that it is a free and [21. Drop-down 1] resource. Opponents of wind energy argue that wind is an unreliable resource and that wind turbines are a danger to [21. Drop-down 2].

Drop-Down Answer Options

21.1 A. exhaustible
B. nonrenewable
C. renewable
D. depleted

21.2 A. airplanes
B. people
C. power lines
D. wildlife

DIRECTIONS: Read the passage and question, and choose the **best** answer.

The National Weather Service (NWS) has created a system of watches and warnings for natural hazards such as tornadoes, hurricanes, flash floods, and blizzards. Tornadoes are a frequent natural hazard in parts of the Midwest and the Great Plains during spring and summer. The NWS issues a tornado watch when atmospheric conditions are right for the development of tornadoes, with advice to stay alert for further information. The NWS issues a tornado warning when a tornado has been seen on the ground or has been spotted on radar. A warning is the signal that it is time to look for shelter from the storm.

22. How do watches and warnings help solve the problem of dealing with strong and dangerous storms, such as tornadoes?

A. They help prevent dangerous storms.
B. They allow people to take cover so that there is less danger of being hurt.
C. They allow meteorologists to study severe storms more easily.
D. They help people understand how severe storms such as tornadoes form.

DIRECTIONS: Read the passage and question, and choose the **best** answer.

The pH of precipitation is changing in some parts of the United States due to the burning of fossil fuels, primarily in electric power plants. The combustion of coal and oil releases substances such as sulfur dioxide and nitrogen oxides into the air. These substances combine with water to make precipitation more acidic than usual. Acidic precipitation harms forests and can cause the release of aluminum from soil into lakes and streams. The higher levels of aluminum and acidity are deadly to some fish species. Acid precipitation also eats away stone and metal in statues and structures.

23. Which argument is **best** supported by the data presented?

   A. The burning of fossil fuels affects all Earth's systems.
   B. The health of all animals is harmed by the burning of fossil fuels.
   C. All across the United States, the burning of fossil fuels is causing acid precipitation.
   D. All important U.S. monuments must be protected from acid precipitation.

DIRECTIONS: Read the passage. Then read each question, and choose the **best** answer.

Agricultural practices can contaminate drinking-water supplies with fertilizers and pesticides. These chemicals can enter water supplies through runoff and precipitation. Modern animal farming also contributes contamination because many animals live in a small area and their wastes build up and then enter water supplies. The wastes can contain disease-causing organisms and traces of drugs given to the animals. Some people think older methods of rotating crops and letting animals graze and spread wastes over larger areas can help reduce the negative effects of agriculture on drinking water. But for these methods to be accepted, they must be as effective as modern practices.

24. What is the main problem that the passage identifies?

   A. Agriculture uses too much water.
   B. Some farming practices pollute drinking-water supplies.
   C. Fertilizers do not increase plant productivity enough.
   D. Crop rotation does not reduce the effects of pollution.

25. What problem must be overcome if the proposed solutions are to succeed?

   A. There must be a larger supply of fertilizers and pesticides.
   B. Cropland must become animal pasture.
   C. Drinking water must come from surface water sources, not groundwater.
   D. New farming methods must produce the same amount of food as the methods they replace.

DIRECTIONS: Read the passage. Then read each question, and choose the **best** answer.

Most energy used in the United States for producing electricity and fueling motor vehicles comes from fossil fuel sources, such as coal, oil, and natural gas. Very little comes from cleaner alternative sources such as wind, solar power, and geothermal power. Unlike these alternative sources, combustion of fossil fuels produces waste gases, such as carbon dioxide. Carbon dioxide is naturally present in the atmosphere as part of the carbon cycle. For example, decomposition of plant material releases carbon dioxide to the air. But the combustion of fossil fuels has increased dramatically since the start of the Industrial Revolution in the late 1700s—along with the concentration of carbon dioxide in the air. Data suggest that this increase is responsible for changes in climate that could have negative effects on Earth's plant and animal life.

26. What is the basic problem identified in the passage?

   A. People have used fossil fuels since the Industrial Revolution.
   B. Excess carbon dioxide is entering Earth's atmosphere.
   C. Too much energy is being used to run electric power plants and motor vehicles.
   D. Carbon dioxide enters the atmosphere from several natural sources.

27. Based on information in the passage, what is a possible solution?

   A. slowing decomposition of plant material
   B. changing the atmosphere to absorb more carbon dioxide
   C. using cleaner alternative energy sources instead of fossil fuels
   D. using more natural gas instead of coal and oil

DIRECTIONS: Read the passage. Then read the question, and answer by marking the appropriate hot spots.

Water is a powerful force that shapes Earth's surface. Flowing water can pick up and carry rock and sediment from place to place. This process is called erosion. Swiftly moving water causes more erosion than water that moves slowly because water that moves fast can carry more rock and sediment.

A river is one body of water that causes erosion, especially in certain places. A meander is a bend in a river. River water moves fastest on the outside curve of a meander. It moves slowest on the inside curve of a meander.

28. Express your understanding of how a river's flow causes erosion. Mark an *X* on each part of the diagram where the river causes more erosion.

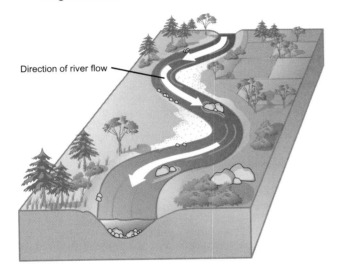

Direction of river flow

DIRECTIONS: Read the passage. Then read each question, and choose the **best** answer.

Glen Canyon Dam blocks the Colorado River in northern Arizona, forming a huge reservoir (Lake Powell) behind it. The waters of the lake rush through the dam, producing hydropower for more than 1 million people. The lake is also a dependable source of water for irrigating arid farmland. But Glen Canyon Dam has changed the characteristics of the river below it, altering its flow rate and temperature and removing sediment. As a result, several aquatic species below the dam are no longer in the area. Still, the biggest controversy has been the loss of beautiful Glen Canyon, now deep beneath the waters of Lake Powell. Glen Canyon was especially magnificent, with exquisite rock formations, unique species, and artifacts left behind by the area's ancient peoples. Several groups want to allow the Colorado to flow freely past Glen Canyon Dam again, draining much of Lake Powell and once again exposing Glen Canyon.

29. Which statement summarizes the environmental effects of Glen Canyon Dam?

   A. It provides power for more than 1 million people, but it has caused a significant controversy.
   B. It has changed the features of the Colorado River, ecosystems, and scenic and historic aspects of the area.
   C. It has formed a lake whose waters are used for producing power and irrigating farmland.
   D. It has drained Lake Powell and exposed Glen Canyon.

30. What are the two opposing arguments about Glen Canyon Dam represented in the passage?

   A. hydroelectric power versus the combustion of fossil fuels to produce electricity
   B. dryland farming with irrigation versus farming with natural precipitation
   C. the value of natural environments versus the needs of a technically advanced society
   D. the importance of lakes for producing electric power versus their value for recreation

Answer Key

UNIT 1 LIFE SCIENCE

LESSON 1, pp. 2–3
1. **C**; **DOK Level:** 1; **Content Topics:** L.d.1, L.d.2; **Practices:** SP.1.a, SP.1.b, SP.1.c, SP.7.a
The labels in the illustration explain the job of each structure shown. The ribosomes are the structures that make proteins. The cell wall is a rigid structure that helps the bacterium keep its shape. The flagellum helps move the cell. The cell membrane encloses the cell and allows waste and nutrients to move in and out.

2. **C**; **DOK Level:** 2; **Content Topics:** L.d.1, L.d.2, L.d.3; **Practices:** SP.1.a, SP.1.b, SP.1.c, SP.7.a
In the illustration, a change in the shape of the cell shows that the cell begins to separate during anaphase, as the sister parts separate. The shape of the cell during prophase and metaphase indicates that the cell has not begun to separate during those phases. The illustration shows that telophase occurs after anaphase, so separation is already under way.

3. **B**; **DOK Level:** 2; **Content Topics:** L.d.1, L.d.2, L.d.3; **Practices:** SP.1.a, SP.1.b, SP.1.c, SP.7.a
The illustration shows the genetic material contained in the parent cell before mitosis and explains that the material is replicated during interphase and then split between two new daughter cells during mitosis. This information indicates that a parent cell having four chromosomes will produce daughter cells that each have four chromosomes. At no point do the cells have two, eight, or sixteen chromosomes.

4. **D**; **DOK Level:** 2; **Content Topics:** L.b.1, L.d.1; **Practices:** SP.1.a, SP.1.b, SP.1.c, SP.7.a
You can determine by studying the shapes and structures of the labeled organelles in the illustration and matching their shapes and structures to the unlabeled organelles that the two unlabeled organelles close to the Golgi complex are a mitochondrion and a lysosome and that neither unlabeled organelle is a nucleus or cytoplasm.

LESSON 2, pp. 4–5
1. **C**; **DOK Level:** 1; **Content Topics:** L.a.1, L.d.2; **Practices:** SP.1.a, SP.1.b
The passage provides many details about how cells are organized in groups and how cells and groups of cells work together to perform certain functions, so the main idea of the passage is that cells specialize to perform specific functions and are organized to perform these functions. If the main idea were that an organism may be made up of millions of cells of many different types, the supporting details would be examples of different types of cells. If the main idea were that the cells in an organism are not all alike and do not have the same jobs, the supporting details would be examples of jobs cells have without explanation of how cells work together to perform specific functions. The statement that organized groups of cells work together to carry out a specific function by forming tissues is a supporting detail of the passage's main idea.

2. **A**; **DOK Level:** 2; **Content Topics:** L.a.1, L.d.2; **Practices:** SP.1.a, SP.1.b, SP.1.c
The detail that axons send messages out from neurons supports the main idea that neurons carry signals through the body to allow a person to move, sense things, think, and learn. It is the only detail that focuses on sending signals. The other details describe the shape of the neuron and its structures and do not support the main idea stated in the question.

3. **D**; **DOK Level:** 3; **Content Topics:** L.a.1, L.d.2; **Practices:** SP.1.a, SP.1.b
The passage presents various roles of bones, which make up the skeletal system, so the sentence that best fits in the passage to express the main idea is "The skeletal system has numerous functions." The statement that some bone cells release calcium into the blood is a supporting detail about functions of bones. The statements about two types of bone tissue and bones being reshaped throughout a person's life do not fit in this passage, which is about functions of the skeletal system.

4. **C**; **DOK Level:** 2; **Content Topic:** L.a.1; **Practices:** SP.1.a, SP.1.b, SP.1.c, SP.7.a
The illustration shows and explains the roles of various organs in the process of digestion from the time one swallows to the time waste passes into the large intestine; therefore, the statement that identifies the main idea of the illustration is "Digestion is a complex process involving several organs." The statement that digestion begins even before a person swallows describes a part of digestion that is not addressed by the illustration. The statement that digestion is mostly complete when the food leaves the small intestine is a supporting detail about digestion being a complex process. The statement that digestion takes place mostly in the stomach is not entirely true because a good amount of digestion also takes place in the small intestine.

5. **B**; **DOK Level:** 2; **Content Topic:** L.a.1; **Practices:** SP.1.a, SP.1.b, SP.1.c, SP.7.a
The illustration indicates that secretions from organs—pancreatic and intestinal juices and bile from the liver—complete digestion in the small intestine, so the detail about the juices involved in digestion in the small intestine best supports the main idea. The other details refer to the small intestine and digestion, but not specifically to secretions from organs.

LESSON 3, pp. 6–7
1. **B**; **DOK Level:** 1; **Content Topic:** L.a.3; **Practices:** SP.1.a, SP.1.b, SP.1.c
Eggs are listed in the "Vitamin B12" row of the table; therefore, they are a food that contains vitamin B12. Black-eyed peas, broccoli, and peanuts are not listed in the "Vitamin B12" row of the table.

2. **B**; **DOK Level:** 2; **Content Topic:** L.a.3; **Practices:** SP.1.a, SP.1.b, SP.1.c
The heading of the first column of a table is a good clue to the information the table is displaying. In this table, the heading of the first column is "Class," indicating that the table lists different nutrient classes. The information in the next two columns is information about the nutrient classes. So the best title for the table is "Major Nutrient Classes." "Vitamins and Minerals" is not an appropriate title because the table provides information about seven nutrient classes, not just vitamins and minerals. "Healthful Eating" is not the best title because the table gives only examples of foods with the different nutrients, not information on eating. "Nutrient Uses" is not the best title because the uses of nutrients is only one part of the table, not the main idea.

3. **A**; **DOK Level:** 2; **Content Topic:** L.a.3; **Practices:** SP.1.a, SP.1.b, SP.1.c
According to the table, the human body needs minerals to build bones. The skeletal system is made up of bones, so a lack of minerals would most affect the skeletal system. Proteins build muscles and the immune system, not the skeletal system. Water is not directly involved in bone building. Carbohydrates give the muscles, nerves, and brain energy.

4. **D**; **DOK Level:** 3; **Content Topic:** L.a.3; **Practices:** SP.1.a, SP.1.b, SP.1.c, SP.3.b
According to the table, vegetables are listed as a source of carbohydrates, vitamins, minerals, water, and dietary fiber. No other item is listed as an example of more nutrient classes. According to the table, eating beans provides only protein and dietary fiber, drinking water provides only nutrients from water, and taking vitamins provides only vitamins.

5. **A**; **DOK Level:** 2; **Content Topic:** L.a.3; **Practices:** SP.1.a, SP.1.b, SP.1.c, SP.3.b
The information in the passage is about good bacteria and how they are helpful. It mentions helpful bacteria in the human body. The table lists good bacteria in the large intestine and how they are helpful, so the idea that some bacteria that live in the digestive tract of humans are helpful is supported by both the passage and the table. The ideas that bacteria break down and recycle nutrients and that production of some foods relies on bacteria are supported only by the passage. The idea that millions of bacteria live inside the human body is not completely supported by either the passage or the table because neither refers to numbers of bacteria.

LESSON 4, *pp. 8–9*
1. **C**; **DOK Level:** 2; **Content Topic:** L.a.2; **Practices:** SP.1.a, SP.1.b, SP.1.c
According to the illustration, the body reacts to histamine by moving blood and fluids to the area and producing swelling. It does not drain blood and fluids from the injured area. The illustration indicates that the body sends white blood cells, not its own bacteria, to the area. The illustration shows that blood vessels in the area expand, not narrow, in response to histamine release.

2.1 **B**; 2.2 **C**; 2.3 **D**; 2.4 **A**; **DOK Level:** 2; **Content Topic:** L.a.2; **Practices:** SP.1.a, SP.1.b, SP.7.a
2.1 According to the passage, signals that stimulate the eccrine glands cause them to secrete sweat onto the surface of the skin. The passage does not mention an increase in heart rate. It discusses salt in the context of being part of sweat, so salt is not being absorbed. Bacteria do not cause odor because of signals sent to the eccrine glands; odor is related to sweat from the apocrine glands.
2.2 According to the passage, the evaporation of sweat from the skin causes the body to cool. At no point in this process does the body break down bacteria. At this point in the sequence of events, the body already has secreted fluid, in the form of sweat.
2.3 According to the passage, the odor associated with sweating is caused by the action of bacteria breaking down sweat. It is not caused directly by the eccrine glands, the body's temperature regulating mechanisms, or body fluids.
2.4. According to the passage, the apocrine glands are responsible for secreting the sweat that bacteria break down, causing odor. The adrenal gland and pituitary gland are not involved in this process. The eccrine glands are those involved in producing sweat that does not have an odor.

LESSON 5, *pp. 10–11*
1. **C**; **DOK Level:** 2; **Content Topic:** L.a.4; **Practices:** SP.1.a, SP.1.b, SP.1.c
As the number of cases increases, the taller the bar is on the graph, meaning that the year in which the largest number of confirmed and probable cases was reported is the year with the tallest bar—2009. The bars for 2007, 2008, and 2010 are shorter than the bar for 2009.

2. **D**; **DOK Level:** 2; **Content Topic:** L.a.4; **Practices:** SP.1.a, SP.1.b, SP.1.c
The key shows the colors for the various categories of geographic spread of the flu. Most states on the map are light green, which the key shows means "widespread." The colors for "sporadic," "local," and "regional" are yellow, beige, and blue, respectively.

3. **A**; **DOK Level:** 2; **Content Topic:** L.a.4; **Practices:** SP.1.a, SP.1.b, SP.1.c
The overall direction of the line on the graph between 2000 and 2010 is downward from left to right, indicating that over time the number of cases decreased. If the number of cases stayed the same, the line would be flat. If the number of cases increased or doubled, the line would go upward from left to right.

4. **C**; **DOK Level:** 3; **Content Topic:** L.a.4; **Practices:** SP.1.a, SP.1.b, SP.1.c, SP.3.b, SP.3.d
The detail in the passage about proper hygiene preventing the spread of hepatitis A and the trend of decreasing numbers of cases over time shown in the graph combine to support the assumption that greater knowledge about how to control the spread of hepatitis A has led to fewer infections. The graph shows that the number of cases of hepatitis A declined significantly, not increased, between 2000 and 2010. Neither the passage nor the graph provides support for the assumptions about the virus becoming weaker or fewer people with hepatitis A seeking treatment from a doctor.

Answer Key

UNIT 1 *(continued)*

LESSON 6, *pp. 12–13*

1. C; **DOK Level:** 2; **Content Topics:** L.c.1, L.c.2; **Practices:** SP.1.a, SP.1.b, SP.1.c, SP.7.a
The direction of the arrow between the "Grasshopper" and "Sparrow" boxes indicates that grasshoppers are food for sparrows. The arrow from the "Sparrow" box to the "Hawk" box indicates that hawks eat sparrows, not grass. The direction of the arrow between the "Grasshopper" and "Sparrow" boxes indicates that sparrows eat grasshoppers, not vice versa. The arrow from the "Sparrow" box to the "Hawk" box indicates that hawks eat sparrows, not grasshoppers.

2. B; **DOK Level:** 2; **Content Topic:** L.c.2; **Practices:** SP.1.b, SP.1.c
The direction of the arrow from the "Soil, air, and water" box to the "Plants" box indicates that soil, air, and water are sources of nutrients for plants. The diagram does not show the number of organisms in any part of the nutrients cycle; it shows only how nutrients flow through the living and nonliving parts of an ecosystem. The direction of the arrow from the "Animals that eat plants" box to the "Animals that eat animals" box indicates that animals that eat plants are a source of nutrients for animals that eat animals, not vice versa. The title of the diagram indicates that the diagram is about the movement of nutrients in an ecosystem; therefore, you can assume that each box in the diagram identifies a part of the nutrients cycle.

3. C; **DOK Level:** 2; **Content Topic:** L.c.2; **Practices:** SP.1.a, SP.1.b, SP.1.c, SP.7.a
All elements of a diagram are included for a reason. The inclusion of five elements in this diagram indicates that all five elements are required for the nutrients cycle to continue. This diagram indicates that nutrients move through a cycle; in a cycle, the same events always occur in the same order. It is impossible to assume from the diagram that plant-eating animals would eat other animals if all plants died. A diagram showing a cycle indicates that eliminating part of that cycle would cause the cycle to end; however, such a diagram does not indicate how individual parts of the cycle would change if one part of the cycle were removed.

4. A; **DOK Level:** 2; **Content Topic:** L.c.1; **Practices:** SP.1.a, SP.1.b, SP.1.c, SP.7.a
The placement of caterpillars directly above ferns in the energy pyramid indicates that caterpillars get energy by eating ferns. Although foxes are above ferns in the pyramid, the placement of foxes directly above birds indicates that foxes get energy by eating birds, not ferns. Although birds are above ferns in the energy pyramid, the placement of birds directly above caterpillars indicates that birds get energy by eating caterpillars, not ferns. The placement of caterpillars below birds in the energy pyramid indicates that caterpillars supply energy to birds, not that caterpillars get energy from birds.

5. D; **DOK Level:** 3; **Content Topic:** L.c.1; **Practices:** SP.1.a, SP.1.b, SP.1.c, SP.7.a
Because the diagram is smaller at each level, its shape reinforces the idea that the amount of available energy decreases as energy passes from organism to organism through the levels of the pyramid. Although the animals shown at higher levels in the energy pyramid are larger in general, the shape of the diagram does not indicate that larger animals in an ecosystem eat smaller animals in the ecosystem. Because plants are at the base of the pyramid, the shape of the diagram may reinforce the idea that plants form the basis for all food chains in an ecosystem; however, the shape of the diagram does not indicate that plants use sunlight to obtain energy. The diagram is not related to where organisms live in an environment, so its shape cannot indicate anything about where organisms live.

LESSON 7, *pp. 14–15*

1. A; **DOK Level:** 2; **Content Topic:** L.c.4; **Practices:** SP.1.a, SP.1.b, SP.1.c
According to the information, the predator-prey relationship is one in which the predator eats the prey. Of the relationships listed, the best example of a predator-prey relationship is that of a bear and a fish. Bears eat fish, so the bear is the predator, and the fish is the prey. Goats do not eat pigs. A bee drinks nectar from flowers but does not actually consume flowers. A barnacle is an organism in the ocean that lives on a whale, but it does not eat the whale.

2. DOK Level: 2; **Content Topic:** L.c.4; **Practices:** SP.1.a, SP.1.b, SP.1.c, SP.6.a, SP.6.c
The canine is a **host** to the tapeworm—the tapeworm lives inside the canine, taking nutrients from food the canine ingests. The tapeworm is a **parasite**—the tapeworm benefits from living inside the canine and harms the canine by taking nutrients from food the canine ingests. The vole is an intermediate **host** in the life cycle of the tapeworm—it hosts the parasite when it hatches from an egg into a larva and develops into a juvenile.

3. DOK Level: 2; **Content Topic:** L.c.4; **Practices:** SP.1.a, SP.1.b, SP.6.c
Commensalism and **mutualism** are the two categories of symbiotic relationships discussed in the passage.

LESSON 8, *pp. 16–17*

1. B; **DOK Level:** 2; **Content Topics:** L.c.3, L.c.4; **Practices:** SP.1.a, SP.1.b, SP.1.c, SP.3.b
The information states and the diagram shows that a community is made up of different populations and that a population is a group of organisms that are all the same species. So if most communities contain all the populations in an area, you can generalize that communities are made up of many different species. The statements that there are different kinds of living things in an ecosystem, that populations in an ecosystem are made up of individual organisms, and that all the organisms in a population are of the same species are facts, not generalizations.

2. DOK Level: 3; **Content Topic:** L.c.3; **Practices:** SP.1.a, SP.1.b, SP.1.c, SP.3.b, SP.6.c
The curve in the graph shows that a population generally **increases in size** until it reaches its carrying capacity.

3. **DOK Level:** 3; **Content Topic:** L.c.3; **Practices:** SP.1.a, SP.1.b, SP.1.c, SP.3.b, SP.3.d, SP.6.c
The steep incline of the curve between years 40 and 60 indicates that the population is increasing rapidly during that time. Based on the graph, the generalization can be made that similar populations in similar ecosystems are **increasing rapidly** between years 40 and 60.

4. **DOK Level:** 3; **Content Topic:** L.c.3; **Practices:** SP.1.a, SP.1.b, SP.1.c, SP.3.b, SP.6.c
If a new competitor were introduced in the ecosystem, the graph would show a generally lower **carrying capacity** for the population it represents because competition for resources affects carrying capacity.

5. **A**; **DOK Level:** 3; **Content Topics:** L.c.3, L.c.5; **Practices:** SP.1.a, SP.1.b, SP.3.b
If an invasive species can make up a large percentage of an ecosystem's biomass, that means it is taking away resources from other organisms in the ecosystem. A valid generalization is that competition from invasive species usually leads to decreased carrying capacity for other organisms because those other organisms will have fewer resources. The other statements are not valid generalizations based on the information. In fact, competition does not typically ensure that the healthiest species survive. A species may be very healthy and still be greatly damaged by competition from an invasive species. The fact that an invasive species can make up a large percentage of an ecosystem's biomass refutes the idea that competition affects the invasive species negatively. Faced with competition from invasive species, an organism that is out-competed will face a decrease in carrying capacity because it is left with fewer resources to support its numbers.

LESSON 9, *pp. 18–19*
1. **C**; **DOK Level:** 2; **Content Topic:** L.c.5; **Practices:** SP.1.a, SP.1.b, SP.1.c
For all groups, the 2012 figure for number of threatened species is higher than the 2006 figure, so the numbers of known threatened species for all groups have increased. By comparing and contrasting the data, you can determine that all groups are alike in that the issue of threatened species remains a problem, that most but not all groups include more than 1,000 threatened species, and that the 2012 figures for most groups are significantly different than the 2006 figures.

2. **DOK Level:** 2; **Content Topics:** L.c.2, L.c.5; **Practices:** SP.1.a, SP.1.b, SP.3.a, SP.6.a, SP.6.c
The characteristics of a healthy ecosystem include **correct proportions of nutrients and sunlight** and **high level of biodiversity**. The correct proportions of nutrients and sunlight allow the nutrient and energy cycles to flow properly. A high level of biodiversity makes an ecosystem more resilient and able to survive change because it has a greater number of species. The characteristics of an unhealthy ecosystem include **nonnative species, loss of habitat**, and **polluted water**. Nonnative species are invasive and upset the balance of populations in an ecosystem. Loss of habitat causes imbalance in the ecosystem because the numbers of certain populations will decline. Polluted water affects an ecosystem negatively in many ways because plants and animals rely on water. A characteristic of both healthy and unhealthy ecosystems is **living and nonliving parts**. All ecosystems are made up of living organisms and the nonliving parts of their surroundings.

LESSON 10, *pp. 20–21*
1. **B**; **DOK Level:** 2; **Content Topics:** L.d.3, L.e.1; **Practices:** SP.1.a, SP.1.b, SP.1.c, SP.7.a
The illustration shows the chromosome pairs in humans and numbers them. The text explains that each species has a certain number of chromosomes in their cells and that chromosomes form pairs. All of this information suggests that humans have 23 pairs of chromosomes in their cells. The illustration shows that the chromosomes are not identical. The text explains that chromosomes make copies of themselves when a cell divides; it does not say that they double in size. No information is given about the number of chromosome pairs in other species.

2. **D**; **DOK Level:** 2; **Content Topic:** L.e.1; **Practices:** SP.1.a, SP.1.b, SP.1.c, SP.7.a
The text explains that each nucleotide contains one of four bases and that the bases form pairs; the illustration shows that the base pairs form different patterns in different parts of a DNA molecule. The sugars and phosphates are described and shown as forming the ladder's sides, but not the middle of a DNA molecule nor the rungs of the ladder. The illustration shows that the sides of the DNA molecule are the same, so one is not longer than the other.

3. **A**; **DOK Level:** 2; **Content Topic:** L.e.1; **Practices:** SP.1.a, SP.1.b, SP.1.c, SP.7.a
The description of a gene in the text and the bracketed portions of the DNA shown in the illustration indicate that a gene is a segment of DNA. There is not enough information to state that all genes have five pairs of nucleotide bases because the illustration shows just a sample gene. Also, there is not enough information to determine how many genes are on one DNA strand. The text explains that genes provide the instructions for building proteins; the nucleotide bases themselves are not proteins.

LESSON 11, *pp. 22–23*
1. **B**; **DOK Level:** 1; **Content Topic:** L.e.2; **Practices:** SP.1.a, SP.1.b, SP.1.c, SP.3.d
The genetics diagram suggests that a trait may reoccur even if it does not occur in a previous generation by showing that the white flower trait occurs in the parent generation, does not occur in the first generation, and occurs in the second generation. The diagram shows that plants with purple flowers produced a plant with white flowers. The information in the genetics diagram has nothing to do with offspring survival rates. A single offspring does not show a blending of the traits of both parents; it has either purple or white flowers.

2. **DOK Level:** 3; **Content Topic:** L.e.2; **Practices:** SP.1.a, SP.1.b, SP.1.c, SP.8.b, SP.8.c
Presence of the dominant allele, represented by P, causes a pea plant to have purple flowers. The dominant allele likely will be present in three out of four offspring, so the phenotype **purple flower color** likely will occur in three-fourths, or 75 percent, of offspring.

Answer Key

UNIT 1 *(continued)*

3. **DOK Level:** 3; **Content Topics:** L.d.3, L.e.2;
Practices: SP.1.a, SP.1.b, SP.1.c, SP.8.b
Molly is the only grandchild who could have short
eyelashes because both of her parents have the recessive
allele *a*. She could inherit the recessive allele from both
parents and, therefore, have short eyelashes. Leslie will
inherit the dominant allele *A* from her mother because her
mother has two dominant alleles, so Leslie cannot have
short eyelashes.

LESSON 12, *pp. 24–25*
1. **B**; **DOK Level:** 2; **Content Topic:** L.e.3; **Practices:**
SP.1.a, SP.1.b, SP.3.b, SP.7.a
The passage says that the mixing of paternal and maternal
genes contributes to genetic variation. From this clue and
others in the passage, you can determine that genetic
variation is the genetic differences, or differences in traits,
among individuals. The segregation of alleles to gametes
contributes to genetic variation but is not what genetic
variation is. Genetic variation is a result of events that occur
during meiosis, not an event itself. Distance between genes
on a chromosome can relate to genes being inherited
together; it is not the definition of genetic variation.

2. **DOK Level:** 3; **Content Topic:** L.e.3; **Practices:** SP.1.a,
SP.1.b, SP.1.c, SP.3.b
Incorrect nucleotide base pairing is one type of mutation.
Correct base pairing in DNA replication is G-C and T-A.
The **illustration of DNA replication on the right** shows
a mutation—a T paired with a G instead of an A. The other
two illustrations of DNA replication show correct base
pairings.

3. **D**; **DOK Level:** 2; **Content Topic:** L.e.3; **Practices:**
SP.1.a, SP.1.b, SP.3.b, SP.7.a
The passage explains that the epigenome is made up of
chemical compounds and restates the language "chemical
compounds" as "epigenetic marks." So an epigenetic mark
is a chemical compound that tells the genome what to do,
when to do it, and where to do it. The epigenome can be
influenced by environmental factors, but environmental
factors are not epigenetic marks. An organism's epigenome
has an influence on the organism's DNA, but it is not itself
DNA. An epigenetic mark is not a genetic mutation, although
it may cause negative results as some mutations do.

4. **C**; **DOK Level:** 2; **Content Topic:** L.e.3; **Practices:**
SP.1.a, SP.1.b, SP.3.b, SP.7.a
The passage describes environmental factors as items an
organism eats or drinks or pollutants it encounters. This
clue tells you that secondhand smoke is an example of an
environmental factor. Chemical compounds on DNA make
up an organism's epigenome. A gene for blue eyes is part
of an organism's DNA, so it is a genetic factor. The trait of
being double-jointed is also a genetic factor.

LESSON 13, *pp. 26–27*
1. **C**; **DOK Level:** 1; **Content Topic:** L.f.1; **Practices:**
SP.1.a, SP.1.b, SP.1.c, SP.3.a, SP.7.a
The passage states that humans, bats, porpoises, and
horses have similar, or homologous, bone structures and
that homologous structures are evidence of a common
ancestor. The living things mentioned use their forelimbs
for differing actions, such as flying and running, so their
forelimbs do not have similar functions. The forelimbs of the
living things mentioned have different functions because
the organisms have different lifestyles. The passage does
not indicate any relationship between habitat and common
ancestry.

2. **B**; **DOK Level:** 2: **Content Topic:** L.f.1; **Practices:**
SP.1.a, SP.1.b, SP.1.c, SP.3.a, SP.7.a
The passage states that similar embryonic development
provides evidence of common ancestry, and the illustration
shows similar embryonic development of the three animals.
The passage and illustration do not address functions of
limbs or bone structure. Although four development stages
are shown in the illustration, organisms go through a growth
and development process that happens continuously, not
just in four stages.

3. **C**; **DOK Level:** 2; **Content Topic:** L.f.1; **Practices:**
SP.1.a, SP.1.b, SP.1.c, SP.3.b, SP.7.a
Moving up a cladogram, each group of organisms has a
new derived characteristic. So the cladogram indicates
that conifers have seeds but that ferns do not. A group of
organisms represented on a cladogram has all the traits
listed before it, so the cladogram indicates that conifers
have vascular tissue and that conifers and ferns share the
trait vascular tissue. On a cladogram, groups of organisms
are listed at the ends of branches, so the cladogram
indicates that flowering plants are a different group of plants
than conifers.

4. **D**; **DOK Level:** 3; **Content Topic:** L.f.1; **Practices:**
SP.1.a, SP.1.b, SP.1.c, SP.3.b, SP.7.a
The evidence represented by the cladogram shows that
flowering plants cannot have come into existence before
conifers because flowering plants have flowers, a derived
characteristic that did not develop until after conifers already
existed. The evidence represented by the cladogram
helps support, not refute, the idea that flowering plants
and conifers have a common ancestor. The format of the
cladogram indicates that flowering plants and conifers share
the derived characteristic seeds. The evidence represented
by the cladogram indicates that flowering plants have only
one derived characteristic that conifers do not have.

LESSON 14, pp. 28–29

1. B; DOK Level: 2; **Content Topic:** L.f.2; **Practices:** SP.1.a, SP.1.b, SP.3.b, SP.7.a

The passage states that individuals having a heritable advantageous trait survive and reproduce to pass that trait on to future generations, thereby causing the trait to become more common in the population. Consequently, you can reason that individuals having a heritable detrimental trait will not survive to reproduce, and the heritable detrimental trait will occur less often in a population over time. The passage and illustration indicate that an individual's environment is significant in relation to traits the individual has, so factors in an organism's environment do have an effect on its survival. The passage explains how natural selection changes a species over time, so natural selection is related to evolutionary change in a species. The passage explains that beneficial heritable traits are passed down; however, the passage does not provide enough information to determine whether this description encompasses all traits. So it is over-generalizing to infer that all beneficial traits are passed on to future generations.

2. DOK Level: 2; **Content Topic:** L.f.2; **Practices:** SP.1.a, SP.1.b, SP.1.c, SP.3.b, SP.3.c, SP.6.c, SP.7.a

The observations that resources available to a population are limited and that a reproducing population which would naturally grow out of control stays balanced support the logical guess (Inference 1) that **competition for resources keeps many individuals from surviving to reproduce**. If the idea that competition for resources keeps many individuals from surviving to reproduce is logical, then it also makes sense to make the inference (Inference 2) that **traits that help individuals acquire and use resources are important to survival**.

3. A; DOK Level: 3; **Content Topic:** L.f.2; **Practices:** SP.1.a, SP.1.b, SP.3.b, SP.7.a

The passage states that the three requirements for natural selection are variation in traits, differential survivability, and heritable advantageous traits. The writer applies these requirements to a beetle population to make the inference about natural selection within that population. The color of an individual and the preferences of its predator are examples the writer uses in the inference, not information used to support the inference. The statement that natural selection can occur whenever organisms in a population have varying traits is an inaccurate statement about the requirements for natural selection. Although it is true that differential survivability occurs when members of a population have a beneficial trait, this statement does not summarize the information used to support the inference.

LESSON 15, pp. 30–31

1. C; DOK Level: 2; **Content Topic:** L.f.3; **Practices:** SP.1.a, SP.1.b, SP.3.b, SP.7.a

The inferences that selection pressures cause natural selection, that adaptations are passed from generation to generation, and that adaptation is related to evolution support the conclusion that evolution is the result of selection pressures, natural selection, and adaptation. The ideas that selection pressures change a species' ability to survive and reproduce and that species develop traits useful to survival in their environment are directly stated facts that support the conclusion, not conclusions themselves. The idea that populations that develop different adaptations always become different species is an over-generalization and, therefore, an invalid conclusion.

2. DOK Level: 3; **Content Topic:** L.f.3; **Practices:** SP.1.a, SP.1.b, SP.1.c, SP.3.a, SP.3.b, SP.6.c, SP.7.a

Possible answer:

(A) Through adaptation, reptiles have developed several traits that allow them to live in environments in which amphibians cannot survive. (B) Reptiles have scaly skin that does not need to be kept moist. Their eggs stay moist because they have shells that hold in their fluids. Reptiles are born with legs to walk on land, and they have claws that allow them to dig land. They have lungs their entire lives, allowing them to obtain oxygen by taking in air. Amphibians have none of these traits and, therefore, cannot survive in the drier environments in which reptiles live.

(A) The first sentence states a conclusion explaining how adaptation has resulted in reptiles' ability to live in environments in which amphibians could not survive.
(B) The rest of the paragraph lists specific examples of traits reptiles have that allow them to survive in drier habitats. The conclusion is supported by information from the passage and table and inferences made using that information.

UNIT 1 REVIEW, pp. 32–39

1. C; DOK Level: 2; **Content Topic:** L.c.3; **Practices:** SP.1.a, SP.1.b, SP.1.c, SP.7.a

When a line on a graph is horizontal, there is no change. The configuration of the line in the graph indicates that at point X, the population stopped growing. If the population had begun to grow more quickly, the line would go up sharply. If it had suddenly decreased, the line would go down sharply. If the population disappeared from the ecosystem, the line would go down to zero.

2. A; DOK Level: 2; **Content Topic:** L.c.3; **Practices:** SP.1.a, SP.1.b, SP.1.c, SP.7.a

Carrying capacity is the maximum number of individuals of a given species that an area's resources can sustain. The graph represents a typical population that grows quickly until it reaches carrying capacity. The introduction of a predator is more likely to make the population decline at point X. Unlimited resources would make the population increase, not stay the same. If adults were unable to find mates, the population would begin to decline.

UNIT 1 *(continued)*

3. D; **DOK Level:** 3; **Content Topic:** L.c.3; **Practices:** SP.1.a, SP.1.b, SP.1.c, SP.3.b, SP.7.a
If the graph were to show that the population had fewer individuals when its growth leveled off, it would mean that the carrying capacity for the population was lower. The most likely reason for a lower carrying capacity would be limited resources. If a disease were introduced, the graph would show a decline in the population. If there were an increase in offspring or an unlimited food supply, the graph would show an increase in the population.

4. D; **DOK Level:** 1; **Content Topic:** L.a.1; **Practices:** SP.1.a, SP.1.b, SP.1.c, SP.7.a
The two body parts involved in the digestion process before food enters the stomach are the mouth and the esophagus, so food must travel through the esophagus before it mixes with digestive juices in the stomach. The digestive system must break down food before nutrients are absorbed in the blood, so the body cannot absorb nutrients from the food until after it has been mixed with digestive juices in the stomach. The large intestine and rectum are body parts involved in the digestion process after food has mixed with digestive juices in the stomach.

5. C; **DOK Level:** 2; **Content Topics:** L.a.1, L.a.3; **Practices:** SP.1.a, SP.1.b, SP.1.c, SP.3.b, SP.7.a
The absorption of nutrients from food takes place after food has been mixed with digestive juices in the stomach, so the conclusion can be reached that the absorption of nutrients occurs in the small intestine. In the mouth and esophagus, food is just entering the digestive system and the beginning stages of digestion. The rectum holds waste after digestion.

6. B; **DOK Level:** 2; **Content Topics:** L.c.1, L.c.2; **Practices:** SP.1.a, SP.1.b, SP.1.c, SP.7.a
Information in the table indicates that the short-billed dowitcher eats the marsh periwinkle and that the marsh periwinkle eats cordgrass, so this is the most likely food chain. The herring gull eats the soft-shelled clam, and the soft-shelled clam eats phytoplankton, so the organisms in the "herring gull-soft-shelled clam-phytoplankton" food chain are in the wrong order. The peregrine falcon eats the herring gull and the snowy egret, so the grouping "peregrine falcon-herring gull-snowy egret" does not represent a food chain. The clam worm eats zooplankton, but the zooplankton does not eat cordgrass.

7. A; **DOK Level:** 2; **Content Topic:** L.c.2; **Practices:** SP.1.a, SP.1.b, SP.1.c, SP.3.b
Because marsh periwinkles eat cordgrass and short-billed dowitchers eat marsh periwinkles, the most likely effect of removing cordgrass from the ecosystem is that these two populations would decrease. Not all consumers would be eliminated because not all consumers eat cordgrass or eat animals that eat cordgrass. Phytoplankton populations would not necessarily increase because some consumers may begin to eat phytoplankton if they cannot eat cordgrass. Peregrine falcons would have fewer food resources because they eat marsh periwinkles, which eat cordgrass.

8. DOK Level: 2; **Content Topics:** L.d.1, L.d.2, L.d.3; **Practices:** SP.1.a, SP.1.b, SP.1.c, SP.7.a
The passage explains that cytokinesis is the division of cytoplasm. Therefore, the illustration shows that the phase of mitosis that coincides with the completion of cytokinesis is **telophase**, when the parent cell splits completely into two daughter cells.

9. A; **DOK Level:** 2; **Content Topic:** L.c.4; **Practices:** SP.1.a, SP.1.b, SP.3.b
The example of the relationship between bees and flowers provided in the passage supports the idea that both species benefit in mutualism, and the example of the relationship between viceroy butterflies and monarch butterflies supports the idea that only one species benefits, but by doing no harm to the other, in commensalism. The incorrect answer choices describe at least one or both of the types of relationships incorrectly.

10. DOK Level: 2; **Content Topic:** L.e.3; **Practices:** SP.1.a, SP.1.b, SP.3.b
Each gene has two alleles. The dominant allele of a gene is the one that is expressed over the recessive allele, meaning that if the dominant allele is present, the associated trait will occur. When a genotype contains both the normal allele and the mutant allele, the human does not have cystic fibrosis, indicating that the normal allele is dominant and **the mutant allele** is recessive.

11. B; **DOK Level:** 1; **Content Topic:** L.a.3; **Practices:** SP.1.a, SP.1.b, SP.1.c
The text explains that the figures in the table represent percentages of total Calorie intake. According to the table, Calories from proteins should make up 10 percent to 35 percent of an adult's Calorie intake. The table also indicates that Calories from proteins should make up 10 percent to 30 percent of the Calorie intake of an older child or adolescent, that fats should make up 20 percent to 35 percent of an adult's Calorie intake, and that carbohydrates should make up 45 percent to 65 percent of an adult's Calorie intake.

12. D; **DOK Level:** 1; **Content Topic:** L.a.3; **Practices:** SP.1.a, SP.1.b, SP.1.c
The text explains that the figures in the table represent percentages of total Calorie intake. According to the table, Calories from carbohydrates should make up 45 percent to 65 percent of the total Calories in an adult's diet, and Calories from fats should make up only 20 percent to 30 percent of the total Calories in an adult's diet. The table also indicates that a young child should not consume a higher percentage of Calories from fats than from carbohydrates and that an older child or adolescent should not consume a higher percentage of Calories from proteins than from carbohydrates. The table specifies that all age groups should be consuming a certain proportion of fat Calories, so to say that they should consume as few as possible is not true.

13. **B**; **DOK Level:** 2; **Content Topic:** L.a.3; **Practices:** SP.1.a, SP.1.b, SP.1.c, SP.3.b

According to the table, the percentage of Calories that should come from fats decreases as a child grows into an adult. From this information, one can conclude that fat is needed for growth. The table does not provide data appropriate for reaching the conclusion that adults burn fat faster than children. The table is based on percentages of Calories, and the number of Calories a person should eat changes based on size, so a person should not eat the same number of Calories of carbohydrates all his or her life. If fats provided more nutrients than carbohydrates or proteins, then the recommended intake for percentage of fats likely would be higher than that recommended for carbohydrates or proteins.

14. **A**; **DOK Level:** 2; **Content Topic:** L.f.3; **Practices:** SP.1.a, SP.1.b, SP.1.c, SP.3.b, SP.7.a

Both boreal forests and tundras have long, cold winters, so the inference can be made that the animals that live in both places have adaptations that allow them to survive in cold weather. The boreal forest gets a fair amount of precipitation, but the tundra gets very little, so animals living in the two types of climates likely do not have the same water requirements. There are no trees in the tundra, so animals living in tundras do not use tall trees for food and shelter. All the animals live in places with long winters, meaning that they have short summers, so they all can survive without long periods of warm weather.

15. **D**; **DOK Level:** 1; **Content Topic:** L.f.3; **Practices:** SP.1.a, SP.1.b, SP.1.c, SP.7.a

The passage indicates that migration is a behavioral adaptation that involves an animal's seasonal movement from one climate to another, so the movement of caribou between the tundra and the boreal forest is an example of migration. The musk oxen's multilayered coat, the ptarmigan's change of color, and the shrub's low growth are adaptations that help the organisms live year-round in one area.

16. **B**; **DOK Level:** 2; **Content Topic:** L.e.2; **Practices:** SP.1.a, SP.1.b, SP.1.c, SP.7.a

To produce the offspring represented by the Punnett square, each parent must have the genotype *Yy*, so both parents carry one dominant allele and one recessive allele.

17. **A**; **DOK Level:** 2; **Content Topic:** L.e.2; **Practices:** SP.1.a, SP.1.b, SP.1.c, SP.7.a

To produce the offspring represented by the Punnett square, each parent must have the genotype *Yy*. Because *Y* is the dominant allele that causes a plant to produce yellow seeds, both parents produce yellow seeds. For both parents to produce green seeds, each would have to have the genotype *yy*. For one plant to produce green seeds, it would have to have the genotype *yy*. According to the information, seed color in pea plants is controlled by one gene, and either green seed color or yellow seed color is produced, depending on the alleles a plant carries.

18. **B**; **DOK Level:** 2; **Content Topic:** L.e.2; **Practices:** SP.1.a, SP.1.b, SP.1.c, SP.7.a, SP.8.b, SP.8.c

The passage explains that green seed color is the recessive trait, meaning that only the genotype *yy* produces the trait of green seed color. The Punnett square shows that the cross represented will produce the genotype *yy* one out of four times, so the probability of producing an individual offspring with green seeds is one-fourth. The incorrect answer choices may result from miscalculation or misunderstanding of concepts.

19. **C**; **DOK Level:** 2; **Content Topic:** L.c.5; **Practices:** SP.1.a, SP.1.b, SP.3.a

The statement in the passage that "the red wolf nearly vanished due to loss of habitat and human persecution" supports the conclusion that the drastic decrease in red wolf populations resulted from the actions of people. Actions such as clearing land for agriculture and development likely are responsible for loss of habitat, and the term "human persecution" likely refers to people's attempts to eradicate the red wolf as a predator of livestock. The statement that the red wolf is one of the most endangered species does not offer information about why red wolf populations dwindled. The detail about the establishment of a breeding program supports the conclusion that people are now making efforts to increase the red wolf population. The statement that humans still cause mortalities among the red wolf population is related to the red wolf's current situation, not the previous conditions that nearly caused its extinction.

20. **B**; **DOK Level:** 1; **Content Topic:** L.a.2; **Practices:** SP.1.a, SP.1.b, SP.7.a

The passage explains how the body works to maintain homeostasis, or remain stable. Stability and balance have similar meanings, so the phrase "tendency toward a balanced state" is closest in meaning to *homeostasis*. The body reacts to maintain homeostasis and has the capacity for fluctuations (changes), but these ideas do not represent the meaning of homeostasis. The condition of being healthy is supported by homeostasis but is not itself homeostasis.

21. **D**; **DOK Level:** 3; **Content Topic:** L.f.2; **Practices:** SP.1.a, SP.1.b, SP.3.b, SP.7.a

The example provided in the passage to explain the three factors necessary for natural selection to occur states that each successive generation of insects has more brown insects than green insects. This detail suggests that inheritability is necessary because organisms must be able to pass on beneficial traits to future generations. The idea that differences must exist in the traits of a population of individuals explains the requirement of genetic variability. The example given addresses the trait of color, but the idea of variation in the trait of color is a specific example of how inheritability is necessary for natural selection, not an explanation of why inheritability is necessary. The idea that individuals must have a trait beneficial to survival and reproduction explains the requirement of differential survivability.

22. **D**; **DOK Level:** 1; **Content Topics:** L.b.1, L.d.1; **Practices:** SP.1.a, SP.1.b, SP.1.c, SP.7.a

The illustration label for the mitochondrion indicates that it is responsible for producing the cell's energy source. The nucleus contains the genetic information and controls cell functions. The cytoplasm holds the cell's organelles. The Golgi complex packages proteins.

Answer Key

UNIT 1 *(continued)*

23. DOK Level: 2; **Content Topic:** L.f.1; **Practices:** SP.1.a, SP.1.b, SP.1.c, SP.3.b, SP.6.a, SP.6.c, SP.7.a
The incomplete parts of the cladogram are boxes for animals that represent the introduction of the derived traits of jaws and hair. The **shark** represents introduction of the derived trait of jaws. A shark has jaws and the previously introduced derived trait of a vertebral column but does not have the derived traits of legs, an amniotic egg, and hair. The **rabbit** represents the introduction of the derived trait of hair. A rabbit has hair and all the previously introduced derived traits. A pigeon has jaws, but it does not belong in the first box because it also has legs—a derived trait represented later in the cladogram. Also, a pigeon does not have hair, so it does not belong in the second box.

24. A; DOK Level: 2; **Content Topic:** L.a.4; **Practices:** SP.1.a, SP.1.b, SP.3.b
The passage states that actions that help people avoid getting dengue fever are using mosquito repellent, wearing protective clothing, and reducing mosquito habitat. From this information, the generalization can be made that recommendations for controlling the spread of the illness involve reducing the risk of mosquito bites. Dengue fever is only an example of an illness caused by a bloodborne virus that occurs in tropic or subtropic regions; this is not enough information to make the generalization that such illnesses are more likely to occur in these regions. The passage does not make any reference to whether a dengue fever patient should see a medical care professional, so such a statement is not a valid generalization. The passage explains what transmission through indirect contact is but does not provide information about whether such transmission is related to more dangerous diseases.

25.1 C; 25.2 C; 25.3 A; 25.4 D; DOK Level: 2;
Content Topics: L.e.1, L.e.3; **Practices:** SP.1.a, SP.1.b, SP.1.c, SP.3.b, SP.7.a
25.1 The passage and illustration indicate that individual nucleotides bind to the nucleotides on an existing DNA strand. Double helixes do not bind to nucleotides, nor do strands or adenines.
25.2 According to the passage, an error in DNA replication causes a mutation. It does not cause a gene, a replication, or a base pairing.
25.3 An error in nucleotide base pairing would be a pair of bases that does not bind together, or a pairing other than A and T or C and G. Therefore, a pairing of C and A is a mutation.
25.4 The passage states that DNA replicates when a cell divides. If a cell divides through the process of meiosis, gametes are produced. Gametes combine during sexual reproduction, with each parent contributing one allele for each gene. So a mutation formed during meiosis could create a gene with an allele that can be passed on to offspring. A mutation is the result of errors in nucleotide base pairings, but a mutation does not create a new nucleotide. A new allele that is created may or may not result in a new trait. Meiosis itself, not a mutation formed during meiosis, creates new cells.

26. B; DOK Level: 2; **Content Topic:** L.c.5; **Practices:** SP.1.a, SP.1.b, SP.3.b, SP.7.a
The passage states that desertification drastically changes ecosystems and that many animals and plants are unable to survive in the new environment, so an effect of desertification is loss of biodiversity. Desertification leads to decreased, not increased, production of crops because the soil is poor. An influx of invasive species is not likely to be associated with desertification because the environment is more hostile to all organisms. Although some areas that experience desertification may be more prone to flooding due to loss of vegetation, areas that experience desertification are generally drier and not prone to flooding.

27. DOK Level: 3; **Content Topics:** L.f.1, L.f.3; **Practices:** SP.1.a, SP.1.b, SP.1.c, SP.7.a
Possible answer:
Ⓐ The passage explains that evolutionary theory suggests that species living today share a common ancestor and that one form of evidence scientists use to support this theory is similarities in stages of embryonic development. Ⓑ The illustration shows that during their embryonic development, both chickens and gorillas have gill-like structures and tails. Ⓒ These traits are evidence that both animals have an ancestor that had gills and a tail, suggesting that the animals share a common ancestor.
Ⓐ The first sentence describes a general type of evidence identified in the passage that scientists use to support the idea that species living today share a common ancestor.
Ⓑ The second sentence notes that the illustration provides specific examples of this type of evidence.
Ⓒ The third sentence draws a conclusion based on the first two sentences.

28. B; DOK Level: 2; **Content Topic:** L.d.2; **Practices:** SP.1.a, SP.1.b, SP.1.c, SP.7.a
According to the information provided in the passage, cells make up tissues, tissues make up organs, and organs make up body systems. So both organs and body systems are made up of tissues that are made up of cells. The passage states that the combining of cells into tissues, tissues into organs, and organs into body systems leads to levels of organization that become more complex. Therefore, the organization of organs and body systems is more complex than that of both cells and tissues. Also, organs and body systems represent the most complex, not the least complex, levels of organization in an organism. The passage explains that tissues, organs, and body systems are all made up of specialized cells produced by cell differentiation.

UNIT 2 PHYSICAL SCIENCE

LESSON 1, *pp. 42–43*
1. D; DOK Level: 2; **Content Topic:** P.c.1; **Practices:** SP.1.a, SP.1.b, SP.1.c, SP.7.a
Based on the key, the model shows that hydrogen has one proton and helium has two protons. The model also shows that a helium atom has the same number of protons and electrons (as do all atoms). The nucleus of any atom contains only protons and neutrons, never electrons. The number of protons and neutrons in the helium atom nucleus, not the number of protons only, is four.

2. **A**; **DOK Level:** 2; **Content Topic:** P.c.1; **Practices:** SP.1.a, SP.1.b, SP.1.c, SP.7.a
The model shows that each individual atom has one electron, for a total of two electrons, and that the molecule has two electrons. So the total number of electrons remains the same; it does not double. Electrons do not become protons, and electrons are not destroyed during the process of covalent bonding.

3. **B**; **DOK Level:** 3; **Content Topic:** P.c.1; **Practices:** SP.1.a, SP.1.b, SP.1.c, SP.7.a
A hydrogen atom has one proton, and the model shows atoms each having one proton. All atoms, not just hydrogen atoms, have a nucleus in the center and electrons that move around the nucleus. From the passage, it can be inferred that hydrogen is not the only element whose atoms form molecules.

4. **D**; **DOK Level:** 2; **Content Topic:** P.c.1; **Practices:** SP.1.a, SP.1.b, SP.1.c, SP.7.a
The model's labels indicate that the ammonia molecule has one nitrogen atom and three hydrogen atoms. Although only one hydrogen atom is labeled, two other atoms look the same, meaning that they also are hydrogen atoms. The molecule has three hydrogen atoms, but it also has one nitrogen atom. Ammonia is not an element, so there cannot be an atom of ammonia.

5. **B**; **DOK Level:** 2; **Content Topic:** P.c.1; **Practices:** SP.1.a, SP.1.b, SP.1.c, SP.7.a
The structural formula includes two Cs and six Hs, indicating that an ethane molecule contains two carbon atoms and six hydrogen atoms. So the chemical formula for ethane is C_2H_6. The other answer choices may result from incorrect counting or misinterpretation of the model.

LESSON 2, *pp. 44–45*
1. **C**; **DOK Level:** 2; **Content Topic:** P.c.2; **Practices:** SP.1.a, SP.1.b, SP.1.c, SP.7.a
In the visual, the pullout illustrations representing magnified views of water molecules show that solids have the least space between molecules. Gases have the most space between molecules. Liquids are between solids and gases with regard to space between molecules. Molecules are not equally spaced across all states of matter.

2. **DOK Level:** 3; **Content Topic:** P.c.2; **Practices:** SP.1.a, SP.1.b, SP.1.c, SP.6.c, SP.7.a
The diagram has a *y*-axis like a graph, indicating that examining the diagram from bottom to top tells you what occurs as energy is added and examining it from top to bottom tells you what occurs as energy is released. According to the diagram, then, energy must be **added** to melt a solid or to evaporate a liquid.

3. **DOK Level:** 3; **Content Topic:** P.c.2; **Practices:** SP.1.a, SP.1.b, SP.1.c, SP.6.c, SP.7.a
Examining the *y*-axis on the diagram tells you what occurs as energy is released. If enough energy is removed from a liquid, it will freeze, or its state will change **from liquid to solid**.

4. **DOK Level:** 3; **Content Topic:** P.c.2; **Practices:** SP.1.a, SP.1.b, SP.1.c, SP.6.c, SP.7.a
According to the *y*-axis, the top of the diagram represents the greatest amount of energy, so particles move the fastest in the state of matter shown at the top of the diagram: **gas**.

5. **B**; **DOK Level:** 3; **Content Topic:** P.c.2; **Practices:** SP.1.a, SP.1.b, SP.1.c, SP.3.b, SP.7.a
The graph shows that water's melting point is 0°C. Because a substance's melting point is the same as its freezing point, liquid water freezes to become ice at the same temperature that ice melts to become liquid water. The temperature −20°C is below the point at which liquid water freezes to become ice. The temperature 100°C is the point at which liquid water boils to become gas. The temperature 130°C is above the point at which liquid water boils to become gas and, therefore, well above the point at which liquid water freezes to become ice.

LESSON 3, *pp. 46–47*
1. **D**; **DOK Level:** 1; **Content Topic:** P.c.2; **Practices:** SP.1.a, SP.1.b, SP.1.c, SP.7.a
The entries in the "Boiling Point" column indicate that the highest boiling point shown is 2,239°C, which is the boiling point for magnesium fluoride. The "Formula" column shows that the chemical formula for magnesium fluoride is MgF_2. Sodium chloride, or NaCl, has the second-highest boiling point at 1,413°C. Hydrogen fluoride, or HF, has the second-lowest boiling point at 20°C. Calcium iodide, or CaI_2, has the third-highest boiling point at 1,100°C.

2. **DOK Level:** 2; **Content Topic:** P.c.2; **Practices:** SP.1.a, SP.1.b, SP.1.c, SP.3.b, SP.6.a, SP.7.a
The passage states that metals conduct electricity and heat, and the table shows that Substances B and C conduct electricity and heat. An *X* in the **"Yes" column for Substance B** and an *X* in the **"Yes" column for Substance C** identify the substances that are metals.

3. **C**; **DOK Level:** 2; **Content Topic:** P.c.2; **Practices:** SP.1.a, SP.1.b, SP.1.c
The footnotes to the table indicate that extensive properties depend on sample size, and the table shows that length is an extensive property. The table shows that hardness, melting point, and taste are intensive properties, which do not depend on sample size.

4. **B**; **DOK Level:** 3; **Content Topic:** P.c.2; **Practices:** SP.1.a, SP.1.b, SP.1.c, SP.3.a, SP.7.a
The conclusion that a chemical reaction occurs when silver tarnishes is supported by the statement in the passage that a chemical reaction causes a new substance to be formed and the observation in the table that the silver developed a dark-colored coating when it tarnished. The conclusion that solid silver can become liquid silver relates to a change in state, not a chemical reaction. The statement that silver can be melted or tarnished is based on information in the table but does not provide any support for the conclusion that a chemical reaction occurs when silver tarnishes. The conclusion that no new substances are formed is incorrect because a dark coating forms when silver tarnishes.

Answer Key

UNIT 2 *(continued)*

LESSON 4, pp. 48–49
1. D; DOK Level: 2; **Content Topics:** P.a.2, P.c.3; **Practices:** SP.1.a, SP.1.b, SP.1.c, SP.7.a
Magnesium oxide is the only substance on the right side of the equation, indicating that it is the product of the reaction. It is not a reactant in the reaction. Magnesium and oxygen are on the left side of the equation, so they are the reactants.

2. B; DOK Level: 1; **Content Topic:** P.c.3; **Practices:** SP.1.a, SP.1.b, SP.1.c, SP.7.a
In the equation, the coefficient 1 is assumed for carbon dioxide, and the coefficient 2 is included for water, so the proportion of carbon dioxide molecules to water molecules is 1:2. The state symbols indicate that the reactants are two gases, not a gas and a liquid. Mass is always conserved in a chemical reaction, so the products cannot contain fewer atoms of hydrogen than the reactants. The directional arrow goes only one way, so the products cannot react to produce the reactants.

3. D; DOK Level: 1; **Content Topic:** P.c.3; **Practices:** SP.1.a, SP.1.b, SP.1.c, SP.7.a
In the general form equation for a single displacement reaction, AC is on the right side of the equation, so it represents a product. AC does not represent an atom or an element because it represents two substances, A and C. AC does not represent a reactant because it is on the right side of the equation, not the left.

4. C; DOK Level: 2; **Content Topic:** P.c.3; **Practices:** SP.1.a, SP.1.b, SP.1.c, SP.7.a
The passage explains that a limiting reactant is a reactant that can limit the amount of product formed if it is not present in a large enough quantity. The reactants in the chemical reaction represented by the equation are benzene and oxygen, so either can limit the amount of product formed if it is not present in a large enough quantity. Carbon dioxide and water are products in the reaction represented by the equation, so they cannot be limiting reactants. If benzene and oxygen occur in the appropriate amounts in a chemical reaction, neither will limit the reaction.

LESSON 5, pp. 50–51
1. C; DOK Level: 3; **Content Topic:** P.c.4; **Practices:** SP.1.a, SP.1.b, SP.1.c, SP.3.c, SP.3.d, SP.7.a
Sodium is an alkali metal, and sodium chloride is a compound formed from sodium. The passage explains that one rule of solubility is that compounds formed from the alkali metals are soluble in water. Sodium chloride will dissolve in the water, so the substance produced will be a solution, not a new chemical compound. Different parts of solutions have the same properties.

2. B; DOK Level: 3; **Content Topic:** P.c.4; **Practices:** SP.1.a, SP.1.b, SP.1.c, SP.3.c, SP.7.a
The passage explains that a dilute solution has a lower ratio of solute to solvent. When the student adds more water, or solvent, the ratio of solute to solvent lowers. So the solution will be more dilute, not more concentrated or concentrated to the point of saturation. The ratio of solute to solvent will change, so the concentration will change, not remain unchanged.

3. A; DOK Level: 3; **Content Topic:** P.c.4; **Practices:** SP.1.a, SP.1.b, SP.1.c, SP.3.c, SP.7.a
The graph shows that solubility of $KClO_3$ increases as temperature increases. If the temperature of the solution increases, the solubility will increase; therefore, more solute can be dissolved in the solution, meaning that it will no longer be saturated. The solubility of the solution will increase, not remain the same. Heating a solution does not change the ratio of solute to solvent or the concentration of the solution.

4. B; DOK Level: 3; **Content Topic:** P.c.4; **Practices:** SP.1.a, SP.1.b, SP.1.c, SP.3.b, SP.3.c, SP.3.d, SP.7.a
The passage explains that a strong acid ionizes completely in solution, meaning that it is soluble in water. It does not retain its molecular structure, and it does not dissociate only partially.

5. D; DOK Level: 3; **Content Topic:** P.c.4; **Practices:** SP.1.a, SP.1.b, SP.1.c, SP.3.c, SP.7.a
The passage explains that an acid ionizes to form H^+ in water, so the equation that shows a reaction that produces H^+ represents the outcome that occurs when an acid is dissolved in water. The other equations represent what occurs when salts or bases are dissolved in water.

LESSON 6, pp. 52–53
1. C; DOK Level: 1; **Content Topic:** P.b.1; **Practices:** SP.1.a, SP.1.b, SP.1.c, SP.7.b, SP.8.b
The commuter traveled 4 miles in 20 minutes. By plugging these numbers into the formula for speed, $s = \frac{d}{t}$, you get $s = \frac{4}{20}$. To find the speed in mi/hr, you multiply 20 by 3 to get 60 minutes, or 1 hour. When you multiply the denominator of a fraction, you also must multiply the numerator by the same number, so you also multiply 4 by 3 to get 12. So her average speed is 12 mi/hr. The incorrect answer choices might be reached through incorrect calculations or formula application.

2. C; DOK Level: 2; **Content Topic:** P.b.1; **Practices:** SP.1.a, SP.1.b, SP.1.c, SP.7.b, SP.8.b
Speed is distance (100 mi) divided by time (5 hr), so the bird's speed is 20 mi/hr. Velocity includes a direction. Point B is east of Point A, so the velocity is 20 mi/hr east. The incorrect answer choices might be reached through incorrect calculations or formula application.

3. A; DOK Level: 2; **Content Topic:** P.b.1; **Practices:** SP.1.a, SP.1.b, SP.1.c, SP.7.b, SP.8.b
Velocity is calculated by dividing displacement by time of travel. Because the bird ends up at its starting point, its total displacement is 0, and, therefore, the corresponding average velocity is 0 mi/hr. The incorrect answer choices might be reached through incorrect calculations or formula application.

4. A; DOK Level: 2; **Content Topic:** P.b.1; **Practices:** SP.1.a, SP.1.b, SP.1.c, SP.7.b, SP.8.b
The line graph shows that from 0 to 40 seconds, for every 10 seconds that pass, the object's velocity increases by the same amount: 10 m/s. Therefore, its acceleration is increasing at a steady rate. If the acceleration were constant, the line would be flat, as it is between 40 and 90 seconds. If its acceleration were decreasing, the line would be falling, as it is between 90 and 110 seconds. If its acceleration were increasing and then decreasing, the line would change from going upward to going downward.

5. **D**; **DOK Level:** 2; **Content Topic:** P.b.1; **Practices:** SP.1.a, SP.1.b, SP.1.c, SP.7.b, SP.8.b
The flat line between 40 and 90 seconds shows that the object is traveling at a constant velocity of 40 m/s. At 90 seconds the line goes downward, indicating a change to negative acceleration, not a change to positive acceleration. The object's velocity does not stop at 90 seconds and then increase; rather, its velocity begins to decrease from 40 m/s. From 40 to 90 seconds, the object's velocity is constant, not increasing, so the description that increasing velocity turns to acceleration is not accurate.

LESSON 7, pp. 54–55

1. **B**; **DOK Level:** 1; **Content Topic:** P.b.2; **Practices:** SP.1.a, SP.1.b, SP.1.c, SP.7.a
The length of each arrow indicates the magnitude of the force. The second shortest arrow represents the second smallest force, 7 N. Force A equals 2 N, Force C equals 9 N, and Force D equals 15 N.

2. **D**; **DOK Level:** 1; **Content Topic:** P.b.2; **Practices:** SP.1.a, SP.1.b, SP.1.c, SP.7.a, SP.7.b
Force equals mass times acceleration, so in this case, 3 kg times 5 m/s^2 equals 15 N. The incorrect answer choices might be reached through incorrect calculations or formula application.

3. **B**; **DOK Level:** 3; **Content Topic:** P.b.2; **Practices:** SP.1.a, SP.1.b, SP.1.c, SP.7.a, SP.7.b
The force applied would be the same, so the arrow showing force would not change. However, because force is calculated by multiplying mass by acceleration, if mass becomes greater, acceleration must become smaller for force to remain the same. Therefore, the arrow representing the acceleration vector would be shorter than in the original diagram.

4. **D**; **DOK Level:** 2; **Content Topic:** P.b.2; **Practices:** SP.1.a, SP.1.b, SP.1.c, SP.7.a, SP.7.b
The arrows representing the direction and magnitude of the forces are the same size. This indicates that the force the floor is applying is equal in magnitude to the person's weight. The incorrect answer choices might be reached through incorrect calculations or formula application.

5. **C**; **DOK Level:** 2; **Content Topic:** P.b.2; **Practices:** SP.1.a, SP.1.b, SP.1.c, SP.7.a, SP.7.b
A person with a mass of 65 kg has a weight of 637 N (65 kg times 9.8), and the upward force from the floor is equal to the person's weight. The incorrect answer choices might be reached through incorrect calculations or formula application.

LESSON 8, pp. 56–57

1. **C**; **DOK Level:** 2; **Content Topic:** P.b.2; **Practices:** SP.1.a, SP.1.b, SP.1.c, SP.7.a
The attraction objects have for one another is inversely proportional to the distance between them. So the shorter the distance between two objects, the greater the gravitational force between them is. The rocket is closer to the center of Earth at Point A than at Point B, so the gravitational force between the rocket and Earth is greater at Point A.

2. **DOK Level:** 3; **Content Topics:** P.b.1, P.b.2; **Practices:** SP.1.a, SP.6.c, SP.7.a
Scenario A represents the **law of universal gravitation**. Because the attraction objects have for one another is inversely proportional to the distance between them, the farther people are from Earth's surface, the less of a pull Earth's gravity has on them. Scenario B represents the **third law of motion**. The rocket creates great amounts of thrust that push downward against the ground under it. That force downward creates an equal and opposite reaction force upward from the ground that pushes the rocket into the air. Scenario C represents the **second law of motion**. The force applied by the 5-year-old is much less than the force applied by the 14-year-old to the same mass. This law applies because it shows that the change in motion of the object, the ball, is directly related to the size (and direction) of the force acting on it. Scenario D represents the **first law of motion**. Newton's first law says that objects will continue in the same state of motion (or rest) until some outside force acts on them. In this case, the car and box continue moving forward until the brake is applied. The brake is the force that stops the motion of the car. But the box is not tied down, so it continues its motion forward until it is acted on by another force, the dashboard.

3. **B**; **DOK Level:** 2; **Content Topic:** P.b.1; **Practices:** SP.1.a, SP.1.b, SP.7.a, SP.7.b, SP.8.b
The total momentum for the system (both carts) before the collision is +40 kg • m/s, or 40 kg • m/s moving east. According to the law of conservation of momentum, the momentum of the system after the collision must be the same as the momentum before the collision, or +40 kg • m/s. If the total momentum of the full cart after the collision is +26.25 kg • m/s, the momentum of the empty cart must be 40 kg • m/s minus 26.25 kg • m/s, or 13.75 kg • m/s. Because the result is a positive number, the cart is moving east. So the cart's momentum is 13.75 kg • m/s moving east. The incorrect answer choices might be reached through incorrect calculations or formula application.

LESSON 9, pp. 58–59

1. **C**; **DOK Level:** 1; **Content Topic:** P.b.3; **Practices:** SP.1.a, SP.1.b, SP.1.c
Using your knowledge of vector diagrams, experience with levers, and the information provided, you can determine that the advantage of using a lever is that doing so makes work easier by changing the size and direction of the force. Using a lever to lift an object differs from using one's arms because using a lever changes the direction of the force. The vector diagram shows that the input force is smaller than, not equal to, the output force. The passage states that if an object is moved, work has been done.

2. **DOK Level:** 2; **Content Topic:** P.b.3; **Practices:** SP.1.a, SP.1.b, SP.1.c, SP.7.a
Using your knowledge of vector diagrams and the explanation in the passage about how a wedge works, you can determine that the **arrows pointing out from the ax blade** represent output forces. The arrow pointing to the base of the ax blade represents the input force.

Answer Key

UNIT 2 *(continued)*

3. **D**; **DOK Level:** 2; **Content Topic:** P.b.3; **Practices:** SP.1.a, SP.1.b, SP.1.c, SP.7.b
Using your knowledge of math and forces along with the equation for work, you can determine that an explanation of a relationship between amount of work done and force applied is that the value of work is zero if the object does not move (any number multiplied by zero equals zero). According to the equation, the value for work cannot be smaller if the size of the force is greater and the distance over which the force is applied remains unchanged. The value for work is related to the meter, a unit used to measure distance. Greater force is required to move a heavier object, so more work is done when the heavier box is moved.

4. **A**; **DOK Level:** 2; **Content Topic:** P.b.3; **Practices:** SP.1.a, SP.1.b, SP.1.c, SP.7.b
Using your knowledge of math along with the equation for mechanical advantage, you can determine that if the output force of a machine is 100 N and the machine provides a mechanical advantage of 4, the input force equals 25 (100 divided by 4). The other answer choices might be reached through incorrect calculations or formula application.

5. **A**; **DOK Level:** 2; **Content Topic:** P.b.3; **Practices:** SP.1.a, SP.1.b, SP.1.c, SP.7.b
Using your knowledge of math along with the equation for power, you can determine that if the amount of work is 19,600 joules and the time required to perform the task is 10 seconds, the power exerted is 1,960 watts (19,600 divided by 10). The other answer choices might be reached through incorrect calculations or formula application.

LESSON 10, *pp. 60–61*

1. **D**; **DOK Level:** 2; **Content Topics:** P.a.1, P.a.3; **Practices:** SP.1.a, SP.1.b, SP.1.c, SP.3.b, SP.7.a
Container B is holding twice the amount of water; therefore, it can be assumed that it has about twice the number of water molecules. More particles moving means a greater total kinetic energy. Thus, Container B has more thermal energy than Container A. Both containers have the same temperature, but temperature is a measure of average kinetic energy, not total kinetic energy. So although Container B has a higher volume of water, the temperature of the water is the same as that in Container A.

2. **DOK Level:** 2; **Content Topics:** P.a.1, P.a.5; **Practices:** SP.1.a, SP.1.b, SP.1.c, SP.3.b, SP.7.a
Conduction occurs by direct contact. Therefore, the **green arrows** where the pot touches the burner represent conduction (D). Convection occurs as currents in a liquid or gas. Therefore, the **blue arrows** over the pot where the steam is rising and in the water where currents are represent convection (V). Radiation is transferred without the need for currents or contact. Therefore, the **yellow arrows** where waves are radiating from the side of the pot represent radiation (R).

3. **B**; **DOK Level:** 3; **Content Topic:** P.a.1; **Practices:** SP.1.a, SP.1.b, SP.1.c, SP.3.b, SP.7.a
The metal feels colder than the wood because it is a good conductor of heat. Therefore, thermal energy is transferred out of the student's hand (which is warmer than either the wood or the metal) more quickly by the metal, leaving her hand with a feeling of cold. Although both objects are at the same temperature, the metal conducts heat more quickly and thus leaves the student's hand feeling cooler.

LESSON 11, *pp. 62–63*

1. **A**; **DOK Level:** 2; **Content Topic:** P.a.3; **Practices:** SP.1.a, SP.1.b, SP.1.c, SP.3.b, SP.7.a
The curves in the graph showing that potential energy decreases at the same rate that kinetic energy increases represent the idea that the total energy of a system is always the same. All things can have both kinetic and potential energy; however, as the graph shows, as one decreases, the other increases.

2. **A**; **DOK Level:** 2; **Content Topic:** P.a.3; **Practices:** SP.1.a, SP.1.b, SP.1.c, SP.3.b, SP.7.a
As the passage and diagram indicate, some of the wind's kinetic energy is changed to electrical energy by the wind turbine; therefore, the wind has greater kinetic energy before it passes through the turbine, not after. The wind is in motion, so it has kinetic energy, not potential energy.

3. **B**; **DOK Level:** 2; **Content Topic:** P.a.3; **Practices:** SP.1.a, SP.1.b, SP.1.c, SP.3.b, SP.7.a
As long as there are materials in the battery to keep the reaction going, chemical energy will be released and changed to electrical energy and then to heat and light energy as the current passes through the filament of the light bulb. This energy dissipates into the space around the bulb, heating the air and illuminating nearby surfaces; it does not return to the battery as chemical energy as stated in the incorrect answer choices.

4. **C**; **DOK Level:** 2; **Content Topic:** P.a.3; **Practices:** SP.1.a, SP.1.b, SP.1.c, SP.3.c, SP.7.a
Once the flow of electricity stops, the changing of one form of energy to another stops. Any electrical energy in the system has been changed to heat and light energy before the wire is disconnected and will not change back to potential chemical energy once current stops flowing through the wire. It can be inferred from the paragraph that the chemical reaction in the battery goes in only one direction. That is, disconnecting the wire does not permit the reaction to reverse and reconstitute the metals in the battery.

LESSON 12, *pp. 64–65*

1. **B**; **DOK Level:** 2; **Content Topic:** P.a.5; **Practices:** SP.1.a, SP.1.b, SP.1.c, SP.7.a
Crests and troughs represent the distances between the resting positions of particles and the farthest positions to which they move. Wavelength can be measured not only from crest to crest but also from trough to trough. The passage and diagram indicate that the particles are moving up and down whereas the wave is moving sideways.

2. DOK Level: 2; **Content Topic:** P.a.5; **Practices:** SP.1.a, SP.1.b, SP.1.c, SP.3.b, SP.6.a, SP.6.c, SP.7.a

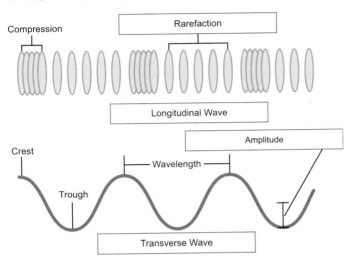

3. D; **DOK Level:** 2; **Content Topic:** P.a.5; **Practices:** SP.1.a, SP.1.b, SP.1.c, SP.7.a
The bulleted list states that visible light is a form of electromagnetic radiation, and the illustration shows that visible light is made of colors. Therefore, it can be inferred that humans can see only visible light. Humans do not see other waves of the electromagnetic radiation spectrum.

LESSON 13, *pp. 66–67*
1. B; **DOK Level:** 2; **Content Topic:** P.a.4; **Practices:** SP.1.a, SP.1.b, SP.1.c, SP.3.b, SP.5.a
The flowchart shows the steps in the formation of coal in sequence. Therefore, the origin of coal is shown in the first box of the flowchart: plants. Once plants are identified as the source material for coal, the passage can be used to determine that plants store solar energy as the result of photosynthesis. Therefore, the energy in coal, a substance formed from plant material, comes from the sun. Peat is a product of an intermediate step in coal formation. Sediment is not a source of energy for plants; it is an agent acting on the plants. Like sediment, burial and pressure act on plants; they are not energy sources for plants.

2. D; **DOK Level:** 2; **Content Topic:** P.a.4; **Practices:** SP.1.a, SP.1.b, SP.1.c, SP.3.b, SP.5.a
Only states with air pollution levels above the national standard must submit plans to bring down those levels. The graphs show that levels of only lead and ozone were at or above the national standards levels in 2010. Therefore, states with ozone and lead at or above these levels had to submit plans for those pollutants.

3. C; **DOK Level:** 3; **Content Topic:** P.a.4; **Practices:** SP.1.a, SP.1.b, SP.1.c, SP.3.b, SP.4.a, SP.5.a
One can infer by the trend downward shown by the graphs for all the air pollutants that it is likely that there has been a decrease in health problems and deaths associated with these pollutants. There is no information in either the passage or the graphs about the cost of implementing the CAA's air monitoring program or which pollutant is the most serious problem for the United States. Also, there is no basis in the materials for concluding that the United States no longer will monitor the identified pollutants.

LESSON 14, *pp. 68–69*
1. B; **DOK Level:** 1; **Content Topic:** P.c.1; **Practices:** SP.2.b, SP.2.d, SP.5.a, SP.7.a
If an investigation does not validate a hypothesis, the researcher should look for errors in the investigation design or modify the hypothesis. In the case of Rutherford's investigation, the results support the action of modifying the hypothesis to state that atoms have positively charged nuclei. Indeed, Rutherford and other scientists tested this modified hypothesis and in so doing, increased understanding of atomic structure. It is unethical to modify the results of an investigation. A researcher should not abandon an investigation because the results do not support the hypothesis; instead, he or she should attempt to learn more by modifying the investigation design or the hypothesis itself. Nothing in the results of Rutherford's investigation suggested that he should assume that atoms do not have electrical charges.

2. C; **DOK Level:** 2; **Content Topic:** P.b.2; **Practices:** SP.2.b, SP.3.b, SP.7.a
The fact that the researcher is using a specified distance and a specified time interval means that the researcher is holding acceleration "constant" in relation to the equation $F = ma$, so the objective of the investigation is to look at the relationship between force, mass, and acceleration. Specifically, the investigation is looking at how changing the mass of an object affects how much force is necessary to move it over a specific distance in a specified time; it is not related to amount of work done, relationships between forces, or acceleration due to gravity.

3. B; **DOK Level:** 2; **Content Topic:** P.b.2; **Practices:** SP.2.e, SP.3.b, SP.7.a
Force changes in response to a change in mass, so it is dependent on the independent variable (mass). Mass is the variable that the researcher is changing, meaning that it is the independent variable. Friction and distance are held constant, so they are controlled factors.

4. A; **DOK Level:** 2; **Content Topic:** P.b.2; **Practices:** SP.2.e, SP.3.b, SP.7.a
Mass is the variable that the researcher is changing, meaning that it is the independent variable. Force will change in response to a change in mass, so it is dependent on the independent variable. Although friction is a force in the setup, it will be held constant, and so will distance.

Answer Key

ANSWER KEY

UNIT 2 (continued)

5. B; DOK Level: 2; Content Topic: P.a.4; Practices:
SP.3.d, SP.8.a, SP.8.b
The passage states that the mean of a data set is the average, so the mean is calculated by adding the values in a data set and then dividing the sum by the number of values in the data set. In this case, you divide 73.7 by 6 to arrive at 12.3. The figure *11.1* is one of the values in the middle of the data set. The figure *15.0* is the highest value in the data set. The figure *73.7* is the sum of the values in the data set.

6. A; DOK Level: 3; Content Topic: P.b.2; Practices:
SP.2.a, SP.3.b, SP.7.a
If an effort had been made to minimize friction on the surface of the ramp, little or no opposing force would have worked against the movement of the lids down the ramp. They would have arrived at the bottom together. As long as the total mass of the objects was recorded and accounted for, the mass of each washer was irrelevant. A steeper ramp or more mass actually might have made it more likely that the lids would have arrived at the bottom at the same time.

LESSON 15, pp. 70–71
1. B; DOK Level: 2; Content Topic: P.c.4; Practices:
SP.2.b, SP.7.a
The hypothesis that adding salt to salt water lowers its freezing point is testable and aligns with the observation. The hypothesis that adding salt to salt water raises its freezing point does not agree with the observation. The hypotheses that state whether an action has or does not have an effect without specifying the effect are too vague.

2.1 A; 2.2 D; 2.3 D; 2.4 A; DOK Level: 2; Content Topic:
P.c.2; **Practices:** SP.1.a, SP.1.b, SP.1.c, SP.2.c, SP.3.b, SP.4.a, SP.7.a
2.1 The diagram indicates that all the liquids have a pH less than 7; therefore, they are acidic. None have a pH greater than 7. Only milk has a pH near 7 and is, therefore, nearly neutral. In addition, bases release hydroxide ions into the water, and all the liquids are acids.
2.2 The diagram shows that the investigation tested the effects of acidity on several species. If the investigation had included only one species, the conclusion that the liquids tested threaten aquatic life would not have been supported by the data. The investigation identified the pH levels of several substances, but for the purpose of finding out how several species react to different levels of acidity, not because pH levels of the substances were in and of themselves integral to the investigation. The investigation did not prove that milk is not a threat to wildlife. The information gives no indication that the investigation has been repeated.
2.3 The table shows that trout are the first to react to an increase in acidity.
2.4 The data show the effect of increasing acidity on members of the bottom of most food chains. There is no relation between the investigation and the human digestive system. The table shows that tomato juice is acidic enough to kill many aquatic organisms and as such would not be appropriate as a nutrient source for them. Finally, the data in the table deal with toxicity, not food preferences.

UNIT 2 REVIEW, pp. 72–79
1. A; DOK Level: 1; Content Topic: P.c.1; Practices:
SP.1.a, SP.1.b, SP.1.c, SP.7.a
The excerpt from the periodic table shows that the atomic number for silicon is 14. An element's atomic number identifies the number of protons in one atom of the element, so each atom of silicon has 14 protons. The number of protons in the atoms of an element does not vary, so protons are not averaged. The average atomic mass of silicon, not the number of protons in an atom of silicon, is 28.09. The periodic table does not indicate how many neutrons are in one atom of an element because number of neutrons can vary.

2. A; DOK Level: 2; Content Topic: P.c.1; Practices:
SP.1.a, SP.1.b, SP.1.c, SP.3.b, SP.7.a
Atomic mass varies among atoms of an element because the number of neutrons in atoms of an element can vary. The number of protons and electrons in an atom of an element is fixed, meaning that the mass of protons or the mass of electrons is not variable.

3. C; DOK Level: 1; Content Topic: P.b.3; Practices:
SP.1.a, SP.1.b, SP.7.a, SP.7.b
MA is calculated by dividing the output force by the input force. The output force required to move an object weighing 1,800 N would be 1,800 N, and 1,800 divided by 600 equals 3. The incorrect answer choices might be reached through incorrect calculations or formula application.

4. C; DOK Level: 2; Content Topic: P.c.1; Practices:
SP.1.b, SP.1.c, SP.7.a
Rods or lines in a model of a molecule indicate covalent bonds between atoms, so the structure of the model indicates that it represents the covalent bonding of one carbon atom with two oxygen atoms. Covalent bonding occurs when atoms share electrons, so the model shows that one carbon atom and two oxygen atoms share electrons. Covalent bonding involves sharing electrons, not losing and gaining electrons, so neither the carbon atom nor the oxygen atoms lose or gain electrons. The lines in the model are representative of a covalent bond, not literal representations of structures in a molecule.

5. DOK Level: 3; Content Topic: P.c.2; Practices: SP.1.a, SP.1.b, SP.1.c, SP.3.a, SP.3.b, SP.6.c, SP.7.a
Possible answer:
Ⓐ The investigation shows that Powder A is sodium chloride because when added to water, this powder does not undergo a visible chemical reaction, only a physical change. The investigation shows that Powder B is copper sulfate because when added to water, it undergoes a chemical change.
Ⓑ Evidence of the chemical change includes the visible changes in physical properties: change in color and change in temperature.
Ⓐ The answer identifies which powder is sodium chloride and which is copper sulfate.
Ⓑ The conclusion about which substance is which is supported by observations identified in the table.

6. B; DOK Level: 2; Content Topic: P.a.2; Practices:
SP.1.a, SP.3.b, SP.7.a
When the student combines citric acid and baking soda in a plastic bag, the bag feels cooler because this is an endothermic reaction. The reaction is absorbing heat from the hand of the student. The chemical reactions that produce a campfire, heat hand warmers, and occur when sugar, water, and sulfuric acid are combined give off energy in the form of light or heat, so they are exothermic reactions.

7. **B**; **DOK Level**: 2; **Content Topic**: P.a.1; **Practices**: SP.1.a, SP.1.b, SP.2.b, SP.3.b, SP.7.a

Working backward from the student's observation and investigation design, you can determine her hypothesis. Her observation of wax dots melting in order from the dot closest to the heat source to the dot farthest from the heat source indicates that heat flows from warmer matter to cooler matter, and her investigation design included the use of a metal (copper) rod, so you can determine that she was testing the hypothesis that heat flows from warmer parts of a metal object to cooler parts of a metal object. The investigation design does show heat transfer in a solid; however, the hypothesis that heat flows from warmer parts of a solid to cooler parts of a solid is not as specific as the hypothesis about heat transfer in a metal. The student does not compare copper to any other matter, so she is not testing a hypothesis about how metals compare as conductors of heat. The type of heat transfer that melts the wax is conduction, not radiation, so the student's hypothesis is not related to radiation.

8. **D**; **DOK Level**: 3; **Content Topic**: P.a.1; **Practices**: SP.1.a, SP.1.b, SP.2.a, SP.2.c, SP.3.b, SP.5.a, SP.7.a

It is likely that the student failed to control the size of the dots and that the dot of wax farther from the flame appears to melt sooner because it is smaller than the dot of wax closer to the flame. Heat transfer within the smaller dot is causing it to melt more rapidly. Even if the flame produces higher heat later in the investigation or the student used a longer metal rod for the investigation, either situation would not necessarily produce the result observed by the student; if the dots of wax were the same size, they still would melt in order from the dot closest to the heat source to the dot farthest from the heat source. The student used a candle to produce the dots of wax, so the dots are the same type of wax.

9. **A**; **DOK Level**: 3; **Content Topic**: P.c.2; **Practices**: SP.1.a, SP.1.b, SP.2.d, SP.7.a

To compare conductivity of metals, an investigator would have to use different types of metals (independent variable) and then observe changes in their temperatures (dependent variable) over time. To compare conductivity of metals, the investigation would involve rods of different metals, not two rods of the same metal or one metal rod and one glass rod. Regardless of how the conductivity of two metals compares, wax dots placed on rods of different metals will melt in order from the dot closest to the heat source because of the way heat is transferred within a solid.

10. **B**; **DOK Level**: 2; **Content Topic**: P.c.2; **Practices**: SP.1.a, SP.1.b, SP.3.a, SP.3.b, SP.7.a

The giving off of a violet cloud is evidence of a chemical reaction because there is a release of energy and a change in color. The touching of the feather seems to prompt a chemical reaction, but is not evidence of it. The qualities of being made of two different elements and maintaining chemical makeup are not evidence of chemical reactions.

11. **D**; **DOK Level**: 1; **Content Topic**: P.c.3; **Practices**: SP.1.a, SP.1.b, SP.1.c, SP.3.b, SP.7.a

The reaction described is represented by an equation that shows nitrogen triiodide (NI_3) as the reactant and is balanced by having the same number of nitrogen atoms (two) and iodide atoms (six) on each side. Incorrect answer choices identify incorrect reactants or products or are not balanced.

12. **A**; **DOK Level**: 2; **Content Topic**: P.c.3; **Practices**: SP.1.a, SP.1.b, SP.6.c, SP.7.a

The description is of a decomposition reaction because one substance (nitrogen triiodide) undergoes a reaction and becomes two substances (nitrogen and iodine). A synthesis reaction occurs when multiple substances combine. Single displacement and double displacement reactions involve the substituting of one substance for another.

13. **A**; **DOK Level**: 3; **Content Topic**: P.c.4; **Practices**: SP.1.a, SP.1.b, SP.1.c, SP.3.c, SP.3.d, SP.7.a

The passage states that solubility generally increases as temperature increases, so the student can predict that the solution heated to a higher temperature will have greater solubility. The amount of KNO_3 in the solution does not change based on change in temperature. At higher temperatures, more KNO_3 can be dissolved in the solution because the solution has greater solubility. The passage states that the student will heat the solution in Beaker B to a higher, not lower, temperature than the solution in Beaker A.

14. **D**; **DOK Level**: 2; **Content Topic**: P.a.4; **Practices**: SP.1.a, SP.1.b, SP.1.c, SP.3.b, SP.7.a

The flowchart shows that heat and pressure transform kerogen into oil. Therefore, kerogen itself has not been subjected to enough heat and pressure to become oil. The passage explains how kerogen is transformed into oil, so kerogen has the ingredients required to be oil, and as such, can be used in practical applications. The fact that kerogen is in solid form when it is mined is not what is meant by the phrase "not as fully cooked."

15. **C**; **DOK Level**: 2; **Content Topic**: P.a.4; **Practices**: SP.1.a, SP.1.b, SP.1.c, SP.3.b, SP.7.a

The passage explains that kerogen is contained in oil shale, so the flowchart suggests that oil shale is formed at step 5 as the result of moderate heat and pressure that turns dead organisms into kerogen.

16. **A**; **DOK Level**: 3; **Content Topic**: P.a.4; **Practices**: SP.1.a, SP.1.b, SP.1.c, SP.3.b, SP.7.a

The flowchart shows that kerogen undergoes heat and pressure to become oil, and the passage states that the process of retorting transforms kerogen into an oil, so it can be deduced that retorting also involves these processes. The formation of oil involves dead organisms, but the process of retorting does not. The process of retorting liquefies kerogen (through the use of heat and pressure), but the passage explains that refining happens after retorting. The process of retorting begins with oil shale and ends with oil, but the process itself involves the use of heat and pressure.

17. **DOK Level**: 2; **Content Topic**: P.b.1; **Practices**: SP.1.a, SP.1.b, SP.6.b, SP.7.a, SP.7.b, SP.8.b

The car's acceleration is **+6 m/s²**, the result of performing the calculation for acceleration or deceleration: subtracting initial velocity from final velocity and then dividing the result by amount of time.

18. **DOK Level**: 2; **Content Topic**: P.b.1; **Practices**: SP.1.a, SP.1.b, SP.6.b, SP.7.a, SP.7.b, SP.8.b

The car's deceleration is **−2 m/s²**, the result of performing the calculation for acceleration or deceleration: subtracting initial velocity from final velocity and then dividing the result by amount of time.

UNIT 2 *(continued)*

19. DOK Level: 2; Content Topic: P.b.1; **Practices:** SP.1.a, SP.1.b, SP.6.b, SP.7.a, SP.7.b, SP.8.b
The car's acceleration is **0 m/s²**, the result of performing the calculation for acceleration or deceleration: subtracting initial velocity from final velocity and then dividing the result by amount of time. A constant velocity means that no acceleration is occurring.

20. DOK Level: 2; Content Topic: P.a.5; **Practices:** SP.1.a, SP.1.b, SP.1.c, SP.7.a

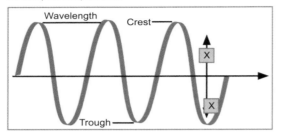

21. DOK Level: 2; Content Topic: P.a.5; **Practices:** SP.1.a, SP.1.b, SP.1.c, SP.7.a

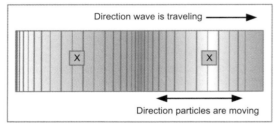

22.1 A; **22.2 C**; **22.3 D**; **22.4 C**; **DOK Level: 2; Content Topic:** P.a.3; **Practices:** SP.1.a, SP.1.b, SP.1.c, SP.3.b, SP.7.a
22.1 Kinetic energy is the energy of motion. Chemical energy is a form of stored energy found in matter. Thermal energy is heat energy. Electrical energy is made available by the flow of electrical charges through a conductor, such as a wire.
22.2 Potential energy is in an object because of its position, and the car is at the highest position at Point A. Chemical energy is a form of stored energy found in matter. Mechanical energy is a combination of kinetic and potential energy. Kinetic energy is the energy of motion.
22.3 As an object falls, its energy changes from potential to kinetic. So as the car falls, it is losing potential energy and gaining kinetic energy. Momentum is found by multiplying an object's mass by its velocity and is not related to changing forms of energy. The energy of an object changes from potential to kinetic, not from kinetic to potential, as the object falls. Gravitation is a force, not a type of energy.
22.4 At its lowest point on the track, or Point C, the car has the least potential but the most kinetic energy.

23. B; DOK Level: 2; Content Topic: P.c.2; **Practices:** SP.1.a, SP.1.b, SP.1.c, SP.7.a
The passage states that at room temperature, carbon dioxide changes from a solid to a gas, and the phase diagram indicates that sublimation is what occurs when a substance changes directly from a solid to a gas. So the information supports the conclusion that solid carbon dioxide (dry ice) sublimates at room temperature and under standard pressure. Dry ice is solid carbon dioxide, and water vapor is gaseous water—they are two different substances, so dry ice cannot evaporate into water vapor. The passage explains that dry ice does not change to fog; instead, when dry ice changes to a gas, fog is observed. The phase diagram indicates that dry ice sublimates at room temperature and under standard pressure; it does not melt.

24. D; DOK Level: 2; Content Topic: P.c.2; **Practices:** SP.1.a, SP.1.b, SP.1.c, SP.7.a
The phase diagram indicates that of the pressure and temperature pairings listed, carbon dioxide is a liquid only when pressure is 100 atm and temperature is −20°C. At all other combinations of pressure and temperature, carbon dioxide is a solid or a gas.

25. DOK Level: 2; Content Topic: P.a.1; **Practices:** SP.1.a, SP.1.b, SP.1.c, SP.6.a, SP.6.c, SP.7.b

Increase in Kinetic Energy	Decrease in Kinetic Energy
Particles speed up.	Temperature drops.
Heat is transferred in.	Particles slow down.
Volume is increased.	Heat is transferred out.
Temperature is raised.	Volume is reduced.

26. A; DOK Level: 1; Content Topic: P.b.2; **Practices:** SP.1.a, SP.1.b, SP.1.c, SP.3.b, SP.7.a, SP.7.b
The net force acting on the crate is determined by adding the values for all the forces acting on the crate: 500 N plus 500 N minus 600 N equals 400 N. The incorrect answer choices might be reached through incorrect calculations or formula application.

27. C; DOK Level: 2; Content Topic: P.b.2; **Practices:** SP.1.a, SP.1.b, SP.2.e, SP.3.b, SP.7.a
Frequency of oscillation is the dependent variable because it is the variable that is expected to change in response to manipulation of the independent variable. The length of the string is the independent variable (the one that is changed on purpose). The mass of the pendulum and the angle of oscillation should be held constant and are, therefore, neither dependent nor independent.

28. A; DOK Level: 2; Content Topic: P.b.2; **Practices:** SP.1.a, SP.1.b, SP.2.e, SP.3.b, SP.6.a, SP.7.a
The length of the string is the independent variable because it is the one that is changed on purpose. The mass of the pendulum and the angle of oscillation should be held constant and are, therefore, neither dependent nor independent. The frequency of oscillation is the variable that is expected to change in response to changing the independent variable.

29. **C**; **DOK Level:** 2; **Content Topic:** P.a.3; **Practices:** SP.1.a, SP.1.b, SP.1.c, SP.3.b, SP.7.a
The passage and illustration indicate that the turbine turns, causing the generator to produce electricity. The turning action of the turbine represents kinetic energy because it is moving. Chemical energy in the coal is released as heat. The generator produces electrical energy.

30. **A**; **DOK Level:** 2; **Content Topic:** P.a.3; **Practices:** SP.1.a, SP.1.b, SP.1.c, SP.3.b, SP.7.a
The chemical energy in the coal is released as heat (or thermal) energy; heat is used to produce the mechanical energy of the turning turbine system; and electrical energy is released by the spinning of the generator shaft. The incorrect answer choices present the energy transformations out of sequence.

31. **DOK Level:** 2; **Content Topic:** P.b.1; **Practices:** SP.1.a, SP.1.b, SP.6.b, SP.7.a, SP.7.b, SP.8.b
Momentum is equal to mass multiplied by velocity, and because it is a vector quantity, it must also specify direction. So the momentum of the object described is **2,500 kg • m/s eastward**.

32. **DOK Level:** 2; **Content Topic:** P.b.1; **Practices:** SP.1.a, SP.1.b, SP.3.b, SP.6.b, SP.7.a, SP.7.b, SP.8.b
Momentum is conserved; therefore, the second object also has a momentum of 2,500 kg • m/s eastward. Momentum is mass multiplied by velocity. The mass of the second object is 20 kg. The velocity of the object is, therefore, the object's momentum divided by its mass: $\frac{2,500 \text{ kg} \cdot \text{m/s eastward}}{20 \text{ kg}}$, or **125 m/s eastward**.

33. **B**; **DOK Level:** 1; **Content Topic:** P.b.1; **Practices:** SP.1.a, SP.1.b, SP.7.a, SP.7.b, SP.8.b
Speed is the total distance traveled divided by the time required to travel. In this case, distance is 600 meters and time is 600 seconds; therefore, average velocity is 1 m/s. The incorrect answer choices might be reached through incorrect calculations or formula application.

34. **A**; **DOK Level:** 2; **Content Topic:** P.b.1; **Practices:** SP.1.a, SP.1.b, SP.7.a, SP.7.b, SP.8.b
Velocity is total displacement divided by the time required to travel. In this case, displacement equals 0; therefore, average velocity is also 0. The incorrect answer choices might be reached through incorrect calculations or formula application.

35. **B**; **DOK Level:** 1; **Content Topic:** P.b.2; **Practices:** SP.1.a, SP.1.b, SP.1.c, SP.3.b, SP.7.a
The arrows in the diagram indicate that the upward and downward forces on the box are balanced and that the force acting on the box from the right (represented by the left-facing vector arrow) is larger than the force of friction (represented by the right-facing vector arrow). So the result of the unbalanced net force on the box is that the box will move to the left.

36. **D**; **DOK Level:** 2; **Content Topic:** P.a.4; **Practices:** SP.1.a, SP.1.b, SP.3.d, SP.8.a, SP.8.b
The mean of a data set is the average, calculated by adding the values in a data set and then dividing the sum by the number of values in the data set. In this case, you divide 3,280 (the sum of the values in the data set) by 7 (the number of values in the data set) to arrive at 468.57, which can be rounded up to 469. The figure *3,280* is the sum of the values in the data set. The figure *520* is the highest value in the data set. The figure *475* is the median of the data set, or the middle value in the data set.

UNIT 3 EARTH AND SPACE SCIENCE

LESSON 1, *pp. 82–83*
1. **C**; **DOK Level:** 2; **Content Topic:** ES.c.1; **Practices:** SP.1.a, SP.1.b, SP.3.b, SP.7.a
An explosive Big Bang would have caused galaxies to fly apart, meaning that they are farther apart now than they were 50 years ago. There is no indication in the passage that the Milky Way is the center of the universe, and, in fact, other scientific findings prove this notion false. The Big Bang would have caused galaxies to move apart not closer together. Facts presented in the passage do not support the idea that a second Big Bang will occur.

2. **C**; **DOK Level:** 2; **Content Topic:** ES.c.1; **Practices:** SP.1.a, SP.1.b, SP.1.c
The data line on the graph indicates that, under Hubble's theory, velocity increases with distance. The data line on the graph does not show that all galaxies move at the same velocity or that galaxies closer to Earth move more rapidly. The graph does not portray a relationship between velocity and mass.

3. **A**; **DOK Level:** 2; **Content Topic:** ES.c.1; **Practices:** SP.1.a, SP.1.b, SP.1.c, SP.3.a, SP.4.a
Red-shifted energy indicates movement away, and a Big Bang would have propelled the galaxies away from each other. The term *red shift* refers to speed and direction of movement, not temperature. The red shift observed by Hubble did not indicate the age of the galaxies. Also, it did not indicate that the galaxies were moving toward each other, but just the opposite.

4. **B**; **DOK Level:** 1; **Content Topic:** ES.b.4; **Practices:** SP.1.a, SP.1.b, SP.1.c, SP.7.a
The first sentence of the passage states that plate tectonic theory explains Earth's structure. The incorrect answer choices list subjects—composition of Earth's layers, density of Earth's crust, formation of the oceans—that are not addressed in detail in the passage.

LESSON 2, *pp. 84–85*
1. **C**; **DOK Level:** 2; **Content Topic:** ES.c.1; **Practices:** SP.1.a, SP.1.b, SP.1.c
The main point of the passage is that the universe is organized into several types of galaxies. The passage also describes the major elements of a galaxy. Therefore, an appropriate summary would do so as well. The incorrect answer choices restate information that is interesting but represents extra details in the passage.

2. **D**; **DOK Level:** 2; **Content Topics:** ES.c.1, ES.c.2; **Practices:** SP.1.a, SP.1.b, SP.1.c, SP.7.a
A title should reflect the main idea of a passage. The passage identifies the sun's structure and provides details about the layers that form this structure. Although the temperature of the sun's core is mentioned, this is not the main idea of the passage. Moreover, the passage does not fully explain the details of how nuclear fusion works, and the sun is the only part of the solar system discussed in detail in the passage.

UNIT 3 (continued)

3. B; DOK Level: 2; **Content Topic:** ES.c.1; **Practices:** SP.1.a, SP.1.b, SP.1.c, SP.7.a
The statement that accurately identifies the main idea and key details of the passage and illustration is the most appropriate summary. The incorrect answer choices contain interesting details but not key ideas that should be part of a summary or make a statement that does not relate closely to the text of the passage.

4. A; DOK Level: 2; **Content Topic:** ES.c.1; **Practices:** SP.1.a, SP.1.b, SP.7.a
The passage is about the life cycle of a star. Therefore, the point about how stars form would be the most important piece of information to include because it explains the beginning of a star's life cycle. The incorrect answer choices contain facts about stars. However, they are facts that do not help explain a part of a star's life cycle, the main idea of the passage.

5. B; DOK Level: 2; **Content Topic:** ES.c.1; **Practices:** SP.1.a, SP.1.b, SP.7.a
The best title is "Life Cycle of a Star" because the passage describes the entire sequence of a star's life. The title about the death of a star refers to just one stage in a star's life cycle. Also, the passage is not mainly about a star's energy, although that topic is briefly discussed. The title about the birth of a star refers to just one stage in a star's life cycle.

LESSON 3, pp. 86–87

1. B; DOK Level: 1; **Content Topic:** ES.c.2; **Practices:** SP.1.a, SP.1.b, SP.1.c, SP.7.a
By showing how the rotation of Earth on its axis causes different parts of Earth to get sunlight at different times, the diagram indicates that the rotation of Earth on its axis creates the pattern of night and day. Nuclear fusion in the sun's core provides energy that lights Earth during the day, but it does not create the pattern of night and day. Although the apparent daily movement of the sun across the sky is caused by Earth's rotation, it does not create night and day. The revolution of Earth around the sun creates a yearly, but not daily, pattern.

2. A; DOK Level: 2; **Content Topics:** ES.c.1, ES.c.2; **Practices:** SP.1.a, SP.1.b, SP.1.c, SP.3.a, SP.7.a
The difference in temperature between the inner and outer parts of the solar system influenced the substances that coalesced into the planets. The size of the galaxy was not a factor in this aspect of the formation of the planets. There is no indication from the passage that one set of planets had more time to develop than the other; if all the planets developed from the same disk of gas and dust around the newly formed sun, it is logical to assume that they all developed at about the same time. Temperature increases, rather than decreases, from the outer to the inner part of the solar system.

3. D; DOK Level: 2; **Content Topics:** ES.c.1, ES.c.2; **Practices:** SP.1.a, SP.1.b, SP.1.c, SP.3.b, SP.7.a
The labels of the illustration indicate that the outer planets are composed of lighter, less dense substances than the inner planets. Based on the illustration comparing a typical inner planet and a typical outer planet, the core represents a much larger percentage of an inner planet than an outer planet. The passage states that inner planets are small, rocky bodies. Outer planets are much larger than inner planets, a fact that is reinforced by both the illustration and the passage.

4. A; DOK Level: 3; **Content Topic:** ES.c.2; **Practices:** SP.1.a, SP.1.b, SP.1.c, SP.3.a, SP.7.a
The diagram shows two ocean bulges on opposite sides of Earth. As each bulge passes over an area, there is high tide. The areas between the bulges are troughs, and as each of these troughs passes over the same area, there is low tide. The incorrect answer choices are supported by neither the diagram nor the passage.

LESSON 4, pp. 88–89

1. A; DOK Level: 2; **Content Topic:** ES.b.4; **Practices:** SP.1.a, SP.1.b, SP.1.c, SP.3.b, SP.7.a
The lithosphere is thicker than the crust because, according to the diagram, the lithosphere consists of both the crust and the upper mantle. The diagram does not address the temperature of the inner core. Although the outer core is liquid (melted substances), the text states that the mantle is solid rock. The diagram shows that the lithosphere and the asthenosphere have different compositions—cooler rock and hot, soft rock, respectively.

2. A; DOK Level: 2; **Content Topic:** ES.c.3; **Practices:** SP.1.a, SP.1.b, SP.1.c, SP.3.b, SP.7.a
In the diagram, the jawless fish fossil is in the part of the rock layers labeled "Paleozoic Era." More precisely, it is shown at about halfway through the Paleozoic layer, indicating that the animal came into existence in the middle of the Paleozoic Era, not at the end of the Paleozoic Era, in the Mesozoic Era, or in the Cenozoic Era.

3. B; DOK Level: 2; **Content Topic:** ES.b.4; **Practices:** SP.1.a, SP.1.b, SP.1.c, SP.3.b, SP.7.a
The diagram label describing the melting of rock in the lithosphere indicates that volcanoes form when the lithosphere melts. The diagram indicates that volcanoes occur where one plate sinks and moves under another. The volcanoes in the diagram are close to, not far from, the ocean (the blue part of the diagram). Nothing in the diagram indicates that the material in a volcano comes from the lowest part of the mantle.

LESSON 5, pp. 90–91

1. D; DOK Level: 2; **Content Topic:** ES.b.2; **Practices:** SP.1.a, SP.1.b, SP.1.c, SP.7.a
Arrows pointing to organisms in a food web indicate what the organisms feed on. Producers in an ecosystem are those organisms that can make their own food. No arrow points to the phytoplankton in this food web, meaning that phytoplankton produce their own food. Cod, killer whales, and zooplankton are consumers; they get food and energy by eating other organisms rather than producing it themselves.

2. C; DOK Level: 2; **Content Topic:** ES.a.3; **Practices:** SP.1.a, SP.1.b, SP.1.c, SP.3.b, SP.7.a
The energy of the water's movement, or kinetic energy, is transformed into the energy of electric current produced by the generator. Tidal energy is kinetic energy because it is the energy of the moving water; it is not potential, electrical, or thermal energy.

3. **B**; **DOK Level:** 2; **Content Topic:** ES.a.3; **Practices:** SP.1.a, SP.1.b, SP.1.c, SP.3.b, SP.7.a
A renewable energy source is one that will never be used up and constantly renews itself. As part of Earth's continuous water cycle, ocean waters will never be used up. A nonrenewable energy source is finite. The movement of ocean waters does not release carbon dioxide. Power produced by ocean waters can be used only in certain coastal areas.

4. **C**; **DOK Level:** 1; **Content Topic:** ES.a.3; **Practices:** SP.1.a, SP.1.b, SP.3.b. SP.7.a
Nuclear fusion involves uniting atoms; therefore, the nuclear fusion discussed in the passage requires that atoms of deuterium and atoms of tritium unite to release energy. Splitting atoms is fission rather than fusion. Heating a substance to its boiling point produces a change in state; it does not fuse atoms. There is no indication from the information provided that tritium can produce deuterium.

LESSON 6, pp. 92–93
1. **D**; **DOK Level:** 1; **Content Topic:** ES.b.1; **Practices:** SP1.a, SP.1.b, SP.1.c
Carbon dioxide makes up 0.0387 percent of Earth's atmosphere, and methane makes up 0.00015 percent of Earth's atmosphere. So together, they comprise less than 1 percent of Earth's atmosphere. The incorrect answer choices might result from incorrect interpretation of the graph.

2. **D**; **DOK Level:** 2; **Content Topic:** ES.b.1; **Practices:** SP.1.a, SP.1.b, SP.1.c, SP.7.a
In the diagram, some arrows representing energy from the sun touch Earth, and others bend where they touch Earth's atmosphere, indicating that some of the sun's energy reaches and is absorbed by Earth's surface and some is reflected by the atmosphere. The diagram shows that not all the energy from the sun reaches Earth.

3. **A**; **DOK Level:** 2; **Content Topic:** ES.b.1; **Practices:** SP.1.a, SP.1.b, SP.7.a
The passage explains that some of the infrared energy that emits from Earth is contained within Earth's atmosphere by greenhouse gases, so the arrows that point away from but then bend back toward Earth represent the effect of greenhouse gases. The arrows from the sun to Earth's surface represent energy from the sun that reaches Earth's surface. The arrows from the sun that bend at Earth's atmosphere represent energy from the sun that is reflected by Earth's atmosphere. The arrows that point away from Earth's surface without bending represent infrared energy that emits from Earth and is not contained within Earth's atmosphere.

4. **B**; **DOK Level:** 2; **Content Topic:** ES.b.3; **Practices:** SP.1.a, SP.1.b, SP.1.c
The map shows that the westerlies blow across most of the continental United States. The incorrect answer choices might result from incorrect interpretation of the map.

5. **B**; **DOK Level:** 2; **Content Topic:** ES.b.3; **Practices:** SP.1.a, SP.1.b, SP.1.c, SP.3.b
All arrows in the map point from areas marked "High" to areas marked "Low," indicating that air moves from areas of high pressure to areas of low pressure. The map indicates that only some air moves toward Earth's equatorial low and that air does not move to areas of high pressure.

LESSON 7, pp. 94–95
1. **A**; **DOK Level:** 2; **Content Topics:** ES.a.1, ES.a.3, ES.b.3; **Practices:** SP.1.a, SP.1.b, SP.3.a, SP.4.a
The passage states that soil is essential for plant life and, therefore, animal life. So soil is necessary for our survival. The facts that intensive farming increases erosion and drought conditions can kill plant cover are contributing factors to the problem of soil loss, but they do not explain most pointedly why it is critical that people care about soil loss. The statement that no soil conservation methods exist is not supported by the passage; in fact, the passage discusses soil conservation methods.

2. **DOK Level:** 3; **Content Topics:** ES.a.1, ES.a.2, ES.b.3; **Practices:** SP.1.a, SP.1.c, SP.3.a, SP.3.b, SP.3.c, SP.6.c
Possible answer:
Ⓐ Rebuilding in New Orleans could be a problem if a disaster such as Katrina occurs again. Ⓑ People trying to decide whether to rebuild should take into account what has been done to protect the city from future storms as strong as or even stronger than Katrina. A new system of flood walls and pumps has been set up to shield the city, but is it strong enough? Ⓒ Some businesses might be reluctant to return to the city because the new protective system could still be inadequate. The new system is built to withstand a storm as strong as Katrina but could be overwhelmed by stronger storms that might become more frequent in the future. The loss of wetlands between New Orleans and the Gulf of Mexico continues as well. As this protective barrier against storms disappears, it will be easier for storm waters to surge into the city. A business owner could make a good case for being reluctant to return without additional protective measures.
Ⓐ The first sentence explains the problem associated with rebuilding in New Orleans, based on information from the passage. The passage states that although rare in the past, conditions brought about by climate change could make storms as strong as or stronger than Katrina more common in the future. The passage also states that parts of the city were well below sea level at the time of Katrina, and they still are.
Ⓑ The second and third sentences introduce the solution that has been devised. The diagram shows and the passage states that a new system of flood walls and pumps has been built around the city to protect it from a storm such as Katrina in the future.
Ⓒ The rest of the answer evaluates the solution, based on information from the passage.

Answer Key

UNIT 3 (continued)

LESSON 8, pp. 96–97
1. **D; DOK Level:** 2; **Content Topics:** ES.a.1. ES.a.3;
Practices: SP.1.a, SP.b.1, SP.1.c, SP.3.a, SP.3.b, SP.4.a
The renewable resources mentioned in the passage—water, the sun, and the wind—do not release carbon dioxide in the production of electricity. The passage does not discuss the relative cost of various energy sources. Renewable sources such as wind and the sun have an unlimited supply. The graph shows that very little electricity in the United States is produced today through the use of renewable energy resources.

2. **DOK Level:** 3; **Content Topic:** ES.a.3; **Practices:** SP.1.a, SP.b.1, SP.1.c, SP.3.b, SP.5.a, SP.6.a, SP.6.c
By using the information in the passage and diagram, you can draw conclusions about which statements would be useful in constructing an argument for mountaintop-removal coal mining and which statements would be useful in constructing an argument against it. The following statements would be useful in constructing an argument for mountaintop removal: **it provides jobs in an area that badly needs them; it is safer than mining in deep shafts; it increases domestic supplies of coal, which are preferable to imported oil**. The following statements would be useful in constructing an argument against mountaintop removal: **diverse forest ecosystems are destroyed and cannot be re-created after mining; removal of forests increases erosion on steep slopes, and flooding results; blasting, mining, and washing the coal can emit unhealthful amounts of coal dust into the air.**

UNIT 3 REVIEW, pp. 98–105
1. **C; DOK Level:** 1; **Content Topic:** ES.c.2; **Practices:** SP.1.b, SP.1.c, SP.3.b, SP.7.a
The diagram shows Earth rotating, such that half of it is constantly moving in and out of the sun's rays, creating night and day. To show the cycle of seasons, the diagram would have to show Earth at different positions in its orbit at different times of the year. The diagram does not indicate tides or lunar phases.

2. **A; DOK Level:** 2; **Content Topic:** ES.c.1; **Practices:** SP.1.a, SP.1.b, SP.3.a, SP.3.b
A summary relates the most important idea or ideas of a passage. In this passage, the most important idea to summarize is that Hubble has given scientists a view of the most distant galaxies ever seen. The passage does not state that the most distant galaxies are 13.2 billion light-years away; it states that these are the most distant galaxies seen so far. In addition, even if this fact were true, it would be no more than an interesting detail, not the main point of the passage. The other incorrect answer options are interesting facts, not main points that summarize the passage.

3. **B; DOK Level:** 1; **Content Topic:** ES.b.4; **Practices:** SP.1.b, SP.1.c
The diagram shows that the asthenosphere is made of hot, soft rock. The crust is the uppermost layer, and it is made of cooler, hard rock. The lithosphere includes both the crust and the topmost part of the mantle.

4. **B; DOK Level:** 2; **Content Topic:** ES.b.4; **Practices:** SP.1.b, SP.1.c, SP.3.b
The diagram shows that the crust is the uppermost layer. The thickest layer cannot be determined from the diagram because it shows only a portion of Earth's interior. The diagram shows the asthenosphere as part of the mantle, not the lithosphere. There is nothing in the diagram to suggest that the crust and mantle ever change places.

5. **B; DOK Level:** 2; **Content Topics:** ES.a.3, ES.b.4; **Practices:** SP.1.b, SP.1.c, SP.3.b, SP.7.a
Based on the part of the diagram that shows volcanoes forming, volcanoes form above the area where two plates meet and one slips under the other. The volcanoes in the diagram are near the ocean, but formation of volcanoes does not result from ocean waters warming air. The volcanoes in the diagram are forming above the asthenosphere, not within it. Finally, the two plates are not pulling apart at the boundary where volcanoes form; the arrows show that they are meeting.

6. **DOK Level:** 3; **Content Topic:** ES.b.3; **Practices:** SP.1.b, SP.1.c, SP.3.b, SP.6.c, SP.7.a
Possible answer:
Ⓐ The water that drops to the bottom of the falls wears away the rock at the bottom of the cliff. Ⓑ The harder cap rock at the top of the falls does not wear away as quickly as the softer rock under it, creating a ledge of harder cap rock that juts out. Ⓒ Eventually, the harder cap rock breaks off, pushing the falls slightly upstream.
Ⓐ The description in the first sentence is supported by the first and second illustrations in the diagram. The diagram shows that the water plunging over the falls is eroding the softer rock under a layer of harder cap rock.
Ⓑ The description in the second sentence is supported by the second illustration in the diagram. The diagram shows that as the softer rock underneath is worn away, the harder rock remains in place as a ledge over the top of it.
Ⓒ The description in the last sentence is supported by the third and fourth illustrations in the diagram. The diagram shows that the harder cap rock ledge eventually collapses and forms a pile of sediment at the base of the falls. However, with the removal of the harder cap, the falls moves a slight distance upstream.

7. **C; DOK Level:** 2; **Content Topic:** ES.c.1; **Practices:** SP.1.a, SP.1.b, SP.3.b, SP.4.a, SP.7.a
A huge explosion would propel all matter in the universe outward, flying away from one spot. Therefore, the fact that galaxies are moving apart rapidly supports the Big Bang theory. The incorrect answer choices are statements that do not provide evidence related to the theory or that make invalid claims.

8. **DOK Level:** 1; **Content Topic:** ES.b.4; **Practices:** SP.1.a, SP.1.b, SP.1.c, SP.6.c, SP.7.a
The plates shown on the map are the **tectonic** plates that make up Earth's surface.

9. **DOK Level:** 1; **Content Topic:** ES.b.4; **Practices:** SP.1.a, SP.1.b, SP.1.c, SP.6.c, SP.7.a
The theory that explains the structure of Earth's crust is the **plate tectonic** theory.

10. **DOK Level:** 1; **Content Topic:** ES.b.4; **Practices:** SP.1.a, SP.1.b, SP.1.c, SP.6.c, SP.7.a
As the plates move and jostle against each other at their edges, this movement creates various **landforms** on Earth's surface.

11. **B**; **DOK Level:** 2; **Content Topic:** ES.b.3; **Practices:** SP.1.a, SP.1.b, SP.3.b, SP.7.a
Wind is the movement of air from areas of higher pressure to areas of lower pressure. The passage states that the ITCZ is an area of low pressure, so winds moving into that area would originate in areas of higher pressure. Because wind moves from areas of higher pressure to areas of lower pressure, winds moving into an area of low pressure would not originate in areas of lower pressure or move to areas of higher pressure. The passage states that storms are associated with lower air pressure and that the ITCZ is an area of low pressure, so winds in that area likely produce storms.

12. **C**; **DOK Level:** 2; **Content Topic:** ES.c.1; **Practices:** SP.1.a, SP.1.b, SP.3.b
Through descriptions of how main-sequence stars of different sizes die, the passage indicates that regardless of their original sizes or how they die, all these stars follow the pattern of ending up as small, dense bodies. The statements that the universe has many types of stars and that stars use hydrogen as fuel do not describe patterns. The statement that all stars explode in supernovas is inaccurate.

13. **C**; **DOK Level:** 3; **Content Topic:** ES.c.3; **Practices:** SP.1.a, SP.1.b, SP.3.b
The passage suggests that the calculations scientists make in radiometric dating involve rate of decay of an isotope, so the rate of decay of the particular isotope being measured must be known. Scientists use radiometric dating so that they do not need to know the order in which layers of rock were deposited to determine the ages of rock. Scientists must use radioactive isotopes because radiometric dating involves measuring the decay, or loss of radioactivity, of an isotope. The passage gives no indication that radioactive isotopes destroy rock.

14. **DOK Level:** 3; **Content Topics:** ES.c.1, ES.c.2; **Practices:** SP.1.b, SP.1.c, SP.3.b, SP.6.c, SP.7.a
Possible answer:
Ⓐ The fusion reaction starts with two atoms of hydrogen. Ⓑ The atoms fuse to produce one atom of helium. Ⓒ In addition to the helium, the fusion reaction produces one neutron and energy.
Ⓐ The first sentence identifies the reactants in the fusion reaction, based on information from the model. The model shows two different forms of hydrogen atoms fusing together.
Ⓑ The second sentence identifies the new element produced in the fusion reaction, based on information from the model. The diagram shows that the fusion of the two hydrogen atoms produces a helium atom and some additional by-products.
Ⓒ The third sentence identifies the by-products produced in the fusion reaction, based on information from the diagram. The diagram shows that the additional by-products of the fusion reaction are a neutron and energy.

15. **D**; **DOK Level:** 1; **Content Topic:** ES.c.2; **Practices:** SP.1.b, SP.1.c
The left column of the table identifies a repeating quality of all four inner planets and indicates that all the inner planets are small, rocky bodies. Only one inner planet has large amounts of surface water; no inner planet has rings; and only half of the inner planets have moons.

16. **D**; **DOK Level:** 1; **Content Topic:** ES.c.2; **Practices:** SP.1.a, SP.1.b, SP.1.c
In the column for outer planets in the table, the text states that all outer planets have several moons. The table also indicates that the outer planets are mostly, not completely, gaseous; that the inner planets, not the outer planets, have hard surfaces; and that the outer planets all have rings.

17. **DOK Level:** 3; **Content Topic:** ES.b.2; **Practices:** SP.1.a, SP.1.b, SP.1.c, SP.3.b, SP.6.a, SP.6.c, SP.7.a
The passage explains that water in the ocean changes state, and you have learned that heating water results in a change of state from liquid to gas, or evaporation. So when water in the ocean is heated by the sun, **evaporation** occurs.

18. **B**; **DOK Level:** 2; **Content Topic:** ES.c.2; **Practices:** SP.1.a, SP.1.b, SP.1.c, SP.7.a
The lunar phases are a cycle. To show a cyclical pattern, some part of the cycle must be shown to repeat. Therefore, the complete pattern of lunar phases is the sequence that begins and ends with the new moon phase. The incorrect answer choices indicate only parts of the cycle.

19. **C**; **DOK Level:** 2; **Content Topic:** ES.b.1; **Practices:** SP.1.b, SP.1.c, SP.3.b
The graph shows that oxygen makes up about 21 percent of the atmosphere and that nitrogen, the most plentiful gas in the atmosphere, makes up more than 78 percent of the atmosphere. So together, they make up more than 98 percent of the atmosphere. Nitrogen, not oxygen is the most plentiful gas in the atmosphere. The percentage of the atmosphere that oxygen makes up is much greater than the percentage made up by carbon dioxide and methane, which are the only two greenhouse gases listed. Together these two greenhouse gases make up less than 1 percent of Earth's atmosphere. The atmosphere has more nitrogen than oxygen, and it has more oxygen than carbon dioxide.

20. **A**; **DOK Level:** 2; **Content Topic:** ES.b.1; **Practices:** SP.1.a, SP.1.b
A summary of scientific information identifies the main points from the information, so the best summary of the information presented in the graph should indicate the main points that Earth's atmosphere is made up mostly of nitrogen and oxygen and should include the important detail that Earth's atmosphere also contains small percentages of other gases. The statements that nitrogen is the most prevalent gas in Earth's atmosphere and that nitrogen and oxygen are the two primary gases in Earth's atmosphere give important ideas conveyed by the graph but do not fully summarize the information provided by the graph. The statement about specific gases that occur in less plentiful amounts in Earth's atmosphere is a detail that does not belong in a summary.

Answer Key

UNIT 3 *(continued)*

21.1 C; **21.2 D**; **DOK Level: 2**; **Content Topics:** ES.a.3, ES.b.3; **Practices:** SP.1.a, SP.1.b, SP.1.c, SP.3.a, SP.7.a
21.1 The table states that wind energy is both free and renewable. Wind is renewable, or available in an endless supply that is constantly replenished, meaning that it is not exhaustible, nonrenewable, or capable of being depleted.
21.2 Because the table states that bats and birds are sometimes struck by wind turbines, the argument can be made that wind turbines are a danger to wildlife. There is no indication in the table that airplanes, people, or power lines are in danger from wind turbines.

22. B; **DOK Level: 2**; **Content Topics:** Es.a.2, ES.b.1, ES.b.3; **Practices:** SP.1.a, SP.1.b, SP.3.b, SP.7.a
From information in the passage, you can infer that the watches and warnings allow people to take cover as a severe storm approaches, thereby decreasing the number of injuries and deaths. It is illogical to think that a tornado watch or warning would prevent a storm—especially since warnings are given only after a storm has been spotted. Warning people of a storm's approach does not change the conditions under which meteorologists study severe storms or explain how they form.

23. A; **DOK Level: 2**; **Content Topics:** ES.a.1, ES.b.1; **Practices:** SP.1.a, SP.1.b, SP.3.b, SP.7.a
The passage explains that the burning of fossil fuels releases into the air gases that increase acidity of precipitation, meaning that Earth's atmosphere and hydrosphere are affected, and that the acid precipitation that is produced harms forests and fishes and eats away at stone, meaning that Earth's biosphere and geosphere are affected. Therefore, the data support the argument that the burning of fossil fuels affects all Earth's systems. The passage mentions only fish; therefore, the data presented support only the argument that fish are affected by the burning of fossil fuels (although other animals, including humans, are affected in various ways). The passage states that pH of precipitation is changing in some parts of the United States, not necessarily all across the United States. Because the passage does not indicate that pH of precipitation is changing in all parts of the United States, there is not support for the argument that all important U.S. monuments must be protected from acid precipitation.

24. B; **DOK Level: 2**; **Content Topics:** ES.a.1, ES.a.3; **Practices:** SP.1.a, SP.1.b, SP.3.a, SP.3.b
The passage gives several examples of how farming practices pollute drinking water, making it clear that the main problem being conveyed is that farming practices can pollute drinking-water supplies. The passage does not discuss whether agriculture uses too much water or fertilizers are effective enough. The passage suggests that crop rotation could reduce the effects of pollution.

25. D; **DOK Level: 2**; **Content Topics:** ES.a.1, ES.a.3; **Practices:** SP.1.a, SP.1.b, SP.3.a, SP.3.b, SP.4.a
The passage identifies the use of older farming methods as a possible solution to the problem but states that these methods must be shown to be as effective as modern methods for this solution to work, suggesting that they must produce as much food as newer methods. The incorrect answer choices describe situations not addressed in the passage.

26. B; **DOK Level:** 3; **Content Topics:** ES.a.1, ES.b.1; **Practices:** SP.1.a, SP.1.b, SP.3.a, SP.3.b, SP.7.a
The passage states that most of the energy we use is produced by the combustion of fossils fuels, which has been pouring carbon dioxide into the atmosphere for hundreds of years. Therefore, the problem identified in the passage is that an excess amount of carbon dioxide is entering the atmosphere. The fact that people have used fossil fuels since the Industrial Revolution is not the most direct statement of the problem, which is excess carbon dioxide in the atmosphere. There is no mention in the passage of the need to conserve energy, and natural sources of carbon dioxide are never identified in the passage as a problem.

27. C; **DOK Level: 2**; **Content Topic:** ES.b.1; **Practices:** SP.1.a, SP.1.b, SP.3.a, SP.3.b, SP.7.a
The passage identifies the problem as the increasing amount of carbon dioxide entering the atmosphere due to the combustion of fossil fuels. The passage also states that several alternative energy sources that are not widely used do not produce carbon dioxide as a waste gas. The passage is suggesting that using more of these alternative sources is a possible solution. The ideas of altering the natural processes of decomposition of plant material and absorption of gases into the atmosphere are not logical solutions and are not mentioned in the passage. Natural gas is a fossil fuel, so it can be assumed that the use of natural gas is part of the problem.

28. DOK Level: 2; **Content Topic:** ES.b.3; **Practices:** SP.1.a, SP.1.b, SP.1.c, SP.3.b, SP.6.c, SP.7.a
The text explains that flowing river water causes erosion and that the water moves fastest on the outside of a meander, or bend in a river. Therefore, the river represented in the diagram causes more erosion in the **areas that are on the outside of its meanders**.

29. B; **DOK Level: 2**; **Content Topic:** ES.a.3; **Practices:** SP.1.a, SP.1.b, SP.3.a
The passage explains that the dam has caused the flow rate, temperature, and sediment of the Colorado River to change; that it has caused certain aquatic species to no longer live in the area; and that it has filled Glen Canyon, covering the canyon's scenic beauty and ancient artifacts. An effective summary conveys all of this information. The other answer choices identify information from the passage that is not a summary of the environmental effects of the dam or misstate information from the passage.

30. C; **DOK Level:** 3; **Content Topic:** ES.a.3; **Practices:** SP.1.a, SP.1.b, SP.3.b
The passage basically contrasts the negative effects on the natural environment of the river below the dam and the land that was flooded to create the reservoir behind it with the advantages of the dam for farmers and for electricity production. The two opposing arguments, then, are about the value of natural environments and the needs of a technically advanced society. The incorrect answer choices identify potential arguments related to Glen Canyon Dam but do not identify the arguments presented in the passage.

ANSWER KEY

Index

INDEX

Index

INDEX

Index

Index

S

Salt as component of sweat, 9
Salts, 51
Saturation, 51, 74
Saturn, 87
Science concepts, applying, 90–91
Scientific evidence, understanding, 26–28
Scientific information
    evaluating, 70–71
    expressing, 92–93
Scientific investigation
    design, 69–70, 74, 78
    predicting outcomes, 50–51
    techniques, 68–69, 74, 78–79
Scientific laws, 54–55, 56–57, 69
Scientific laws, applying, 56–57
Scientific method, 62, 68, 70, 74, 78–79
Scientific models, understanding, 42–43, 48
Scientific theories, understanding, 82–83
Scientific theory, 68, 82–83. See also Big Bang theory; Cell theory; Evolutionary theory; Plate tectonic theory; Scientific theories, understanding
Screw, 58
Sedimentary rock, 75
Segregation of alleles, 24
Selection pressures, 30
Sexual reproduction, 20, 22, 24
Simple machines, 58–59, 72
Single displacement reactions, 49
Skeletal system, 5
Skin, 4, 8–9
Small intestine, 5, 32
Sodium, 50
Soil, 12–13, 19, 94
Soil chemistry, 19
Soil conservation, 94
Solar eclipse, 85
Solar system, 85, 87
Solids, 44–45, 61, 77
Solubility, 50–51, 74
Soluble substances, 50
Solute, 50–51
Solution, identifying problem and, 94–95
Solutions, 50–51
Solvent, 50–51
Sound, 60
Sound waves, 65
Source information in tables, 6
Speciation, 30
Speed, 52–53, 79
Spinal cord, 5
Spiral galaxies, 84
Spotlighted Items
    drag-and-drop, 19, 29, 37, 57, 65, 97
    drop-down, 9, 71
    fill-in-the-blank, 15, 17, 45
    hot spot, 23, 25, 47, 59, 61
    short answer, 31, 95

Spring tides, 87
Stars, 84–85, 100
States of matter, 44–45, 77
Statistics as supporting details, 4
Stomach, 5, 32
Strong acids, 51
Strong bases, 51
Structural formulas, 43
Sublimation, 77
Subscripts, 49
Sugars
    in DNA, 21
    photosynthesis, 66
Sulfur dioxide, 104
Sun
    day and night on Earth, 86, 98
    layers of, 85
    nuclear fusion, 85, 101
    as source of energy, 12, 19, 66, 85
Sunspots, 85
Supernovas, 85, 100
Supporting details, 4
Sweat glands, 9
Sweating, 9
Symbiotic relationships, 14–15, 34
Symbols
    in chemical equations, 48–49
    for dominant and recessive alleles, 23
    for elements, 42, 49
    for nucleotide bases, 21
    as scientific models, 42
    for states of matter, 49
Synthesis reactions, 49
Systems of human body, 4–5, 32, 39

T

Tables
    for comparing and contrasting, 18
    complex tables, 46
    interpreting, 6–7, 46–47
Tectonic plates, 83, 89
Telophase, 3, 33
Temperature
    in ecosystems, 19, 35
    effect on solubility, 51, 74
    heat transfer and, 61, 77
    measurement of, 60
    regulation of on Earth, 92–93
    regulation in human body, 9
Testable hypotheses, 70
Test-Taking Tech
    accessing on-screen calculator, 52
    answering multiple-choice and hot spot items, 22
Test-Taking Tips, xiv
    accessing prior knowledge, 58
    answering multiple-choice questions, 70
    categorizing and classifying, 14
    determining answers from diagrams, 12
    determining best answer, 4
    identifying arguments, 96
    interpreting arrows in vector diagrams, 54
    interpreting graphs, 10

    interpreting illustrations, 2
    interpreting observations, 62
    interpreting tables, 6, 46
    interpreting three-dimensional diagrams, 88
    recognizing key words in generalizations, 16
    relating text and visuals, 20
    understanding language of questions, 48
    using data from diagrams, 56
Text and visuals, relating, 20–21, 64
Thematic maps, 10
Thermal energy
    in chemical reactions, 73
    defined, 60
    temperature and heat, 60, 77
    transfer of, 47, 61, 74, 77
Thermal equilibrium, 61
Thermometers, 60, 77
Thiamin (vitamin B1), 6
Threatened species, 18, 36
Three-dimensional diagrams, interpreting, 88–89
Thymine, 21, 25
Tidal ecosystems, 33
Tidal power, 91
Tides, 87, 91
Time, 52–53
Tissues, 4, 39
Titles
    of complex visuals, 44
    of graphs, 10
    of maps, 10
    of scientific models, 42
    of tables, 6, 46
    of text, 58
Tornadoes, 103
Trade winds, 93, 100
Traits
    adaptation, 30–31
    grouping in cladograms, 27, 37
    inheritance of, 20, 22–25, 38
    mutations, 25, 34, 38
    natural selection of, 28–30, 36
    selection pressure, 30–31
    speciation, 30–31
Transform boundaries, 83
Transverse waves, 64–65, 76
Tritium, 91
Troughs of waves, 64–65
Tundras, 35
Turbines, 63, 78, 91

U

Ultraviolet light, 65
Unicellular organisms, 2
Universal gravitation, law of, 56–57
Universe
    Big Bang theory, 82, 99
    galaxies, 82–84, 98
    solar system, 85, 87
    stars, 84–85, 93, 100
Uranus, 87
Urea, 9

Using Logic
evaluating answer choices, 82
identifying conclusions, 30
identifying main idea, 84
interpreting complex visuals, 44
interpreting flowcharts, 66
making inferences, 28
using context clues to determine meaning, 24

V

Vaccines, 11
Valid generalizations, 16
Vaporization, 45
Variables, 50, 69–70
Vector diagrams, understanding, 54–55, 58
Vectors, 54–55
Velocity
acceleration and, 53, 75
calculation of average velocity, 79
momentum and, 57, 79
speed and, 53
Venus, 87
Viruses, 11
Visible light, 65
Visuals
cladograms, 27
complex tables, 46
complex visuals, 44
content-based tools, 22
developing summaries from, 84
diagrams, 12, 54, 56, 64, 86, 88
energy pyramids, 13
flowcharts, 12, 66

food chains, 12
food webs, 90
genetics diagrams, 22
graphs, 10, 62, 92
illustrations, 2, 38, 44
interpreting, 2, 6, 10, 12, 22, 42, 44, 46, 54, 88
maps, 10
with numeric values, 52
pedigree charts, 23
phase diagrams, 77
Punnett squares, 23
relating to text, 20–21, 64
scientific models, 42
tables, 6
vector diagrams, 54
Vitamin B6, 6
Vitamin B12, 6
Vitamins, 6–7
Volcanoes, 89
Volume, 47

W

Waning crescent moon, 102
Waning gibbous moon, 102
Waste products, 4, 13
Water
change of state, 44–45
as component of sweat, 9
in ecosystems, 12–13, 19
erosion by, 38, 99, 105
need by human body, 7
in photosynthesis, 66
Water cycle, 102
Watt, 59

Wavelength, 64–65, 83
Waves, 64–65, 76
Waxing crescent moon, 102
Waxing gibbous moon, 102
Weak acids, 51
Weak bases, 51
Weather
air pressure, 93, 100
blizzards, 103
hurricanes, 95, 103
tornadoes, 103
wind zones, 93, 100
Weathering, 99
Weather warning system, 103
Wedge, 58–59
Weight, 55–56
Westerlies, 93
Wheel and axle, 58
White dwarf stars, 85, 100
Wind energy, 103
Wind, erosion by, 38
Windmills, 63
Wind turbines, 63
Wind zones, 93, 100
Work, 58–59, 72

X

X-axes, 10
X-rays, 65

Y

Y-axes, 10